THINKING
INSIDE
THE BOX

THINKING INSIDE THE BOX

Written by
LOUIS SAHA

Edited & translated by
GEORGIA DE CHAMBERET

VSP

Published by Vision Sports Publishing in 2012

Vision Sports Publishing
19-23 High Street
Kingston upon Thames
Surrey
KT1 1LL

www.visionsp.co.uk

ISBN: 978-1-907637-53-7

Originally published in French under the title
Du Quartier aux Étoiles: Le Safari du Footballeur
by Editions Anne Carrière, Paris, 2012

Written by Louis Saha
Edited & translated by Georgia de Chamberet
UK edition edited by: Jim Drewett
Copy editor: Alex Morton
Cover design: Neal Cobourne
Back cover artwork: Darren Baker

Typeset by Palimpsest Book Production Limited, Falkirk, Stirlingshire

Printed and bound in Great Britain by TJ International Ltd, Padstow, Cornwall

A CIP Catalogue record for this book is available from the British Library

This book is supported by the Institut Français as part of the Burgess programme.

INSTITUT
FRANÇAIS
ROYAUME-UNI

CONTENTS

A MESSAGE FROM CHARLES BIÉTRY

journalist and director of Al Jazeera Sport, France

Louis Saha is a footballer, and a very good one at that. However, what you are about to read is not a book about football, but a book about life. Of course, it will tell you about Manchester United, Everton, Tottenham Hotspur and the French national team, Les Bleus [The Blues]. Of course, you will discover the secrets of a world with a silver-sequined lining. Those of you who are nuts about football will also find plenty to savour. In this book, Louis Saha takes you on a journey that is out of the ordinary.

It is impossible not to be moved by his words, his worldview, his passion and his trenchant truths. His style is original, his ideas strike deep, his intuition disturbs, and his heart beats hard and fast.

It would be an inaccuracy to say that his narrative reads like a novel. This book is more than reportage, or a collection of anecdotes. It is a slice of life that will surprise and excite you, arouse your curiosity and inflame your passions. Most of all, it will make you think

FOREWORD BY PATRICE EVRA

I have never read anything quite like *Thinking Inside The Box*. This book really shows how footballers live and think, and describes how it is. It's as though you are walking in a footballer's shoes.

Louis Saha has been through a great deal, and always bounces back stronger. He is a fighter. His account of missing the Champions League final due to injury -- and not just because the coach made a choice as I had thought -- and his anguish are immensely moving.

Stories about his family, such as his father's arrival in France and eating Dijon mustard for the first time when he was used to Caribbean scotch bonnet peppers, made me smile. You find yourself laughing one minute and almost crying the next. It's more than likely you will experience a range of intense emotions as you read.

I know Louis Saha from way back, yet thanks to this book I rediscovered a great guy who is strong albeit modest. He is the only player I know who truly savours football from one moment to the next. For other players it may be all in a day's work to win titles, but he feels and appreciates every minute. Not only does he live his passion, but he observes and understands what is going on around him.

Thinking Inside The Box is crucial reading for young guys hoping to break into a game that is beautiful yet which is, more often than not, beset by sharks.

Patrice Evra, Manchester United

AUTHOR'S PREFACE

My little brother was the inspiration for this book, which took nearly four years to write.

Football educated me and made me grow up.

I watched and listened, and now pass on what I learned the best I can.

When you sign as a professional, you take on and accept the responsibility.

I've been lucky enough to be a player in a sports universe that has an overabundance of wealth, prestige and pressure to bring out the best in you.

At times, football has disconnected me from real life.

Football teases me and there's nothing I can do about it.

I'm hooked. Love makes me blind.

Sometimes football doesn't care about me, but I just have to accept it.

The game demands that I do my best, and even a little bit more.

I'm as dependent on football as man is on the air he breathes.

Football feeds me, clothes me, gives me shelter and makes me feel beautiful.

Football spoils me with gifts, money and rewards.

I have become blind to its excesses.

Jealous people accuse me of being arrogant because I'm bold.

I appreciate being able to live a privileged life.

Football gives me a lot, but from one day to the next it can take back everything.

Sometimes I believe I have the upper hand, but in reality football is my master.

I no longer have any control over my time, my image, or my personality.

I just about control my money and what I do for fun.

Football has aged me, and people see me as old, but I'm still just a carefree kid.

Football is more than just a ball bouncing on the ground; for me it's the entire world going nuts for it.

Football is a religion which, like music or film, can trigger intense and uplifting emotions.

Football is a gift from God in all his glory.

I live the dream and hate to sleep.

When my little brother told me he wanted to become a footballer, I thought: "Is he crazy? Does he realise what he'd get himself into, or what he'd have to go through to succeed?" He needs to understand what a player's career actually involves and have some real reference points before venturing into that world.

The beautiful game has become an immense global reality TV show. The world of football spins on an axis of money and sex. Players are under great pressure to play to the best of their ability, and win. If a player does well, he stays on the back pages, but if he puts a foot wrong in his private life, he becomes front-page headline news. A player must be all things to all men, women and supporters; his coach and team-mates; his wife . . . But what lies behind the sensational tabloid headlines that hit us every day? How does it feel to be attacked in this way? How does a player who is about to start a career as a professional footballer cope with it all? What help and advice is he given? If a world-class player makes a mistake, how does it affect him? What can he fall back on? Does he have a good support network? The arrogant footballer is now a familiar image, but isn't this a misconception developed by the public and the media?

Many players, like me, come from the inner city. Unfortunately, not everyone reaches the stars. A player will be affected by the family and environment he grows up in. Later on, whether he is married with kids, or single, this will also influence his behaviour on the pitch and off it. Daily life moulds a footballer. A family man is more likely to be responsible whereas a young, single guy can easily be destabilised, or worse, corrupted by the trappings of success. Lots of little, but crucial, elements mix into his daily life: does he go home after training and rest? Or does he go out and party into the small hours? Is he eating properly, or living off takeaways (and putting on weight)? Does he blow his pay cheque in casinos and shopping malls, or is he investing for his future?

I have managed to stay grounded thanks to my parents, my wife and a strong attachment to my roots. When the cashier reads my name on a credit card, it's not usually the Iranian airline, Saha Air, that first comes to mind, but football. This is a source of pride for me. But representing the family name so publicly is also a big responsibility.

What's more, Saha in Arabic means "health". The significance of this in relation to my name is a real paradox. Me: plagued by injury. This name is my destiny, my talisman, because apart from my talent, I am lucky. I am injury-prone, yet each time I come back fighting stronger. It is a miracle. Life, like sport, is not without contradictions.

St Protais St Anne, a little town on the island of Guadeloupe – a small piece of France in the middle of the Caribbean – is the true starting point of my story. My parents were born on these beautiful islands which ceased to be a French colony after 1946. When I go there on holiday, I try to soak up the energy of my ancestral family, their strong character, the island's heavenly land-scape and its bewitching scents. I always return from Paradise with my belly, as well as my luggage, a few pounds heavier. I savour the flavours of good Caribbean food. I love talking with and listening to my grandparents. I admire the efforts and sacrifices they have endured to build a great, close-knit family. Me, just a kid from the 'hood: I was lucky not to be born in an under-developed country where you don't live: you survive. I am fortunate to be under the roof of a Saha – although when I think about it, to be a Jordan (Michael) or Smith (Will) would be cool.

Even though my personal experience forms the core of this book, I have used an eclectic approach. I am writing for young people like my little brother who are looking for guidance, as well as for fans or curious punters. I take readers on a unique safari to show them the beauty and the dangers of the magical world of football. I have chosen to write about important issues in football today. I have talked to my friends in the beautiful game about their triumphs and their disappointments, as well as the destabilising effects of large salaries and the trappings of wealth and fame. Patrice Evra, Zinédine Zidane, Carlos Tevez, Tim Cahill, Thierry Henry, William Gallas, Ji-Sung Park, Sylvain Distin, Sir Alex Ferguson and others have given me their personal insights. Many come from extraordinary countries, far away. Their ancestors would be proud to have such descendants elevating their family name. They have become part of history, along with the culture, traditions and true grit of their ancestors. They talk about how to handle pressure, victory and the burning desire to win trophies. How to protect their private life from media intrusion. How to keep a cool head and make balanced decisions. How to stay true to yourself and not lose the plot in the soccer circus. Like me, they have succeeded despite setbacks and risen to the top. They reach for the sky, but the day will come when their vitality and brilliance is gone. Like that of a beautiful shooting star, our journey is one of extraordinary and ephemeral moments.

I hope that this book serves as an opportunity to see the lifestyle and the world of a privileged sportsman from the inside looking out. It gives an HD image of football and the footballer. I am proud you have opened this book. I hope to show what it is like to be part of this universe that is the stuff of dreams.

My wife has also written a special chapter bringing together the observations and anecdotes of the wives and girlfriends of players, offering a different view to the usual one.

More than likely, people who are quick to criticise will say that the profits of this book are a way to give myself a better retirement, or the trip of a lifetime. I would answer that half of them are being donated to the charity ELA, which fights against the degenerative brain disorder leukodystrophy. Zinédine Zidane is one of its patrons, along with other notable personalities.

My name is Louis Saha. I still see myself as that inner-city kid who succeeded without really asking. I'm neither a journalist, nor a referee. I just recount what my mates and I have experienced. I write with my guts and hope that fans and novices will come to better understand the complicated yet sensational career of a professional footballer.

My journey has taken me from Metz to Newcastle; from Fulham to Manchester United and Everton. Today I play for Tottenham Hotspur. I have experienced public success and personal disappointments. I have played locally, nationally and internationally in a career spanning Euro 2004, the 2006 World Cup and the Champions League. For this book, my mates and I have come together to reflect on the game which is our life.

Louis Saha, April 2012

I

GOOD LUCK, BAD LUCK

1
KICK-OFF

I can see us not so long ago. My brother is describing his dreams. For a while now, I have noticed there is something special about him and realise how much he loves this sport; my sport. He talks about it all the time and wants to know everything. He knows all the players and their qualities. When I grasp the Playstation controller I notice he has spent all night re-designing the shirts, boots and hairstyles of the players on his favourite game, FIFA 12, so they are exactly right. I sense how my shy little brother comes into his own when our talk turns to football and his idols' goals. I can see that he wants to become a pro and that he will need help, as I did. The world I broke into has changed and is tougher now.

I say to him, "What you see on TV is not a realistic representation of what it's like if you manage to break through." I shift our conversation towards the virtual world and my generation, asking if he knows about, *Olive et Tom, Champions de Foot*, a Japanese cartoon by manga artist Yôichi Takahashi (in Japan it was called *Captain Tsubasa* and in English *Flash Kicker*). It was hugely popular in France and I never missed it when I was a kid. This cartoon made a real impression on us back in the 1980s, especially young football fans like Thierry Henry, who I talked to the other day about that mythical bird, the Phoenix, and its multiple resurrections in Masami Kurumada's manga film, *Saint Seiya: Knights of the Zodiac*. I always refer back to it when I get injured, when my body snaps like wood. A few days after our conversation, Thierry displays a picture of Olivier Atton, the hero of *Olive et Tom*, in a Barça shirt, on his BlackBerry profile.

Thierry Henry: "Petit Louis, of course it was an inspiration, so cool. I didn't have much say when it came to my old man – he was ultra-strict and going out wasn't allowed. So TV was like going out to play. Olivier Atton v Marc Landers, or else that unbeatable goalie, Thomas Price."

The sight of Olivier dribbling up the pitch in a series of creative, skilful moves remains etched in my memory. As does the way the players seemed to take 10 minutes to cross the pitch as if it were a never-ending hill. A shot at goal could take so long that it would leave you in gut-wrenching suspense until the next episode. I'd go to school and two days later come back to the exact same moment with the goalie blocking the shot: swirling, super-powerful and unstoppable. "Wait . . . !" When I started to kick a ball myself, I was disappointed to realise it was only in a cartoon that you could ever make such a fierce impact and get away with such over-the-top gestures after scoring a goal. Fifteen years later, my brother grew up with the next series of *Olive et Tom*, and he had a similar experience to me as he too watched manga and gradually moved into professional football.

My brother and I are 12 years apart. So we are not close, despite the blood tie that is as strong between us as it is between all our relatives. The exponential rallying point in our family is sport. Competition is the pillar of success in life. Being different is one thing; to do the best with what we are given is everything.

My brother has lost that carefree quality which was always the source of my strength, and that of many of my team-mates back in the day. Wherever he goes, he will have to deal with the legacy of his family name, even if it isn't that of the great Pelé! Since I started to play football, everything in the game has changed: mentality, technology, respect, opinions, everything about the daily working life of a footballer has become tougher. The simplest things are often the hardest to do.

My brother and I talk through all that and more. We discuss the yellow card I received at a crucial point in my career. This example illustrates certain key points that I want him to understand. It was the 2006 World Cup quarter-final, France v Brazil. First yellow card: a warning. Then the semi-final, France v Portugal. Second yellow card: suspension. I am banned from the World Cup final. I try to express how that knot festering in your gut symbolises immense frustration, disappointment, shame, anger, pressure and desire all at once. What's all important in dealing with it is that unknown element, the "it" factor, which you have to find inside yourself. If you can master it, you've done half the job.

I describe to my brother how nauseous I felt as Lilian Thuram yelled angrily at me after my awkward tackle on Figo. My ears had disconnected. All I could see was a hazy silhouette and a wildly contorted mouth. The message did not get through. It was as if the carrier pigeon had hit the skyscraper in full flight.

Twelve thousand volts hit me with that second yellow card, but I could not lose face. I was supposed to be a professional and had to deal with any problematic situation and win. I lost the ball, yet was unable to react in my usual way. My throbbing head was trapped in the referee's pocket.

When the final whistle sounded, I became aware of the great tension that had been saturating my entire body during that World Cup semi-final. The pressure dropped, France had won the match and qualified for the final, but I was overwhelmed by disappointment which played havoc with my usually calm, controlled temperament.

The yellow card was stupid, but it showed how eager I was. I wanted to do too much, too well, because I was so frustrated at not being able to play regularly, having come off the bench in those two crucial games. I was super-motivated and determined. I was aggressive and boiling over with too much of everything. In a flash, I was looking for excuses for this incident.

At the time, I almost resented my team-mate Sylvain Wiltord for not telling me how he had felt as he watched me during our warm up before the Portugal semi-final. He was convinced I would get another card. But I don't hold it against him at all now. On the contrary, this incident was part of my apprenticeship, and I'm sure if he had warned me it would not have changed much, if anything. I had been stupid. So I ruminated in silence.

The two days before the final were bad, even though I was sure I would become a world champion. Everyone was focused on last-minute preparations, except me. In just a few days I had become a sidekick. For me, the dream was over. I would be up in the stands for the final, France v Italy. To this day, the match and the penalty shoot-out are still atrocious episodes in my memory. The worst thing, for me, was to see the Italians glorified. That was the greatest injustice of all.

Exactly seven days after my second yellow card, I slumped into depression at my mother-in-law's house. I may have been on holiday, but it was hard to smile. I love my mother-in-law, but my head lolled like a lead balloon while my soul went for a stroll in a ditch. My body moved like Casper the ghost. I spoke, but no one understood the vowel-less words that came out of my mouth. I finally snapped out of it 72 hours after the final, thanks to the second best moment of my life – when I became a father for the second time.

The birth of my son saved me from my torment. Enzo was my final; my trophy. There is no victory more beautiful than a child, but it was hard. This time it was up to my wife to choose the name. And she could do no better than pick an Italian one! Put it this way: had she called him Marco, I would have left the love of my life (it was Marco Materazzi who scored Italy's equaliser in the final and was then involved in the incident which ended with Zidane head-butting him and being sent off). How not to feel bitter about an Italian name for your kid? It's a tough call. Fortunately, the boy is handsome. I laugh about it today with my friend Domenico. His little one is called Vincenzo and mine Enzo Vince.

I was barely knee high to a grasshopper when I became a real football fan sometime between 1992 and 1995, thanks to the Paris St Germain team featuring George Weah, David Ginola and Raí. Watching them play, I saw everything I loved about the game: dribbling, goals and a burning desire to win. I have long believed that professional football should be based just on these three elements. Before you can have fun on a professional pitch you have to master these. It takes a lot of work, but I never want to forget that football is a game.

I made my professional football debut for Metz one evening in 1997. Tensions were running high. Nobody really knew how I'd get on alongside the professionals; the seniors; the elite. When a coach tells a young player he will be baptised in Ligue 1, the Bundesliga, La Liga or the Premier League, it's as though he will end up in front of his examiners. Every young player faces his destiny at some point. They were all waiting for us, ready to pass judgement on the true potential of our future careers. There might be other opportunities, but it is always wise to do your best because there are plenty of others lining up to have a go. Having the public as jury and the coach as supreme judge can be frightening, intimidating and paralysing. Everything could be over by the end of the night. In a few hours, me, the guy who didn't normally dare to talk too much or attract attention when we sat down for meals as a team, would have to become an exhibitionist.

I remember praying in my hotel room before the game. I had

the privilege of not having to share a room with another team-mate. I was uncertain but excited. In just a few hours I would be surrounded by thousands and might receive my diploma, my badge, my baptism. I remember coming on in the 90th minute and scoring in the 91st. It felt as though it was all happening in slow motion, allowing me to savour every second, every move-ment, in this very particular matrix which can only be understood when you've experienced it. I had scored my first goal as a young pro.

Each player lived it differently, but no one could say that those hours before our baptism lacked that special taste of privilege. The chance to play professional sport is a gift, but do not wait for it like you wait for Santa Claus.

I will never forget following the FIFA Confederations Cup on TV in 2003. My main recollection of this tournament is not France's victory thanks to Thierry Henry's goal in the 98th minute of the final against Cameroon, but an agonising image of a gentle yet incredibly powerful man collapsed on the ground, his eyes rolled back, in the middle of the semi-final. He was an exceptional football player. He had the face of a good man, with an angelic smile that you couldn't take your eyes off. His sudden death deprived us all from getting to know him. He left us aged 28, during a game when his Cameroon national team met Colombia at the Stade de Gerland in Lyon. Marc Vivien Foé left behind a wife and children and a football community in shock. Strangely, during half-time of this, his last match, he said these poignant words: "Guys, even if we have to die on the field, we must win this game." It's grim when a strong, young man out having fun on a football field dies of a heart attack. We all cried, and I remember my little brother was traumatised for a long time after this brutal incident.

A few years later I was actually on the pitch when Fabrice Muamba collapsed during an FA Cup match between Spurs and Bolton. We were all focused on the action, then I turned around and saw him lying still on the ground. My mind flashed back to that image of Marc Vivien Foé all those years ago. It was a shocking scene that makes you feel powerless – intensified by the sudden silence in the stadium followed by Bolton fans chanting 'Fabrice Muamba'. Thanks be to God that the cardiologist, Dr Andrew Deaner, happened to be sitting in the front stand and could help the club's doctors. What a miracle! The way they took control infused us with confidence and helped us to keep calm. On the pitch all we could do was pray as we held our heads in our hands. Pray 4 Muamba on twitter was a show of humanity, support and love, uniting everyone in our sport.

A professional player, rich or not, is a man like any other. At times fragile, alcoholic, angry, naïve, childish, depressed, sick, flamboyant, shy and more. His genes and his salary can spoil him, but he is far from being a robot. Illness and death have no frontiers. They strike when and where they like.

The suicide of that inspirational man, Gary Speed, was shocking. I found it hard to accept the death of such a well-respected, nice guy. He helped me when I was a kid freshly arrived on loan at Newcastle. I had a flash of awareness that I was being bullied with a 'welcome to England' tackle in one of my first games. A split second later I saw Gary Speed and Dietmar Hamman flying in with massive tackles as a warning to the opposition, "Don't touch the kid!" I will never forget it.

I salute those young players who died suddenly: French international David Di Tommaso, Cameroon's Marc Vivien Foé, Spain's Antonio Puerta, Hungary's Miklós Fehér, along with other deceased sportsmen. I want to remember them all and the immense distress caused, since, ultimately, football is just a game.

I see myself brought back to earth by that yellow card. I remember running around mindlessly, realising I would not take part in the final. I see everything and nothing. It's terrible, but it's not the end of the world.

2
INNER-CITY LIFE: BACK TO MY ROOTS

There are at least 190 countries, with around 6,000 languages, on our beautiful planet. Many customs and cultures to be discovered. Millions of beautiful postcards to send to friends. There are also less-glamorous spots with no greenery and tower blocks that almost tickle the clouds.

Countless council estates and rural villages in France and other countries are full of potential young prodigies. Great musicians, singers, businessmen and athletes emerge from these narrow streets screaming with frustration. The mean streets that are snubbed, ignored and left wanting. The underprivileged are hamstrung by difficult conditions. Some of the lucky ones who are more talented, more athletic, or more motivated and who are better supported will one day discover magnificent sites and stadiums around the world. Their stories are different other than for one detail; they have a single passion. For me it was for a football, for others it may be for a tennis ball, or a piano.

From Carlos Tevez who comes from Fuerte Apache in Argentina, to Ji-Sung Park, the Korean from Suwon's tropical landscape, like me they derive intense feelings of pleasure from this spherical object waiting to be mastered. For a young person constantly searching for an identity and new friends, the camaraderie underpinning the game is extraordinary. It's a never-ending sharing of skill and pleasure with his team-mates and his opponents. Being from the inner city intensifies all this and helps forge those special links that create a perfect synergy for a footballer.

Affluent, leafy, smart suburbs like Versailles, Le Vésinet, or Neuilly-sur-Seine (where Nicolas Sarkozy served as Mayor from 1983 to 2002) which surround the heart of Paris with its 20 *arrondissements* are a world away from the low-income housing of the *banlieue* (suburbs on the outer edge of the city) where *Les Cités* (high-rise estates) sprang up in the 1960s, each with a population of around 17,000 inhabitants. Eight million people live in the *banlieue* on the outskirts of Paris: its 'outer' rather than 'inner' city. They are similar to low-income neighbourhoods in the United States like Cypress Hills in east New York and Compton in Los Angeles. Genuine opportunities for ambitious young people are hard to come by, which is particularly problematic since a high proportion of kids and adolescents live in *Les Cités*. The commune of Sarcelles in the northern *banlieue* of Paris has high unemployment and a rough reputation, but it is wrong to assume all high-rise estates are the same.

The French inner city has a caricature image. Graffitied tower blocks and subterranean walkways. Cliffs of grey concrete. Violence, cars burning, public buildings torched, schools vandalised. It's all played up by the media and used by politicians. What's the reality? In my neighbourhood in south-west Paris, Soisy-sous-Montmorency, tower blocks of around eight to 20 floors. Here you will find an entire community trying to move forward in the face of serious problems. Some struggle to make ends meet and feed their families. Some make headway regardless of the law and the dangers involved. Money is tight. These difficulties are hard to think about or understand from afar. Sometimes people do things that cannot be approved of or justified, however tough life is, even if it's understandable in the circumstances. But the inner city has its success stories. Famous or not, these people set an example which can also embellish the image of a rough estate. Meanwhile, the vast majority battle on unnoticed. It's the minority which smashes up the place and make headline news. That's how it is.

In today's inner city, respect for the elders has all but disappeared, so it's important for parental authority to be fair and coherent. A child has to learn respect when they're young, later on it's too late. My parents didn't do too badly in their choice of neighbourhood; others had no alternative. For Pat Evra, Thierry Henry and Sinik, the rapper, it was Les Ulis in the south-western *banlieue* of Paris. For Zinédine, it was Castellane in northern Marseille. For Ji-Sung born in Seoul, Korea's teeming capital, it was Suwon in the south; for Steven Pienaar, it was Westbury, a township on the outskirts of Johannesburg in South Africa.

Patrice Evra: "Louis, for me the neighbourhood was like a second family which enriched and shaped me. It's thanks to her that I have a strong character. Hard-knock life prepared me for the professional world. The spirit of the streets is what has given me my strength; without it I wouldn't have sweated blood. Nothing came for free, nothing came easy, except solidarity. I learned not to throw in the towel. I was sometimes surprised by the cheap shots you have to bear in the world of football. When I left Les Ulis, the anger on the streets came with me, I was hungry and full of an inner rage to succeed."

Zinédine speaks to me in that legendary Marseille accent we all love: "Me, Petit Louis? I had a group of 15 mates. We all had the same burning desire to play football. In Marseille's northern district, you could be tempted to do stupid things, but not us; no one smoked, or did any funny business. All we wanted was to play football. I'd say to myself that for inner-city kids like us, it was the only escape. I didn't do great at school and didn't really want to, although I regret it now that I have kids. I had one thing in mind: get out and play football. For that, I had an inner rage to succeed."

For me, lovely Soisy-sous-Montmorency was my refuge, my yardstick, my stability, my prison at times, and at others a source of embarrassment when I had to say its name. Picture yourself making eyes at a girl from one of the chic *arrondissements* of Paris and telling her: "I live in Noyers-Crapaud," (which literally means "Toads Under the Walnut Tree"). That was the name of the high-rise estate I lived on. Things had looked promising, but with this little announcement you have just cut your chance of success by 30 per cent. Unless you were a dead ringer for Brad Pitt, you would be given the vicious elbow. I wonder if the people who chose the name of this estate despised the people who settled there. I've heard that the name has been changed now. Could it be because of local pressure? We were spoiled with a fairly modern community & sports centre. I have other reasons to believe that the community was disrespected, given the name of that venue: "Campanules", which means "Camp for the Hopeless". It's better than, say, "The Happy Pig", but it's irritating, given the number of talented, beautiful, funny and intelligent people who live in the area, even if it's a while since I went back.

The crime rate is about 54 incidents per 1,000 inhabitants; the lowest in the Val d'Oise département which extends westwards from the north east of Paris. Soisy-sous-Montmorency was and still is far from being the Bronx, Manchester's Moss Side, or even Sarcelles. For those who know the Val d'Oise, we were five minutes from Montmorency forest, 25 minutes from Charles de Gaulle Airport, five minutes from Lake Enghien-les-Bains, and 20 minutes from the Champs Elysées if there were no traffic jams.

I wonder if those in power – such as those who are elected to office or become CEOs – are reassured somehow by the misfortune of others, as though it helps bolster their success. I'm almost afraid that I have behaved like this myself. Perhaps I have not done enough for my neighbourhood, or for the people living there. I certainly did what I could for my parents after being signed up by FC Metz: I got them to leave Noyers-Crapaud to live in a semi, close to our local football stadium. Then, thanks to my transfer to Manchester United, I moved them on again to

Enghien-les-Bains, the well-to-do suburb north of Paris developed in the 19th century around the pretty lake of Enghien, with its spa, casinos and beautiful walks. I have done what I could for the wellbeing of my family, but I have not done much for the place where I grew up, especially when it comes to young people. For them, perhaps, I have forgotten my childhood. But I haven't. If I told you everything I can remember it would make a series of short stories or comic films.

There are the good people; there are the not so good. Crime exists everywhere in France, but we're talking here about the inner city. We all judge without knowing and let prejudice do its damage. The neighbourhood and its impulsive, fearless spirit has served all of us footballers from the inner city. It has meant we could play without hang-ups or doubts. At times, thanks to this bullish mindset, we managed to raise our game and turn a situation to our advantage, but this spirit is not without its flaws. Sometimes you can get caught up in a high-pressure or complex situation whether you're in training, or during a major tournament. Being stubborn and unwilling to compromise can be disruptive for the team and coaching staff. Unlike a showdown in the inner city, in football sticking to your guns can backfire, so sometimes it's best to put the gun down. Of course, we all have our faults, regardless of whether we are from the inner city, or a beautiful place.

The route followed by Patrice Evra from his neighbourhood to France's national football team is a source of great pride to him. He says: "Despite the temptations and vices of the mean streets, I don't want my image to be 'bad boy saved by football.' I see guys sweating blood under the tower blocks, and I tell myself 'don't mess up this good thing because I'm bored or satisfied to excess'. I respect where I come from and keep my feet on the ground because of it. I'm still hungry for what the neighbourhood led me to discover."

I can still see myself, aged six or seven, waiting alone on a bench in front of the icy ground of my local team, Soisy-Andilly-Margency. The stadium was a 10-minute stroll from my estate, where the tower blocks were often too high to enjoy the beautiful blue sky from the ground. I stayed at least an hour on this uncomfortable cold stone seat, before finally deciding to take the first step as my father had instructed, and ask Madame Sylvestre for a club registration form. I was extremely shy and reserved, but found what courage I could in my small frame, and went for it. I was impatient to join my friends, Domenico and Stéphane Divol, and play on the rough, red cinder pitch. This gritty, unstable surface must have been the worst nightmare for all those parents whose kids came home with grazed legs or faces. But it was worth it if it meant I could practise my favourite sport. Whatever the surface or space, we played. Beautiful pitches with a soft synthetic surface, causing fewer injuries, have since become popular in place of the rough surfaces we played on back then.

The first years you're signed up to your local club are usually the most fun and carefree. You play without worrying about objectives and issues. There is no better way to have a laugh and build relationships than to be with a bunch of mates on a sports ground. This stays with you for life. Players sharing their feelings – that is the essence of team sport. Running and yelling. Choosing sides and going for it so your team-mates see how much you're part of the group. Dummying defenders. Scoring so half-time is more fun. This mindset must stay in the head of all players, no matter what age or level.

At this time there is no pressure, unless parents push their little prodigy. Since the magnificent occasion of France winning the 1998 World Cup, parents have realised that success can be found in a stadium. The secret dream of all French fathers who are football supporters is to see a crowd of fanatical fans waving the tricolore surrounding their son in a bus covered with ticker-tape and party streamers, escorted by the police.

A boy's love for the game can be judged by the number of

hours he talks about it, plays with his ball and watches matches to learn new flicks, tricks, special moves and how long he carries on when most of his friends have moved on to something else.

Back in those naïve days, I was so nuts about the game that there was no way I was going to swap my football for the bag of marbles and baseball cap that I wanted so badly. So, instead of my lucky ball, I traded my brand new BMX bike! I remember my father shouting at me, "You jackass!", then running after the guy who had managed to get the bike off me as I stood there happy with my loot.

When I was 10, three or four of us from the team would stay on in the changing room after hours of training where we'd have fun shooting between benches, or playing 2 v 2 games which always ended with me coming home late and getting a telling off. We'd play until the moonlight told us it was time to go home. My parents have always been very tough. They were very strict about my time-keeping and going out; tough about school marks. When I came home late I'd be grounded. When I did so again and again and despite the consequences, I realised I was hooked. Despite my parent's rage I couldn't stop myself. They quickly understood that blackmail worked best. They knew that to deprive me of training or worse, a match, would drive me crazy. Locked in my room, I would get hysterical while my mates who'd come to pick me up waited at the foot of the tower block. Friends pressurised each other's parents to let them off doing homework so they could play football instead. Many friends tell the same story.

Patrice Evra: "On the days our teacher was off sick from eight to nine in the morning, I'd ask my friends to come at eight o'clock anyway to play a six-a-side on the school's synthetic turf. I even trained in the snow when most of my friends were chatting about girls. For me it was football. I was hooked."

My career as a young, inner-city player began with small matches that became more and more exciting. Before that, as was undoubtedly the case for the little Argentine in Fuerte Apache, or the Korean in Suwon's tropical landscape, I would juggle my ball for hours and hours and even sleep with it. It was as though I wanted to hurt it when I smashed it in the back of the net.

I picture a young African in his village playing with no shoes, the arch of his foot thickened. He is unharmed by stones. Like many other future prodigies, he presents his ball to his new friends, but shares it as little as possible. When these boys cannot find a way to pass and dribble across the ground, instead of feeling bad about it they try out Maradona's spin, a Cruyff turn, or a step over. Such are the spirit and rules of street football. These boys feel like they have grown wings when it comes to controlling their ball. As each one tries out the best technical moves he saw on the previous night's TV, he pictures himself in a huge stadium with delirious fans chanting his name, even though he is just playing on a small wire-fenced basketball court at the foot of a tower block. He won't let up until he's in control of his prized pigskin. He dreams of his idol: Zidane, Maradona, Ronaldo, Pelé or even that retired old pro, his father. This little prodigy becomes enthusiastic when football comes up in the conversation and especially when he is told he has the "it" factor. These images remain indelibly strong.

Ah! Those happy memories of tournaments followed by a tasty *merguez* sandwich. This spicy mutton-or-beef sausage was a reward in itself. To go to the cafeteria at half-time at my club, Soisy, was a special moment, especially when I had enough cash on me for a packet of crisps as well. Ways and means to get by were usually found. Everyone can look back and say what fun they had, despite them and their family putting up with years of financial struggle.

Parents play a key role in a player's progression. An example is the phenomenon that is Thierry Henry: the best striker in French football and the Premier League for many seasons. He was formed by the intense discipline of his perfectionist father

who was excessively demanding, but it was these exacting standards that helped shape the King of French football. Watching the
result today, I ask myself if these demands really were so
excessive?

Henry, a.k.a. "Titi", says it himself: "If it hadn't been for him,
perhaps I wouldn't have succeeded. When my friends were out,
I was at home with no choice but to do my homework or go and
train. It was one or the other. But today, I've no complaints."

I'm sure he still would've made it, but perhaps he wouldn't
have been catapulted quite so quickly into world champion status
as he was in 1998. This is what forges that fearless mentality of
steel on the pitch which makes a champion; those special beings
like Maradona and Zidane, or even Gascoigne, despite his
tormented private life.

Titi says: "You know my old man believes in strict Caribbean-
style education. He was the one who took me to training and
brought me home only when he was satisfied with what he had
seen me achieve on the field. He passed on to me his obsessive
perfectionism. Petit Louis, it was a tough call. Bro, you know
what I'm saying. We did it together, although at first it wasn't
really for yourself that you did it. For me, it was just to see a
smile spread across my father's tensed-up face. I quickly acquired
a taste for victory, scoring goals and trophies."

Thierry became an obsessive perfectionist, stubbornly focused
on putting the ball in the back of the net. People who do not
know him say he is arrogant, or does not behave as one should
on the field, but each of us has our own kind of self-expression.
The point is the desire to succeed, not idle talk. People will chat;
nothing can be done about it. Everyone has a different past to
his neighbour. Just look on the internet at some of Henry's 200
goals with the Gunners at Arsenal. You admire the first 70 goals,
but after 150 you begin to wonder when it will all end. You start
to sense the effects of scoring so much, each season. Scoring
masterpieces one weekend after the other, one season after the

other, one international match after the other, victory after victory, trophy after trophy . . . Looking at a Thierry Henry top goals montage on YouTube, I get a sense of the invincibility, of feeling like a super-hero, that must have surged through Titi's veins when he dribbled through Liverpool's defence – which falls away when faced by their worst nightmare – to score one of his famously unstoppable right-foot shots. Or when his friend from the French team, Fabien Barthez, can only stand back and admire Henry's control of the ball as he volleys a lightning-quick shot that smashes home into the top corner of the net, past a defence in disarray.

Had Tony Henry's son had a less robust mindset, his entire career could have been completely different. My father was dismayed that Raymond Domenech showed such disrespect to such a player by not bringing him on for a farewell appearance for his country at the 2010 World Cup. It was baffling. Killer Henry! What a career!

Every Sunday, my father would take me to watch his football team, AS PTT, play. He was a defender. Wherever he played, I always found another kid, a group, or a wall to train against. He took me to practise on the sweeping plain of La Courneuve in the north-eastern *banlieue*, where I'd juggle the ball with both feet or my head. He taught me the spirit of competition by way of simple challenges like doing keep-ups with my weaker foot and other exercises. Without realising, he injected me with a harmless but aggressive virus that developed from year to year.

The love of the game means accepting its challenges as well as its beauty. Success seems to come easily to some. Certain players create an illusion of effortlessness as they go after what others can only dream of, although in reality their goals are achieved by them alone through sheer hard work. The most important quality for a footballer today is the will to succeed. The game has become so popular that the number of competitors vying to show they have what it takes makes the ascent of a good player to the top rung of professional football more difficult and dangerous. Inner cities are full of families with one, or even two, gifted boys who inevitably become increasingly impatient and hot-blooded and are still ruled by the codes of inner-city life. Super-determined kids with a fierce ambition to succeed, they are highly motivated, keen to enjoy the good life that they believe should be theirs, but which they feel is denied them. To have fire in the belly like this is an advantage as it sets these young players apart from the rest, enabling them to break through. But it can also stop them from making the right decisions, or from behaving impeccably, as is required of a footballer today.

It is inspiring to watch the passion of a young neighbourhood player in action, completely unconcerned about his talent or where it could take him. For them, like me, any surface can be played on. I have marks that look like the top of a pizza on the sides of my thighs as souvenirs of time spent playing on a certain rough, red, gritty surface.

In each high-rise estate there is generally a play area in the middle of the complex so kids from any tower block have instant access to it. These young hopefuls may not be technically gifted, but their simple, imaginative actions get the adrenaline going and create a lot of fun and togetherness. The friendships forged here and the feeling of making all the difference to a team are important factors in building self-worth. To tackle is as much fun as playmaking for some. Each to his pleasure.

A young player shows off his technical skills and his temperament on an inner-city sports area. Whatever his state of mind, when he is with his mates, he forgives and forgets, lets go of the pain and the fuckeries of life around him. He forgets about those long nights with no lights or TV and hustling for cash. He almost forgets delinquency, if that's what it is, because the real crime is not always where people say it is.

The real gangsters are all-powerful. They cleverly manipulate the negative image of the inner city and use the brashest kids or youngest rebels to hide their magic tricks. Billions of pounds can go walkabout when it comes to a major scam in the world of big business. But when it comes to a decent family, all you need is a couple of unpaid bills and everyone's on your case.

In the 'hood you think you're invincible: truth is, you're fragile. Things can go wrong even when you aren't looking for trouble. You may not always be the best, but you laugh out loud! Simple things make you happy. All you want is to come back from school and show how well you're doing, how you can control the ball better than anyone. You want compliments, to be first choice in local youth football tournaments; you want a superhero's nickname, and to hear "Wow!" as you dribble past your opponents. All you want is to play and have fun.

Whether you're sweating it or winging it, you'll soon find out if you've got what it takes to beat the competition. More than likely, you'll come up against two or three big guns who are faster and much more powerful than you. To exaggerate, to ridicule and mock opponents typifies the spirit of an inner-city football player. There is fair play, but things can quickly degenerate. Pull a clever trick or a good joke on a player in a bad mood and you will get aggressive tackles and high-kicks coming your way. Improve your game so that one day you can teach the big boys a lesson in football: that is how you deal with them.

From the first to the last in class, the oldest to the youngest, the fattest to the thinnest, the playboy to Quasimodo, the most delinquent to the most virtuous: they're all nuts about football. Back in the day, a computer or a games console was a luxury, so kids had no choice but to pitch up on the small patch of urban land that served as a stadium. Less athletic types ended up in the sandpit.

All or nothing: that's what inner-city life is like. There is no middle ground, as there is in the smart 16th *arrondissement* of Paris or other magnificent parts of the world where the poor are never invited in and are snubbed for not having succeeded.

Inner-city life: everyone becomes attached to the big guns. Their powerful personalities provoke as much laughter as fear.

Inner-city life: as you grow up, you want respect. Some try to get it through violence, others by playing Don Juan. Everybody wants it, one way or another, and to impress. I was neither Quasimodo nor a gangster, sport was my thing. Winning is good, but to win and play brilliantly is the ultimate. I'm a natural-born competitor, which goes with being a bad loser. How I hate to lose! And to play badly. If I had to choose between the two, I'd go for playing badly. Let's say that it's harder to accept losing because I can't do anything about it. But my performance will improve after five or six hours of extra training. Only victory truly satisfies me.

Inner-city life: is being part of a group, united and ready to go to war together. Knowing that nobody will do a u-turn at the crucial moment is an advantage over any adversary. It's accepting very different personalities; different colours, traditions and cultures and making a team.

Back in the 19th century, football was the poor man's sport, whereas the rich played cricket, tennis or rugby. Being a player in the inner city or the slums can be a real advantage for becoming a pro. I'm not suggesting you disinherit your children, treat them mean to keep them keen, but think about it . . .

One day my son, Enzo, checked out the Parisian three-room apartment that we had just finished decorating, and turned to his mother looking very surprised, "Mum," he said. "Where's the games room?" He is already used to luxury. To be so spoiled at just four years old is not great. The teeth of his ambition may well be harder to sharpen than those of a kid from a rough estate.

Back to my Roots

So much misery exists all around the world. We are bombarded with images of slums, famine, destruction and wars in impoverished countries for which the outcome is not always advantageous, even for for their wealthy presidents. People are not living, but just surviving in these societies. Those who can make a difference are anaesthetised by endless dirty, bloody news reports, each more heartbreaking than the last. When I look at the French inner city and compare it to an African or Indian ghetto, I consider myself lucky to have lived in a first-class council estate.

My childhood was super-cool and rewarding, but my family and my story do not begin during a heat wave in Paris on 8 August 1978, but the day my ancestors rebelled against slavery and oppression. And when they decided to form a new language: Creole. They kept this warrior temperament, this fighting spirit, and were ready to face any challenge with pride.

Slavery has left an indelible trauma, but also an undeniable strength and athleticism which can clearly be seen in so many great, talented Caribbean sportsmen. Thierry Henry, Nicolas Anelka, William Gallas, Lilian Thuram, Gaël Monfils, Marie José Perec, Teddy Riner, Philippe Christanval, Jean-Marc Mormeck, Ronny Turiaf, and others. They are the jewels of the Caribbean sporting crown. This impressive array of talent from overseas is a paradox. How come such a small population from just a few islands has produced so many world-class sportsmen? Maybe there are more vitamins in the Caribbean because of the sun? Maybe because life is harder, there is more of an incentive to go and seek your fortune? It's impressive to see so many players of Caribbean ancestry in the French national squad. It's a source of pride to have reached such a level when I picture my parents flying to Paris with nothing but the shirts on their backs. These two young people left Guadeloupe behind them and headed for the big city, feeling proud to work for France. They had left the countryside where for my father, going to the movies meant drilling a hole in the partition wall of the neighbour's house to watch their TV. This mischievous eye peering through a hole in the wall is symbolic of his desire for better things in life. This desire was never expressed through jealous words or behaviour, but by pride, willpower and determination to succeed. This young couple was convinced the good things of life could be gained through hard work. Now my parents have a widescreen TV. One thing is sure, when it comes to strength and staying power, to have the genes of slaves is an asset for today's international players. Research has shown that the genes of a person who suffered trauma during his life can mutate and be transmitted to his descendants. So a man who was humiliated, or was harmed, can pass on a phobia or certain character traits to his children or grandchildren. Ancestral courage and determination enable the black race to flourish, and find that "extra something" in the minds and bodies of these athletes.

I can't imagine the young people of today working from dawn in those vast 19th-century fields of sugar cane, overwhelmed by scorching heat and without modern 21st-century machines. My ancestors worked like animals. I would not have survived, but they did. It's thanks to them that I could have fun on that rough, red, gritty surface. Without them, I would have no right to tell you about my childhood, which is recounted with the utmost respect for their history and that of my parents, as well as a desire not to disappoint. Progress has been made on the road to freedom, but certain scars remain unhealed because of prejudice, as with the Jews who will forever live with the trauma of the Holocaust. It is a sensitive issue and many institutions are fighting to commemorate the horrors inflicted on Black, Jewish, Arab and other races. I fight from the inside out, so that my children never forget that I am black, African-Caribbean and proud of it. Since I've never had a thrashing at the hands of a colonialist, I've got nothing to complain about. I just use the platform built by my ancestors with their blood; the gene of slavery.

Tim Cahill, who plays for Everton, has a work of art tattooed on his right arm, from the shoulder down to the wrist, which illustrates his family history and culture. He was born in Sydney, Australia, to a Samoan mother and an English father of Irish descent and had his tattoo done in Samoa to celebrate his roots.

All his strength and determination come from his family. Samoans are huge with a Herculean strength that has flowed down through the generations. Legendary New Zealand rugby superstar, Jonah Lomu, and Hollywood actor, Dwayne Johnson, whose mother is of Samoan descent, are considered huge when away from their homeland, but in the Polynesian islands they are average-sized men.

Tim Cahill: "I draw all my strength from my family and my roots. Because of all the efforts they have made, I never let up."

Tim is actually not big, or very stocky, but he makes up for the height he gives away to others. Look at him play and you realise the power of his monstrous mentality. He is an example for all young people who want to succeed. Experienced players like him provide important points of reference, whether at school, a football academy, or in the professional world facing the public.

I am proud to be French, but my ancestors are not the likes of General de Gaulle and Louis XVI. Being proud to be French does not mean learning by heart *The Fables of La Fontaine*, the story of Napoleon Bonaparte, or eating *foie gras*, however much I love the French countryside with those small villages and their old stone streets, the charm of the little church and its local legends.

I always burst out laughing when my father describes arriving in France and his story about eating Dijon mustard for the first time. He was used to chillis and Caribbean scotch bonnet peppers, but not familiar with the yellow condiment he noticed on the side of his new co-workers' plates. He was their guest. Polite and friendly, he asked for some mustard like everyone else to accompany his succulent sirloin steak. Everyone seemed to savour this seemingly harmless yellow relish, so he smeared a generous amount on to his first mouthful in front of his new friends – with all the confidence of a man used to Caribbean spices. The mustard burned up his nose and his eyes lost their twinkle, turning an angry red as though about to explode. My old man did not want to lose face in front of his colleagues. For the pride of West Indian spices, he tried everything to contain this internal shock, but the mustard got the better of him. A long drawn-out "Aaaaahhh" surprised the whole table, making everyone smile.

I love watching people play *pétanque* [a form of *boules*] and having a laugh as they enjoy their *apéritif*, and as I have got older I have learned to love music other than zouk, rap, or raï. Francis Cabrel, Daniel Balavoine, Charles Aznavour, Pablo Picasso and many other French artists I like symbolise my attachment to my homeland. Although Charles Aznavour is of Armenian origin and Pablo Picasso Spanish, France was able to adopt them, as she does her athletes.

Here is my dream, today: that my kids succeed in education where I failed because of wasting time messing about with friends and having a laugh. Picture this, a vision of the future as told by my son:

"I was a model student. The girls thought I was a playboy. The teachers thought I was a brainbox. In 5th form, I skipped a class and still passed my exams with flying colours. Today I'm a successful engineer or footballer. I want to thank you, Dad, Mum with this little gift."

I would then say to him, "Thank you, son." This will be, I hope, my children's story.

I was a restless student. Frankly, I had a tough time concentrating. The lack of interesting subjects about the varied origins of French history meant it was hard to get motivated. Although our text books intrigued me, like many of my mates I had that classic question hanging in the air: where are the West Indians, Arabs, or Africans? Did they all arrive as immigrants, or as a result of France having colonies? Why not help school kids from diverse backgrounds better understand their part in French history? This would facilitate true integration. Why not tell us about Toussaint L'Ouverture and the slave revolt in Haiti, or the fate of black people during the Holocaust? What about Aimé

Cesaire, the poet and politician who was one of the founders of the négritude movement in Francophone literature? Or Frantz Fanon, the philosopher and writer – admired by Jean-Paul Sartre – whose work remains influential in the field of post-colonial studies? Or Gisèle Pineau, the award-winning novelist and former psychiatric nurse? These subjects were never covered, thereby creating today's malaise with the French flag which is so often booed at the Stade de France before an international football match. This may be a simplistic explanation, but it has consequences, especially since the far-right party of Jean Marie Le Pen monopolises the national flag as its logo. One cannot see a blue-white-red flag fluttering over the roof of a house without it provoking mixed feelings.

I struggled to understand, so I ended up making the same mistake as most kids. I refused to retain, or memorise and only half listened to what I was taught. I foolishly boycotted the whole process. Fortunately, I had no time to rebel against an inadequate school system which fails to stimulate the enthusiasm of its students. Since I left school I have had no need for geometry or the Pythagoras theory.

Today, I regret my behaviour. Back then I did not have the maturity or benefit of hindsight to appreciate the situation. I regret not having stored up as much information as possible in order to pass it all on to my kids. Now I know I must develop my general knowledge, for them and for me. On my journey from the inner city to the Institut National du Football (INF) de Clairefontaine, I struggled to understand why it was important to be a good student. I made a choice. Today, seeing the failure of some of my friends, I realise I could easily have got burned.

Back then, to talk of defeat and failure was a sign of weakness. Had I lost my gamble that I could succeed in life without a university degree, I would have had to conform to the system. Pat, Cristiano, Wayne, Zizou, Carlos, Titi, me and many others had to take a risk and go for it, without being afraid of returning to sit in the front entrance of our high-rise, as many of our mates did. We took this risk thanks to our confidence and a carefree, reckless attitude. This touch of madness is necessary as it blinds you to the injustice that prevails today in the world of work, and the difficulties of getting a good job which enables one to live properly. Properly, meaning, having just enough money to shop and to eat; being able to afford a good holiday and look in the mirror with pride.

An impoverished little French, Spanish, Swedish, American or other kid in the West still has greater flexibility to get by in life than a young African. Dreaming the impossible dream of becoming a football star means that Africans from Cameroon, Zambia, Togo, Ivory Coast, or elsewhere on that great continent have little other choice than to get wasted. The journey of big chief Didier Drogba is every man's African Dream. This is where misery transforms a young European's Christmas wish list into the dream of a lifetime for a young African. Wealth, priorities, laws, needs and dreams are not the same everywhere. Football is often the only way out. I thank God I was born in the right place for my dreams to come true.

France has a wonderful climate, beautiful monuments, superb landscapes. But France also represents everything to do with 'French Algeria' – the colonial state that ended in 1962 after a long and brutal war – and the plight of *les pieds noirs* (Algerian-born French). It is the country that fought two world wars with Senegalese riflemen fighting for the tricolour flag. It is a paradoxical country with a long history of conquest, yet one that has a culture envied by people around the world, many of whom are jealous of the birthplace of Human Rights.

France adopted me, it's true, but my sporting talent made it easier. I am proud to be French. I speak the language, eat the cuisine, drive on the right and support any French team in international tournaments. The French are considered to be elegant, gourmet, charming and lovers of all that is good in life. My France is: Paris, Metz, Cannes and St Anne in Guadeloupe, which I know a little less, perhaps, than those other cities. I say it with pride to envious foreigners as it is my identity. My France: I love it and would not trade it for anything.

France is an extraordinary country, even if it is flawed. I speak English, but my accent always exposes my origins. My personal France is only 32 years old, but it's a continuation of the story of my parents' generation, which is diametrically opposite to François Mitterrand's, with his devout Roman Catholic, conservative background and mother related to Pope John XXII. There's no way my parents were going to scatter Easter eggs down the stairs of our tower block, or around the cemetery that was considered our garden. In Guadeloupe, pine trees were impossible to find, and no one garlanded palm trees with Christmas decorations. As for a sled, let's not even go there! It's only years later, in France, that my parents would marvel at the gifts we could offer to our children. Truth is, I consider myself to be a child of the world.

Thierry: "I'm going to live in the States but when someone speaks badly of France, I answer frankly and directly, it's stronger than me."

My roots have a very important place in my heart. For this reason, I've never allowed to myself to say to my parents, "I have the right to . . ." because they raised me and cared for me. Everyone has their own way of educating and teaching their children good manners. My father was always given respect in the streets, not just at home. He was friendly yet commanded respect because he was straight-talking and confident. True, he was strong and people were a little scared of him too. He liked to have a laugh and never insulted anybody. Because of that young people left him alone.

It's hard to forget the countless times I had problems at school because a teacher dared to criticise my strict upbringing. It was intolerable to me that my teachers, who I was sure had not gone through as many difficulties as my parents, indulged in harsh criticism while I admired my parent's efforts to build me a future. I was accused of being distracted and talkative. Some teachers even went so far as to say my parents were educating me all wrong and implied they were uncaring. My parents could hardly have been more attentive to my daily life as a schoolboy. Such criticism was unbearable knowing how my father and mother got up so early and worked hard to feed their family; knowing how my mother did back-breaking work lifting old people in and out of their beds all day. For all I knew, those OAPs were related to my teachers!

Life is hard, vicious and sometimes unscrupulous. My parents suffered yet never complained. I was a hyperactive kid bursting with energy and was expected to do certain chores to ease my parents' daily life. During their struggles, they always kept an unwavering faith in God and our family in Guadeloupe, who were even further in the gutter yet managed somehow to send us one or two large notes to get us out of trouble. How could I accept criticism of my parents who slapped me if I was just one minute late? Later, I came to realise that they protected me and enabled me to follow a less tortuous route than many of my peers who I envied at the time.

I got slapped for things that make me laugh now as an adult. Don't believe parents read a so-called "perfect parenting" manual at the birth of their child! As for the little Argentine or Korean footballer, it all depends on family history, character and his understanding of the world around him. My father and mother taught me boundaries. If parents don't do that, their child learns to be a burden to others. Respect for elders and their experience allowed us to grow and evolve. It's a shame that some young people today think they know more than their elders because of the internet; because of Twitter, Facebook and especially Google. The web is a wonderful tool, but no emotions are transmitted through the keyboard.

I recently read a nice story in a newspaper. A man standing in a supermarket queue is idly watching a small boy and his mother ahead of him. The little brat keeps on pushing the shopping trolley into the ankles of the lady in front. After several polite requests to stop, the lady asks the mother to talk to her child. To everyone's surprise, the mother has nothing better to say than the fact that she never forbids her son anything because it's all part of his development. The man observing the incident is furious and longs to box the little brat's ears. He opens a pot of jam and pours it over the mother's head. Enraged, she has no time to complain, as the man explains: "Sorry, but me too! I was never ticked off as a child and was allowed to empty pots of jam on people's heads." The cashier offers the man a new pot of jam.

What do 10-year-old kids dream of today? The new iPhone or the latest computer game? Showing off their latest Nike footwear so they can feel as grown up as the other kids who have their own latchkey to get back in late at night? At that age, details like this make all the difference. You feel like a man and, naïvely, think that you've got one over on your old man. Today, parents are more open-minded and relaxed about the way society and its new gadgets have evolved. Marbles have been replaced by PlayStation 3, and fine collections of beautiful poetry have been bastardised by text messaging. Annihilation with the game "Angry Birds" is preferred to building a Lego model, or a puzzle. It's a shame the way kids living on council estates in Britain are banned from kicking a ball around outside their house or high rise. "No Ball Games" is such a familiar sign that it's even been satirised by graffiti artist, Banksy. Obviously troublemakers smashing the place up with a ball are a no-no, but football on the streets is not a bad thing. Especially as people are worried about kids getting obese and staying indoors playing computer games instead of running around outside.

Parents' views about football have also evolved. My grandfather stopped my father from playing football when he finished working in the cane fields. My old man walked for miles to go to school and laboured in the fields all week, but kicking a pigskin was not allowed, especially on Holy Saturday. Football was considered frivolous. Boys were expected to find a trade not a hobby. At the time, many talented kids were subject to parental authority and abandoned their dreams. All family members, especially the boys, had to bring in the cash.

Today, parents believe in the money and notoriety that football generates. Some sign up their kid and yell at the coach who just lets him have fun. Kids' football has become a very serious business. Parents spend a fortune on their boy, who very likely would prefer to play the game on his Playstation than on a great green field, as there is no need to run. It's much less tiring and there's just as much teasing to do between winners and sore losers. Many people feel trapped by our material culture. Parents feel guilty about not being able to give their children enough. Because of the extra hours of work necessary in order to live decently there is little time to be together as a family. Football, parents and the inner city have changed.

The inner city is bathed in frustration and doubtless will blow up one day. So there are even more emerging talents. New mutants: younger, larger, more insane, more technical, beefier, more informed, more determined than before, but less innocent. They look less cheerful, almost blasé. The neighbourhood may be an economic failure, but it's still a tremendous source of talent.

3
THE STAR
ACADEMY, OR
SC MARSALA?

You got the "it" factor?

Luck. Talent. Lots of hard work. The "it" factor. If you want to become a footballer you need the lot to be spotted by a scout, or a coach from a professional football club. You've got to be as good as it gets on D-Day. That day when the scout has decided to drive 60 miles to see the little guy known as "The Rocket". And then there's the player known for his "sweet left foot", or the defender known as "The Steamroller".

The "it" factor sets the little guy apart from the other players. Aggression, fighting spirit, technique, power, a good mindset and vision of the game; speed and being skilled at passing and tackling; a powerful shot and goal-scoring . . . these are the qualities the experts look out for like gold dust.

Experienced scouts assess young players' potential and decide what will happen. Time speeds by even faster these days, so you have to grab your chance because more and more young hopefuls are trying to break into the very lucrative football market. However much everyone loves sport for its own sake, it's not enough.

At a very young age, I was lucky and honoured to be part of several local and regional squads. I have an extraordinary early memory of the Parc des Princes, home of Paris Saint-Germain. I was selected to play at the world-famous stadium for a team consisting of the best 12 to 13-year-old kids in the Paris region.

The clash between us and the children of former French football legends like Jean Tigana and Jean-Michel Larqué was part of the celebrations for the anniversary of the Variety Club of France – originally the Variety Football Club – which regularly puts on fundraising matches at the legendary stadium off the Boulevard Périphérique, one of the busiest roads in Europe. The VCF has helped out numerous charities and people in need, and participates in around 50 events a year: curtain-raisers for leagues 1 and 2, charitable games, anniversaries, tours across the globe or in deepest rural France.

The chance to perform before a demanding audience on this legendary pitch was a dream come true. I already knew most of my team-mates, having taken part in many youth football trials for the Val d'Oise region. A magical atmosphere filled the stands. The applause resounded. The 20th anniversary of the Variety Club of France was to honour its stars and the golden triangle of French football in the 1980s: Platini, Giresse, Tigana. Who were we? Twenty newbies privileged to be welcomed into the proud stadium of the French capital to play an opener as a respectable opposition for the kids of former French international players.

About three hours before the game, I was with my parents in a coach under police escort. I'd done nothing wrong; neither had my parents. No, I was not dreaming. The driver was allowed to go through red lights and drive on the hard shoulder. On our no-holds-barred trip to the Parc des Princes, I laughed at the surprised stares of passers-by and their gestures when they realised important people were inside the well-protected bus. Yet it was just a bunch of kids nuts about football. I began to appreciate the immensity of the event, despite my way of being laid back and never knowing where I'd be before arriving. I had not said to myself, "I must be in top shape for the match," or "Whoah! In a week's time, my dream will come true. I must do my best to put on a good show." The others were certainly aware of what was going on, though. None of this crossed my mind, although

I did pick up that something special was happening. My father tells me to this day that he was surprised to see me so calm and relaxed. I had the spirit of an insouciant, oblivious child who just loved football and its face-offs.

As we arrived in the changing room we were greeted by the coach of our group. Mr Corfu reminded us all how lucky we were to take part in this friendly; how it was a great opportunity for us to show off those qualities which led to our being selected. The pressure was rising . . . tension built up to a level we would never have imagined.

A bit later on, I remember sitting in front of Mr Corfu and realising that something unpleasant was happening. I had seen him talking to ex-Variety Club players and a few bosses. To see these great footballers pulling wry faces dented my naïvety. They were shocked and surprised by the physique of some of the young players from our impressive Parisian squad. Given my nickname at the time, I did not have much cause for concern. "Petit Louis" referred to my gangly, pint-sized appearance compared to a Philippe Christanval or a Gérard Gnanhouan. These two young phenomena were already sturdier and taller than the rest of us. They were assessed, scrutinised, judged and doomed before even putting on their blue-and-white socks. After a final meeting between our manager and Variety Club old timers, a couple of players considered too big were forced to watch us all get changed. Our team was chosen with the aim of trying not to make the stars' kids look ridiculous or disadvantaged.

Like lots of young hopefuls that day, we soon understood what kind of world would greet us if we landed a career as a pro. Especially since the scandals of the 1990s would burst into public view involving the largest French and foreign clubs – the Olympique Marseille-Valenciennes affair implicating Bernard Tapie and AC Milan and the doping scandals in Italy.

Since our arrival at the stadium, our focus for this match had shifted slightly. In football, as in politics, everyone pulls strings.

If pressure can be applied in some way because of status, an opportunity to wield power is rarely missed. Everybody is confronted by this kind of situation and everyone invariably succumbs to the temptation to use their power. The pre-match pep talk was concluded with a simple piece of advice given by Mr Corfu: "Kids, have fun, but go easy on them."

Mr Corfu's instructions were of little consequence to me, but might well have had an effect had I been like those young African players who have the mature body of a married, family man. In Africa and South American countries, to register a child two or even five years after their birth is common practice. This means that even if a kid's real age is five he is often registered as a kid of three. So he's more physically and mentally developed and is ahead of his mates. Africa is such a huge continent that this is a way of giving a helping hand to young people who want to become professional footballers. To this day, I thank God and my parents for saving me from those filters which weed out young players who are keen to succeed.

I was lucky enough to play in this stadium which was impressive enough for an adult and even more so for a kid. I had a good laugh from beginning to end. If I remember right, I scored direct from a corner kick. I'm not sure if this was cool or crazy, as I was almost afraid of disobeying Mr Corfu's orders. But apparently I caught the eye of certain clubs and a few years later everything picked up speed.

Clairefontaine, or not?

I grew up in the world of football, and from the very beginning I opened my eyes wide.

A la claire fontaine [At the clear fountain]
M'en allant promener [While I was strolling by]
J'ai trouvé l'eau si belle [The water looked so lovely]

Que je m'y suis baigné [I went in for a swim]
Il y a longtemps que je t'aime [I've loved you for so long]
Jamais je ne t'oublierai . . . [I will never forget you]

[This song has been very popular in France since the eighteenth century and there are around 500 different versions of it.]

The Fernand Sastre National Technical Centre, better known by the name of INF Clairefontaine, is 50 miles south west of Paris in the middle of the forest of Rambouillet in the départment of Yvelines. It was a new football academy when I began to take part in the entrance trials. A paradise of 138 acres surrounded by nothing but trees and greenery, the huge estate includes the famous château which is the training base of the French national football team. A replica of the great World Cup trophy stands 15ft high at the entrance. Immaculate green grass training pitches stretch smoothly into the distance, and there are different playing surfaces for all kinds of weather conditions. The medical building is at the cutting edge of sports science. The restaurant and cafeteria offer slap-up meals or light snacks to the many groups who come to train or visit.

The whole selection process kicked off with a number of trials, ending in a tryout involving a day of technical, physical and medical tests at the impressive facilities of the immense academy. Each player had been supervised, encouraged and even indoctrinated throughout their young career, with the ultimate goal of getting into Clairefontaine. Players were monitored to ensure they fit the criteria for admission during small neighbourhood matches and major national youth tournaments. I have no idea when scouts first came to observe me, but I received numerous invitations to play in Val d'Oise trials. My father often spoke to me of scouts who had come to watch me, but I just concentrated on the game and getting the ball in the back of the net. The name "Mr Volpe" rings a vague bell, but that's it.

I began to recognise a few faces as we bumped into each other during the trials. Their potential was obvious. I gave them nicknames while I waited to get to know them. The first, I called "The Rocket". He played with FC Saint Leu, 24km north of Paris. Fast and nimble, he was impossible to contain. Defenders who had the misfortune to mark and tackle him were crushed. Think of Dash, Mr Incredible and Elastigirl's son in the animated film *The Incredibles*. Picture this super-fast boy dressed in red with an "I" in a circle plumb centre of his slim-fit shirt, rather than the sky-blue of Saint Leu and, to top it off, a serious tan and a broad white smile. A Malian black with cool blue undertones and a gleaming shaved head thanks to Gillette's Mach 3 razor. A centre-forward would invariably arrive five seconds after this supersonic winger had crossed the ball. The Rocket loved to mess about and was the spitting image of Tupac Shakur, the famous American rapper who was assassinated. Later, I'd call this player for FC Nantes and PSG, who also played for Manchester City in 2001/02, "The Tower", but fans would know him as Alioune Touré.

The second I nicknamed "The Watchtower", same as you'd see in an airport because he was already way taller than the rest of us. He had a touch of class which, along with his technical prowess, was a talking point amongst scouts and coaches excited by his many footballing qualities. He stood head and shoulders above everyone else, even later as a pro. I remember one particular contest when he was coming through the ranks of AAS Sarcelles in the northern *banlieue* of Paris. It was ludicrous, the way he crossed the pitch and nearly scored into an empty goal because his opponents were so overwhelmed as he hurtled through them on his phenomenal pins. They were in total awe of this future great player's assurance. A former French international defender who played for Barcelona, Monaco and Fulham, he retired in 2009. Alias, Philippe Christanval.

The third, I called "The Panther" because of his agility and his cat-like reflexes when he leapt to save shots that looked destined for the net. He had a style similar to Bernard Lama's, PSG's former goalkeeper. A sprightly guy, he was very flexible and faster than most midfielders. Maybe not as fast as The Rocket, but watch it, once the guy got going he was a force to be reckoned with. A goalkeeper who impresses generally wins a one-on-one over a hesitant attacker. He liked to joke and mess about like The Rocket and always created a vibe. This Ivory Coast international and former goalkeeper for Montpellier HSC and EA Guingamp is Gérard Gnanhouan. Gégé is one of those unfortunates who ended up with all the wrong coaches. Given the right conditions, he could have been a winning force for many teams.

These are the players I came across regularly. As in all trials, they had different styles but were elegant and skilful, and they have stayed in my mind despite my bad memory. All those players with whom I have shared such a wonderful adventure can attest to this!

As I was maturing in a group with players who were older than me, I was always the junior of the team, and so "little" was put before my name. My nickname has stuck with me to this day, and sales of the cheese called "Petit Louis" have gone through the roof because of it!

Criteria number 1 to gain selection into INF Clairefontaine was, obviously, the game of football and your potential for progress. Number 2 was to have a good academic record for a 13-year-old, including acceptable behaviour. Number 3 was to be a French citizen, although exceptions were granted to certain players. I came out OK on the first and third conditions, but the second was a real sweat.

A few months before the final tests to get into Clairefontaine, I realised I had to deliver a good academic record. I struggled with my homework as always. So I set to work to do well in the academic tests and get good marks. I only managed to achieve this in part. My academic record was sufficient, but I failed in my behaviour because I was cheeky and a bit of a prankster. The academy would take me in hand.

As for the football, we had to get stuck in. For one whole day of the process, a hundred kids took endurance and speed tests; technical and medical examinations. Everything was perfectly organised so everyone expressed themselves in all aspects of his game. Mid-afternoon, an 11v11 played in the Pierre Pibarot arena was the final and most crucial part of the trial. This stadium is often used by the French national team for training and has a nice stand. Coaches, scouts from big clubs and parents aired their views on the talent on show. As usual, I did not really care about the crowd, the surroundings, or the pressure. I just went out and tried to have fun.

My father told me the good news a few weeks after our one-day tryout, "Louis! Louuuuiiiiiiis! You've been accepted!"

"Yeah cool, Pa, can I go play outside then?" I said, still in my bubble.

To be accepted at Clairefontaine is not a dream come true, it's just the start of a long set of new challenges. But I was unaware of how difficult it is to get selected. My father certainly knew, but said nothing. Three groups of 20 young people aged 13-17 board at the academy in a well-equipped building. The stage was set for us to develop and bloom. A few years after I left, another building similar to the INF was made available for groups of girls, which must have made the place much livelier, both by day and night. Who knows, maybe that was what training became: making INF Clairefontaine babies!

The academy largely consists of teachers and high-level coaches. Players stay and train for three years with five workouts a week. That's when the serious work starts. As a 13-year-old, you have to grow up fast.

Being a boarder with great players is the best way to learn fresh ways of participating in more competitive matches, not to mention new dribbling techniques. It was like a video game in which I had reached a new level and could try out new tricks. I quickly assimilated what the academy required of me. The rules and rigidity of my parents had suffocated me. I must admit that for a brief moment I was happy to have escaped from their dungeon. But I soon realised that I had underestimated my new gaolers. I was given other conditions, schedules and responsibilities to meet. The place looked like a top summer camp, but this was misleading. I thought that the place would have flaws and would not be disciplinary. I presumed the teachers would succumb to my whims when I gave them one of my cute hangdog looks.

Work, work and more work. We hadn't got this far just to watch someone else step into our boots. It was a question of pride. It was only natural that we made quick progress, since technical basics were drilled into us from the off. We had to apply ourselves. There is nothing better than to work under competitive pressure.

Education and achieving school grades go hand-in-hand with football at Clairefontaine, so we had lessons from 8.30am to 3pm. It was important to have an adequate academic background in case things went belly up. It's simple: if you drop out of school, you're expelled from the academy, no matter how well you are playing. Harsh maybe, but it works.

Despite the constraints and being separated from the people I loved, I had been given a chance to soak up the brilliance on offer so I could forge ahead and absorb the competitive bug, which made my skin itch like crazy whenever I didn't play my best, or when I lost a game. Sleep was disrupted because of flashbacks replaying through my mind showing how the action could have been different. Today, I refer to my educators as spiritual fathers, since they nurtured me the same as my real father.

At the time, I could not stand it when the others taunted me for being the coach's favourite. Now I appreciate that Mr Merelle had already adopted a lot of children. All the guys in my class were like half-brothers. Mr Merelle, my mentor for three years, always protected me and pushed me forward. I always understood what he was trying to do, and focused on the exercises he instructed me to do. He'd often say: "In this first year, I will teach you how to play football." We all knew exactly what he meant. The guys in my class were well aware of their qualities, but they had little notion of tactics. Most still played street football and rarely looked up to assess the position of their team-mates or opponents. This coach was instrumental in changing our approach.

Since this time, I only watch a game to check out how well the players express their desire to produce a beautiful game on the pitch like the greats I watched when I was young, especially George Weah and David Ginola as they were maturing in Paris. I was lucky to have a support structure which allowed me to copy the technical moves of those great footballers. I loved to copy that special way Ginola had of mastering the ball with an inside-outside touch of the foot. I loved his power and elegance. His stunning 85th-minute goal for AC Milan against Verona in 1996, when he picked up the ball in his own penalty area and ran the entire length of the pitch before firing the ball into the bottom corner, captures the spirit of the beautiful game.

Mr Merelle was an admirer of technical skill and of players who had the desire to illuminate the beauty of the game and master the perfectly spherical ball. A lover of the short passing game now mastered by Barcelona, he'd become extremely enthusiastic when watching individuals exploit their talent. This kind of coach is ideal for young players who want to improve and refine their technique. Rumour has it that coaches from Barcelona came to observe him in action. Lol! INF Clairefontaine has the very best masters. Just ask Thierry Henry or Nicolas Anelka.

Nicolas was a rough diamond who shone so bright that it was hard not to watch only him on the pitch. Mr Merelle was like a special tool used on precious gemstones that are very hard to carve. When the work is done with skill and care, the result is outstanding. An exceptional diamond, which travels from one window display to the next because all the top jewel merchants want to have it in their showcase. Some will say Nico is too special and different, but there are always football chairmen prepared to spend big money transfer fees on him.

I had the pleasure of working with Mr Merelle and Nicolas, that 14-year-old phenomenon who was a good player with a tough personality. He hit it off with the coach, and in just a year his progress was dramatic. He was a little warrior with killer dribbling skills and the vision of a veteran. On our first day of communal life in the academy, the captain of the oldest year group made a welcome speech and outlined some basic rules and regulations. We were strangers to each other, but the respect we had for our seniors was automatic. But Nico stood up grumbling and said that no one would force him to do anything if he didn't want to do it. This tenacity, tinged with a touch of madness, can make him unpredictable on the pitch. When no one else is willing to go for it, he will try the impossible and succeed. That's the "it" factor which makes Nico so unique and self-assured. What a character.

In our first year, the training programme was focused on improving technique. The hardest of moves were made simple, and the simplest ones became almost innate. The fundamentals of every kind of passing, technical manoeuvre and ways of controlling the ball were taught. Mastering the basics of high-level football was a must.

In the second year, it was all about picking up information and knowing where your team-mates were. We were taught to slalom through the defence, head held high, all the while seeing the way ahead like all the great players. Now that our muscle mass was well developed, we worked on improving long-distance passing as well as zonal defence and man-to-man marking. Everyone's physical evolution was at the mercy of nature's growth hormones. We only did light running training. Mastery of the ball was the top priority. Working on our physique came later. For now, the coaches knew that if you had to run, you would run even harder with the ball.

In the third year, we learned about team spirit. We were injected with the bad loser virus. After a full week of training, every Saturday we played against an older age group. We were under-16s yet more talented than the players developing in the under-17 national youth team. We had an impressive team: Philippe Christanval, Gérard Gnanhouan, Gregory Proment, Alioune Touré, Nicolas Anelka, Sebastien Piocelle, Yves Deroff and others who are less well known today but who were equally promising back then. To go from being a player who is learning to a player who has absorbed it all so that everything comes naturally is the aim. I was lucky enough to train with the cream of the crop and to succeed where others failed.

The third year was when the real spirit of competition took hold within the team. You had to earn your place and once you were in the team you were expected to win the national youth tournaments. Clairefontaine is the crème de la crème of football training centres with a great reputation. It is the world's most successful football academy after Barcelona. Over 1,500 young French hopefuls try every year to win a place at this talent factory.

Our daytime routine was intense, so at night we messed about and had fun. I remember heavy workouts in the gym as well as racing through the immense forest. We took it in turns to look for each other in games of good old hide and seek. Some listened to R&B, funk and rap, while others read football magazines or watched John Travolta and Samuel L. Jackson in *Pulp Fiction* – this was the days before Playstation, mobile phones and the internet.

We all got a bit down sometimes, but football was ever present like the sun in Dubai and the snow in Siberia. We did stupid stuff and had great times on and off the pitch. During a game of hide and seek I once hid in the trees near the imposing château entrance, with its tall windows. When I was spotted way up in the branches, which were about 30m high, I slid down the trunk and ran into the darkness to escape my pursuers. I was fast: few could catch me now. Then suddenly, in a flash, I realised my life hung by a thread. I knew I had pace, but I failed to grasp why my feet no longer touched the ground. Suddenly there was a void and I had plunged 3m on to stony ground. I had fallen into a huge hole which was completely invisible in the dark. The next day when I returned to see where I'd fallen, I saw what a miracle it was not to have broken a leg, or to have ended up in a wheelchair.

On another occasion there was an unforgettable ruckus which could have ended badly. Two guys, Kalagan and his mate Yapo from Sarcelles, had decided to visit their neighbourhood mates Gérard Gnanhouan, Ernst Atis-Clotaire and Philippe Christanval at Clairefontaine. The two guys took the bus, the tube and the train south to see their friends interned in a certain über-modern football institution in the countryside. What they didn't know at the time was that their arrival would coincide with a fight that had been planned by pupils of a nearby school with which Clairefontaine was partnered, who were jealous of the brash, arrogant footballers strutting around their patch in their tracksuits and stealing their girlfriends – not to mention wound up by a comment made to one of them by yours truly.

A friendly match between us and the local school had been organised and there'd be a party afterwards, at which we'd enjoy some delicious *merguez*. However, the locals had arranged to use the occasion to teach us a lesson. Violence was brewing, although I had no idea as I arrived in the town of Les Essarts le Roi and promptly found myself sprinting down its streets with Sebastian Pendola (who later played for PSG). We were outnumbered by our pursuers, who were tooled up. Run, jump, crawl, hide. We caught our breath and plucked up our courage as we ducked behind a strip of wheat in a field alongside the railway before heading off to join our crew who were partying. They knew a punch up was in the offing.

When we joined our mates, we discovered that Joachim Machado and William Gallas had taken a beating. Despite their aches and injuries, though, I'm sure they managed to land some punches. Joachim was a stocky, tenacious midfielder and William a hot-blooded Guadeloupean like fiery overproof rum. Ready and waiting: we watched the country bumpkins arrive at the stadium. They clearly thought they were the business. What a joke! They were nothing like those tough guys from the Bronx or South Central LA. There were more of them and they were older than us. That's all.

They wanted to take chunks out of us, and me in particular, just because I took the piss out of one of their school mates. I found myself facing not one, but 20 rugby types. Two guys talked to Gérard Gnanhouan who was not one to back down. Then our mates showed up. They'd come all the way to north Rambouillet from a notoriously rough neighbourhood to watch a friendly match in the countryside, only to find two crews eyeballing each other ready to kick-off in a big way.

Yapo and Kalagan saw that the spirit of the streets which they thought they'd left behind had followed them. Kalagan isn't a massive guy, but his calm, powerful aura is impressive and unset-tling. He's always up for it, fights to the max and never bottles out. He left the yokels in no doubt that if they didn't finish him off he'd be back with his crew from Sarcelles to show them what violence was all about.

All it took to sort things out was for the big boys from Sarcelles to have a word with the rugby types from the school. Kalagan is 1m 85cm tall and commands respect. He didn't look like he was only around for the football, but some terrace action too. He told the yokels I was his little brother and if they'd any sense, they'd treat me with respect. "Step out of line and we'll have you."

I smile as I write this because I can remember how it felt to be under the wing of Kalagan. To see this guy almost single-handedly dominate this group of 20 rugby types was impressive. It was like a real-life scene from the TV series *The Wire*. Later, I called my Rottweiler who weighed 55kg "Kalagan", but I had to give him away because of my kids. An adorable dog, but I didn't want to take that kind of risk.

Other stuff happened, like raids into Rambouillet, the nearest town. We were crazy enough to cross a forest several miles long to get there. The lucky ones were generally lighter-skinned; they hitch-hiked. It was a 30 to 40-minute sprint to get to town, which just goes to show how imprisoned we were by the dense jungle around us that was like a green fortress. I've no idea how often I jumped the perimeter fence. Punishments were all part of my adolescence. I was only 14 and had left behind my friends and family and "normal" life. Being a candidate for a bright future can quickly go to your head. Keeping it real for three long seasons was a big ask at that age.

On balance, those three years were a great experience. To end up with a certain status, technical savvy, rigour and determination, fired by the competitive virus, is no bad thing. Add to that a bunch of mates who are enthusiastic, supportive and worldly, and you're on to a winner. We all learned important concepts and definitions of the term "professionalism," regardless of whether we went on to be professional footballers, or not.

My one regret is the timing of my three years' training as it coincided with a period when I would have liked to hang out with my brother and sister. My relationship with them now is not really how I would like it to be. In the eyes of my brother especially, I quickly went from being his older brother to being a famous member of the family. The same goes for the childhood friends I lost touch with. I'm writing this in part as an apology to them.

Many international stars start their careers in an institution that moulds them. There isn't a tried-and-tested formula for a coach to help them choose the youngest hopefuls and detect the traits which show they've got what it takes to be a star. This leads to waste, and many good, young players get overlooked. A coach working in a training centre does not only form footballers, but citizens.

Zinédine: "Petit Louis, aspiring to be part of the professional world means understanding that there are rules, regulations and standards to be learned throughout training and career development. You can't do what you want, like in the street, because there is a certain structure to be respected. Teachers and coaches are especially important when players are evolving as they need to be able to spot those who need freedom to grow and move on; balance giving rigorous advice with keeping the instinct and imagination alert. I've always been lucky to have coaches who let me move and play in a way that felt right. I listened carefully to the instructions given by Jean Fernandez and Guy Lacombe; players who became coaches with this kind of experience like Alex Ferguson. When I think of Cantona, it's when he was under Ferguson's wing that he became *that* player, *that* legend. Ferguson realised that Cantona needed freedom to express himself. I was given that chance too."

Zizou is right, of course, especially given the intense way 10-year-olds are coached today compared to 10 years ago. Gaétan Baudet (physio for AS Cannes) has told me how shocked he is by the increase in muscle tears in kids who should require little warming up because the body is so elastic at that age. Coaches push kids to do more and more sprint and endurance sessions. For kids to complain of a groin strain is a worrying sign. These practices show the need for a rethink of the philosophy of training. Ten to 14-year olds should mainly focus on mastering their technique to help them to understand the matrix of the good footballer.

Believe in yourself

Everything was primed for a high-flying career. I'd only just arrived at Clairefontaine when I signed an Option Agreement with FC Metz. Three years later, aged 17, it was time to move on.

After leaving Clairefontaine, I often heard how confident people were that Petit Louis could break into the professional world. But I had to prove myself. To reach the highest level is one thing, but you need staying power. Carlos Tevez, Sergio Aguerro and Lionel Messi were sure of a great career, despite their small stature. It seems that in Argentina the criteria are not the same as in Germany or France where, who knows, they might have been judged differently. Iniesta, Xavi, Ludovic Giuly and Mathieu Valbuena undoubtedly had to deal with the obsession about physique and strength in a sport requiring technical and mental skills, as well as vision.

Carlos Tevez: "In Argentina, I didn't do much body-building. Training was based on mastering technique and confidence in an offensive game."

So I asked him: "Where does the power that energises you, Agüero and Messi come from? That strength which means you can all stand solid on the pitch on those huge thighs? "

He said: "Papito, *todo es la determinación*. It's determination and self-confidence that mean we don't fail."

Others like Patrice Evra, who is now considered to be one of the best left-backs in the world, have succeeded in spite of a road strewn with setbacks and without going to an academy. Patrice had to stay longer in the neighbourhood and fight alone to find the strength to believe in his dream. He deserves all the more credit for succeeding since his school teachers laughed in his face when he said he wanted to become a footballer. His self-belief was solid as a rock.

Patrice Evra: "Bro, I've nothing against training centres, but I'm living proof you can do it without them."

His willpower and the fact that he had the nerve to go and play in Sicily on his own aged just 17 are a great example for my little brother of how some players have the fire in their belly to succeed, as I'm often critical of how easily he gets bored, or isn't motivated enough.

Patrice: "I see myself just a junior in those early days when I discovered my passion for football, playing in an indoor tournament in my neighbourhood with a burning desire to make my dream come true. I remember a scout telling me I had guts and he offered to take me to Italy for a trial."

Pat is one of those players who'll do anything to make his dream come true. He takes the bull by the horns, no problem. It's impressive to hear about a kid who was so passionate, so young; who is so nuts for the game and so determined that he'll leave for an island known for being rough on foreigners. It takes ambition, motivation, discipline, immense hope and most of all, courage. He is a great example of all these qualities.

Pat describes his incredible journey after being spotted by a scout: "He was called Onofrio Jamarezzi. He called two days after the indoor tournament to confirm that he thought I had something special. Louis, he had to persuade my mother to let me go alone to Turin, aged 17, for a tryout for a Serie B team, and for that I thank my brother. I'd never left my neighbourhood before then. My big brother argued with my mother, saying there was nothing in Les Ulis to allow people to become someone. After two weeks of training with a youth reserves squad in Italy, another agent offered me a professional contract, but this time in Serie C with SC Marsala in Sicily. I went for it."

Pat had always dreamed of being given a chance: "I'll never forget the day I found myself standing in front of the departures board in an Italian railway station showing all the destinations, and missed my train. I was done for as I didn't have a mobile with GPS, or even any basic Italian to ask for directions. I was like a little illegal immigrant from Senegal lost in the middle of Italy."

I was so moved I could almost cry.

He went on: "Frozen to the spot, all alone in this busy station, I believed God would send me a guide. 'Patrice Evra you will become someone. I have decided it must be so.' Surging from nowhere, a Senegalese man spoke to me in Wolof [the language spoken in Senegal] and said he'd put me up for the night. That way I'd catch the train I missed the next day. I found myself sitting with a knot in my stomach, in a small room eating Yassa [chicken with onions and lemon] alongside eight other people. What a beautiful sense of solidarity. God gave me a hand by way of that Senegalese who I'd love to see again, to say thank you. That was my training centre."

Powerful stories like this one have inspired my brother and others too. It takes luck, but most of all a lot of motivation. Pat's story is a real catalyst for kids who want to get ahead in life. To go from rags to riches and reach the top is magic. Naturally, it commands respect.

World-class football may be a real test compared to other disciplines, but other challenges during a man's life can be greater still. I will always be in awe of the legend who is Nelson Mandela. Everything was taken from him; he was given nothing to succeed. It wasn't like a Pelé who was told, "See those 11 guys, go destroy them with your innate technique, your strength and your instinct."

It's easier to work hard with talent and to succeed, as opposed to working hard without a choice even if blessed with a mind and philosophical sensibility well above average. Mandela did not have to stay so long in prison, but he refused to back down on his principles. He did not have to learn the language of his oppressors. He did not have to be incorruptible. He did not have to sacrifice family life for the emergence of South Africa, even if he wanted to succeed and see his dream become a reality. He pursued his goal in the face of immense difficulties. That is why, today, he is such a magnificent symbol of courage and perseverance.

If you go into battle with bravery and determination, you have all it takes to face the tough times. Slog your guts out. Push yourself to get even better. Never be satisfied with what you have, or what you have achieved. It is best to carry these qualities with you as early as you can in life, as these virtues are easily learned during adolescence.

Overcoming difficulties and setbacks triggers genuine learning. The fear of failure is a necessary ingredient of courage and fuels motivation. The fear of failure can be transcended so that the failure never becomes a reality. Beware of developing a defeatist attitude. A training centre like Clairefontaine may increase your chances for success, but if you have the "it" factor and other less-obvious breaks come your way, then go for it!

4
YOU REAP WHAT YOU SOW

Summer 1995. I land in Lorraine, in north-east France, which has the city of Metz as its capital. To choose FC Metz over another club was tricky yet so important. Luckily, my parents got it right. A couple of young players from that club are selected each year for the French national youth team. FC Metz is known for building up emerging talent, although the players don't usually stick around long enough to help their club's first team. Clubs like Metz and Le Havre FC, who gave the world players like Ibrahim Ba and Lassana Diarra, can't do much to stop their best young talent from leaving for top-flight clubs. Incredibly, the great Michel Platini nearly played for "Les Grenats" (The Garnets), as Metz are known, but missed out because he wasn't considered to be in the peak physical condition required by the club. It's in their dark red jersey that Franck Ribéry made his Ligue 1 debut, and Robert Pirès also emerged from their youth academy to become a world champion. A training centre with a reputation for rigour and discipline is particularly important in the eyes of the Metz coaches – a place where exceptional human qualities contribute to a fiercely competitive, but healthy, atmosphere.

Other offers were on the table before we headed to Metz. I was courted by Monaco, PSG and others during my time at Clairefontaine, but I had to go east because of my Option Agreement with Metz which prevented me from signing to another club. So the historic town famous for its football was my destination after three years at Clairefontaine. It proved to be a choice that improved my chances as a young hopeful aspiring to play only at the highest level. My parents thought that for me to join a team focused on developing emerging talent, one which could not afford to buy too many international stars, was more likely to give me a break. The ability to make the right choices on or off the pitch is crucial.

William Gallas: "I'm at Olympique de Marseille and I have a choice: stay, but on an amateur contract because the club already has a full quota of pros in the squad. I have to be downgraded if I want to stay at the club and show that they're wrong. Or I can return to Caen, where I was trained and where I flourished, but I do not want to give such a strong sign of failure. I don't deserve it. So I stayed on. A tough call, but I slogged my guts out."

During the next season this tricky situation took a different turn and he attracted the interest of the biggest clubs. William is stubborn and very brave. He swallowed his sour grapes and his pride. He has done everything to get what he deserves. It's on the playing field that his mindset is exceptional. Maybe he has too much integrity and is sometimes too full on, but he is deeply passionate about football because it's his dream; his life goal.

A person's life is full of complicated and difficult decisions to be made at critical moments. There are so many things to consider: career path, club, financial impact, personal wants and health; the effect of all of these on friends and family. More often than not, sacrifices have to be made. Each person acts according to their principles, their past experiences, their desires and state of mind. Once we learn to evaluate our decisions based on consequences, everything falls into place.

Coaches, scouts, parents, families, girlfriends and even supporters play a key role in the life of a footballer. To master the power of persuasion is all-important. As is finding the right way to engage and influence people to help advance your career in the right direction. Stay away from people who belittle your ambition. Maximise your opportunities and do the right thing. Stay spontaneous, but never lose sight of your dream.

Luck and religion have a special bond in this process that is ambiguous and fragile. When it comes to religion, some say divine intervention is what guides us through everyday life. The word "fate" is used a lot. It's a concept which some find hard to swallow, especially when it comes to poverty. Everything is supposedly already written: "It's fate, *mektoub*, I cannot help it . . ." Yet our actions determine our destiny. You can get it if you really want. If you think you are strong, then you *are* strong, or will be. For me, fate is the most contradictory of concepts, especially if religion can be considered as a straightforward code of good conduct. The idea that your actions or your choices are already written and assessed in advance; to say to yourself that whatever you do is what God has decided; to say it's my destiny, be it good or bad: c'mon, it can't be!?

On the other hand, I believe that God commands people and things. Faith in God is not something to apologise for, it's a sign of strength. Having faith and trust in God and his plan for you on Earth, and in your talents, is critical to achieving personal goals. Accept what life gives you and make the best of it.

Almost everyone can choose which direction to take in life. When I realise how lucky I have been, I wonder if fate is just a timescale in the middle of a blank page with birth at the top and death at the bottom. The blank space is filled up with rungs of good or bad luck depending on how fortunate you are, a bit like the board game, Snakes and Ladders. Possibilities fill the empty spaces between each rung and only here does a person truly hold and shape their destiny. Making the right choices, working hard and avoiding pitfalls weave patterns across the blank page.

Sometimes the life will be scrawled across a filthy, wet page. The choices will be so cruel, you wonder what that person did to deserve them. To have to sleep rough, or to be raped by a stepfather is not a choice. It's abuse; a burden; a scar for life. In such a situation, avoiding sinking into despair and figuring out how best to handle it is the way forward; fighting against temptation or grim situations. It's easy to say, "Work even harder to tempt fate in the right way," but that is the solution.

Of course, it's all too easy for a guy like me to theorise, but I'm a straightforward type and complicated answers aren't my style. I'm still wary of my blank page. I may be one of the lucky ones, but I'm still on the alert.

When I was a boy, in my local team Soisy-Andilly-Margency, there were good players. Had the dice rolled well they would have had a very different life. A guy called Kémaïs springs to mind. He knows I regret that he didn't fight against his joker's nature. He didn't always listen to his coaches. He was strong technically; more robust than me and more confident. But, although he was talented, Kémaïs didn't work out when to take action to achieve success. I was as ignorant as he was about the world of professional football. We weren't bothered about money, fame or responsibility. My great advantage was my father. He breathed down my neck and monitored who I saw and what I did. Dodgy people and dubious influences didn't gain access to where I lived, three floors up in a building at 23 rue du Cimetière. The view from our flat, of lugubrious graves and overgrown mausoleums, was breathtaking. Kémaïs was not surrounded by sufficiently disciplined people focused on grabbing the right opportunity at the right time. He didn't have a forceful authority figure to counter his strong temperament. It is all well and good to mash it up, but sacrificing having a laugh would have been worth it in the end.

One episode in my early career illustrates why it's so important for parents to make constructive choices on behalf of their children. This particular incident changed my life although at the time it felt unbelievable and heartless. My father received a request for me to take part in a trial for the Val d'Oise area team. But it was scheduled for the same day as my local club, FC Soisy, played the semi-finals of the Val d'Oise Cup. The week before we'd argued yet again about my school report. I was warned that

I'd be banned from going out if I made the slightest slip up. When I realised that the trial and the semi-final clashed I had a word with my club coach. I desperately wanted to play in the semi-final with my mates, and he reassured me that I didn't need to worry about the trial since we could write to the organisers asking if I could play in the next one.

I was sure I'd be allowed to choose which game to play in, so I took it upon myself to have a word with the boss, sharpish. I tried to get my old man on side with loaded questions: "Dad, we need to make a decision about my trial," or "How will we get to two games at the same time on Saturday?" I explained that I wanted to play in the semi-final and that my coach said not to worry about the tryout. He listened calmly in his usual poised and reassuring way and nodded his head so I assumed the outcome would be positive. But, sitting in his favourite chair, reading his newspaper, *Le Parisien*, my father told me in a monotone voice that I would not play the semis with my mates. A tingling sensation flooded my body. This was totally unexpected. It was way too harsh!

My father was adamant. I threw a wobbly, but vehement gestures and despairing glances had zero effect. All week, I begged him to change his mind: "Call the coach – he'll tell you I don't need to go to your tryout, please talk to him."

But he refused. It felt like my old man had been on my case ever since my crap school marks. Wailing, tantrums, threatening a hunger strike: all my antics were greeted with silence. So I began to hate him and look at him disdainfully. I couldn't believe he'd carry out his threat. To force me to do something I didn't want to do was spiteful. I cursed and warned him: "I'll never forgive you . . . Why? What've I done? Are you jealous or what?"

My old man was determined to teach me a lesson about authority throughout that long week, with its fruitless negotiations and interminable wait. All my friends were going to be allowed to play in the semi-final. I watched my step, but he wouldn't budge. The tension at home was terrible. My mother was gutted to see me in such a state. Then, to my surprise, he told me that he would allow me to play with my club until half-time. Exhausted like my mother, he had given in, even though there's no father like mine when it comes to teaching respect for authority. It was the first time I'd ever seen him change his mind, but also the first time I had seen him act so unfairly.

After 45 minutes of the semi-final, my team was winning. Stubborn as a mule, my father took me off to the tryout. I could see that he was tense by the way he drove.

The teams for the trial match had already been selected and the game had kicked off. My father barely parked the car. He rushed to the organisers to explain why we were late. The officials looked at me with a kindly eye and said it would be OK for me to join in. The match was 10 or 15 minutes old when a player came off and I walked on to the pitch.

My father likes to repeat this story, emphasising how my entrance into the game was noticed. He also likes to reiterate what the organisers said. It turned out they were considering penalising Soisy for playing me in the semi-final as the club had not been entirely honest about why I would not be taking part in the selection for the Val d'Oise squad. It turned out that this match was in fact the final selection for Val d'Oise before the trials to get into INF Clairefontaine began. Maybe a letter had been mislaid or forgotten. Whatever, missing this match would have cost me dearly.

The boss tells me that had I listened to my coach, I would have been crossed off the list of potential candidates for Clairefontaine. I would have missed the last and crucial selection, the event which ultimately empowered the wings of destiny to carry me to dance with the stars. The father who I had thought was jealous, hateful and dishonest had gone behind my back and carried out his own investigation. He'd inquired about the kick-off times of the two games and discovered the importance of my taking part.

I learned a great many things from that day. My parents had taught me to walk and talk, not so that I'd fetch their baguette for Sunday breakfast, but so I'd realise my true potential. They had not made sacrifices just to watch me sabotage my chances of success. Despite certain flawed decisions, most of the people around me hoped I'd do well, even if I did not always feel loved, or it seemed as though they were in the grip of some demonic power. Nobody's perfect.

That day, I realised that no one could love me or want my happiness more than my parents. To grow up in a family that is too nice, in which anything and everything goes, means a child does worse later in life or becomes overly dependent on others. We tell ourselves that a perfect father cannot be bettered, but obviously he will fail sometimes. That incident also made me realise how easily a child can become ungrateful and rude. I saw how parenting is a constant challenge. If you're not vigilant everything can change in the blink of an eye. I had preferred to believe a stranger rather than my own father. I was gutted.

If everyone had parents like mine and could benefit from their wisdom and knowledge how lucky they'd be. Although I'd have had too many brothers in a small room and too many competitors! Making choices for your children is a responsibility. But there are also times when a kid's instinct is crucial and proves to be decisive.

Pat: "I had a difficult choice: listen to my mother and stay at home like a good boy, or stay in a room with three mattresses and eight Senegalese strangers on the floor in Italy and not go back to my neighbourhood to hang out for who knows how many years."

I picture Patrice 10 years ago in Italy, age 17. The brother, as I call my mates, could easily have ended up inside accused of smuggling or selling counterfeit goods out of his sports bag. Despite everything, he made the right choice.

Ji-Sung Park: "I did all I could to join the South Korean national team because back then professional football was just beginning. I remember a key moment when I'd been turned down by a professional club in Korea, and during that year at university I decided to try my luck far away in Japan. It was a big risk. One thing led to another fast. I took part in the World Cup and here I am now in Manchester. It was a difficult choice, but I had what it took and it was right for me."

An evaluation, a decision, a choice and a journey with a different route. One of the pillars of the great club that is Manchester United had nearly hit the skids too.

Kémaïs was a great kid. Today he is happy, but many others with the same potential have stayed frustrated. They realised too late the importance of choosing between having fun and signing what I like to call the Professional Sportsman's Personal Sacrifice contract. The athlete signs it as proof that he is 100 per cent committed to his goal, which is to become a pro in his favourite sport. Most of all, he seals the deal with himself and must keep the contract in his pocket wherever he goes – alone or with friends. He should also have it on him when he goes to school. The contract must always be with him in case he finds himself in a situation that could jeopardise his goals. Whenever the little devil on his shoulder queries his conscience he should take it out of his pocket and read it aloud.

My Professional Sportsman's Personal Sacrifice contract:

I the undersigned Mr X promise before God and myself to act in the best way possible to achieve my goal to become a professional football player. I will fight temptation on a daily basis by any and all means possible.

I promise always to think twice or even three times before making an important decision. I promise to listen to the advice of experienced advisors and to respect my coaches.

Signed Mr ... ...

Dated ... ...

Not to follow your mates, or indulge in the usual adolescent

silliness is hard, but it's crucial to minimise any consequences that could impact on a promising career. Nowadays, if he messes up, there are more ways for a recognised football pro to bounce back. However, a young player who still has to prove his worth is far less likely to be forgiven by his club.

Something almost carnal and, with hindsight, comic which could have had more serious consequences happened at the end of my first season with Fulham, in 2001. I'd been a pro for nearly four years by then, and it was a lesson in temptation.

She was sleek and black with knobbly bits here and there. She was oh, so sophisticated. I loved her charm, her feline shape and sassy ass which made my jaw drop. Once I'd seen her in the magazines she was always on my mind. For months I waited, eager to devour her as a wolf waits for a sheep to stray from its flock. Did I own up to my obsession? Of course I said nothing to my family; especially not my father as he is so serious and wouldn't have understood. I told my girlfriend and our conversation was electrified. I felt small but gave in to temptation. When I removed the packaging, I let out a little whimper. I was not licensed to drive my beautiful KTM Duke and had less experience with motorbikes than an eight-year-old. I remember how I rode her with a great big smile on my face; my dreads whipped by the wind as I went no more than 20 or 30 miles an hour. What a loser!

The euphoria of the previous year with our promotion to the Premier League and playing against Manchester United at Old Trafford the previous week were too much. I had put my Professional Sportsman's Personal Sacrifice contract in the wrong pocket and let go, literally, as my bike was too wild; too ready to leap ahead from a standstill. She was for someone with a lot of riding experience, so I found myself on the pavement outside my house thanks to taking a tight corner a little off-balance on the super-powerful machine. The bike took off and we flew through the air. Boom! I came back to earth with a bump. Fear didn't even get a look in. For a couple of seconds the realisation and acceptance of what was to come overwhelmed me. All of this on the morning of a big match at home to Sunderland. What a moron!

I spent the morning trying to cook up a valid explanation for my gashed shin and burned leg. I was covered with bumps and scratches, but it seemed nothing was broken. My wrist hurt like hell and I was stunned by my total lack of self-awareness. I'd travelled three metres through the air and bitten the dust like Twit of the Year. I was a long way off cool.

We had to take three points at home after our 3-2 defeat against Manchester United in the first game of the season the previous week. Being newly promoted to the Premier League, we were keen to get points on the board to avoid the bookmakers making Fulham favourites for relegation at the end of the season.

My fiancée, my mate Manu and former French international, Sylvain Wiltord, were all planning to watch the game kick-off at 3pm from high up in the stands. But they all ended up waiting with me in A&E as my gash needed stitches to stop it healing into a thickened, raised scar. I soon saw how the medical system in England is creaking at the seams. Two guys with cut scalps following a punch up were sitting calmly on their best behaviour, clearly used to long waiting times. The battered scalps looked set to hang about for hours. If they weren't considered urgent cases, it was pointless me waiting. I got treatment at home and set off, ready for action. Despite my limited knowledge of Shakespeare's language, my story was well-oiled. I invented words and characters. My burned leg was the unfortunate result of me messing up with a frying pan. It was hard to verify. No way could the team doctor suspect a motorbike crash. I'd see soon enough, during the warm-up, if my damaged legs would be able to keep going at the intensity required of a Premier League match. I was not at my best, but the adrenaline rush triggered by the crash and my will to win did the rest. I held up well. What's more, I played a good match and scored, clinching victory for us.

It could all have ended very differently with irrevocable consequences. For example: I could have broken my leg and got in trouble with my insurers since professional footballers are not allowed to go on two wheels, skis, or do other dangerous sports. Like Matt Jansen and Carlo Cudicini, the former Blackburn Rovers and current Spurs players, I could have ended up laid off, or making limited appearances and struggling to re-establish myself. Almost certainly the chairman, Mohammed Al Fayed, and my coach, Jean Tigana, would have punished me with a heavy fine and I'd have paid the penalty by earning a bad reputation: playing in the reserves, perhaps never getting back to the top level, breach of contract, unemployment, divorce . . . A split-second mistake can mean the end of the dream: never forget this. Everything can change like dominoes falling the wrong way. The choices we make build our future.

Valentino Rossi, multiple Moto GP world champion: "Luck has always played a part in my success. It is the same for everyone. Without it, you're stuffed. Luck is not everything, though – you need to build on it by way of the choices you make and I've always made the right decisions at the right time."

It all goes so fast . . .

It's a coach's job to make decisions and choices ranging from simple to complex. Using collective intelligence effectively is the key to success.

Phil Neville: "Any idea why Sir Alex Ferguson, José Mourinho and Arsène Wenger are the best coaches in the world? They either know or get information about everything to do with football. The elements are therefore in place to make the best decisions. Each has his own philosophy, but one thing is for sure, they sweat blood to get it right. They know the names of every player at their club, their characteristics, the weight of the new official ball, the family problems of a potential new recruit . . . Special individuals who analyse nearly 300 games per year and memorise 10 GB of information a day. They know how to play chess and poker in the world of professional football. All that goes towards making the right choices."

I remember how Sir Alex Ferguson loved to sum up the philosophy of Man United: "I show big respect to the great player who scores or plays well when his team really needs it. If a player is productive when the team is in top form and crushing its opponents he is not particularly impressive, whereas if he takes the lead during a bad patch I am reminded of a Cantona, Best, or Keane. They create success and bring luck." Sir Alex told me that he looks for this type of player throughout the world because they're the ones who make all the difference.

Fergie would ask us to take responsibility as opposed to lying low when our team was in bad shape. My first encounter with this national monument was a surprise because, like a lot of people, I imagined him to be angry and stiff. Not quite a General, more of a Colonel: strict and very much on our case. But I was puzzled by how relaxed I felt when I found myself in front of him alongside my father and my agent. The "Ferguson effect" had already done its job. His competitor's virus was more powerful than any that my other managers ever injected into me. The effect was immediate but painless. Oddly, his iconic aura may have been impressive, but it gave me even more confidence. I wanted to win for him all the time, non-stop; I was full of beans. When I saw him, my body responded and I was ready to go.

Each player is different. Each has his own particular strengths, weaknesses and personality. A good coach can analyse the whole lot. This can even mean trying to find ways of dealing with the narcissism which is characterised by excessive self-esteem, a need for adulation and a lack of empathy. Then there's the avoidant personality which involves not taking risks because of fear of failure. Or else there's the borderline personality disorder with its emotional instability, impulsiveness and mood swings. He must be able to deal with them all.

The best coaches are psychologists and are not only severe, as symbolised by Ferguson's famous "hair dryer" treatment used to trigger a reaction in players and give them a kick-start. A good trainer has several tools in his box and knows which one to use, depending on what he's planning on building.

Philippe Senderos, who has played for Servette, Arsenal, AC Milan, Everton and Fulham: "What was important for me was to know that with Arsène Wenger, whether you were 17 or 32, he'd give you a chance because it's his philosophy. If you're good, you play. That makes you feel very confident."

The philosophy of each coach differs depending on which position he played during his career. An ex-defender-turned-coach will naturally master the defensive aspects of his players and the team and direct attacking play less well. That's why coaches always need an assistant as a sounding-board because no one can know or understand everything about football. So it's easier for a midfielder than for a defender or attacker to gain a comprehensive view of the technical, tactical and fitness levels required. A striker-turned-coach usually relies heavily on instinct when it comes to how best to position his offensive players. The tactics of a coach reflect the man himself – the player he once was, his ambitions and what he would still like to be able to do.

A coach needs to get to know each individual's strengths and evaluate which training drills are best for him. He must do all he can to help the player make the right choices at crucial points of the game. Football can be paradoxical of course. You can train with great diligence, yet your performance goes leftfield, then you take three days off or do light training for a week and you're a winner. It's a puzzle. I say this as an aside; a subliminal message to my coach. To be able to adapt is crucial, since from one month to the next the opposite can happen.

You need to know how to use a group's competitiveness so it excels, grows and stays consistent. To be sidelined is unpleasant for any player. The trick is to learn how to transform that ball of frustration or anger in your belly carefully so that you dominate it, or regain your place. Truth is, hard work pays; it has been proved that it's the best way to change your mood or how the coach sees you. So you want to play? OK then, show you deserve to, on and off the pitch. Your style, your body language and even what you say all reveal your level of confidence. The coach will sense it. He often has to support a player's tensions. Performance on the playing field is by far the best language, but sometimes a strong personality can seem trickier to manage than the others in the team. If you are a lamb you need to become a wolf, as you don't want to be easy prey.

Edwin van der Sar, in his 20-year career, never really had any experience of being a replacement goalkeeper, a number 2, but he still trained like crazy to keep his number 1 spot. Everything he did was high-intensity, focused and ambitious.

Thierry Henry: "You need to be world class for the coach or the fans to truly trust you. Arsène has a lot of confidence in his players. He'd die to protect you. He leaves you to do your thing on the pitch, yet you feel something is going on. It's difficult to pinpoint what makes it all click. The atmosphere there is so special I became a real supporter. Even now when things are going badly for the Gunners I feel flat and when they win I feel lighter than air."

Ottmar Hitzfeld, former coach of Borussia Dortmund and Bayern Munich: "Not everything can be explained in football. A coach has to analyse his opponents, develop tactics and make choices based on that. So he has to think with his head, but also listen to his gut feeling to make decisions that at times may seem surprising viewed from the outside. These unexpected choices make all the difference between a good and a great coach."

To have the ability to always make good choices is the ultimate quality for every human being who wants to win trophies, get involved in politics, build a lucrative business, or just live happily. For the footballer, many things outside the sports arena can further complicate decision-making. In society, as in football, you have to react and act instinctively and efficiently. It's hard because we are often judged too quickly. Confidence and mutual solidarity take time to flourish.

5
ON THE ROAD

Today, I live for much of the year on an island known for its cold climate. The skies are often grey and it rains more than the sun shines. Even the most beautiful beach in Bournemouth will never have the cachet of the Croisette in Cannes. For some foreigners, driving on the left and mastering the round-abouts can be nerve-wracking. Bar billiards, B&B's, car boot sales and bonfire night are Great British oddities. I appreciate the little things that are part of my life in England, not least because they make me appreciate my holidays even more.

One of the best smells in the world is the one that emanates from a French bakery. I wait patiently for a visit to the Champs Elysées or the Côte d'Azur to throw myself at the finest pastries. Yet after a couple of months I miss England because I love its values, its towns with pubs full of people who are proud to wear their national team's jersey. I love their passion for football and the way the St George's Cross flag hangs from car and van windows when there's an international football tournament. I love the way they respect success. It seems they are happy for those who become commercially successful. There are jealous people all over the world, but the Brits know how to use this flaw wisely to evolve and grow. England and its football suit me. I realised this when I landed in Newcastle on loan from Metz to play for the powerhouse of the north.

Newcastle and its Geordies made me fall in love with England

and its football. Everyone in the city works hard and parties hard. They are real football fanatics: happy, relaxed and a joy to behold. And I felt totally at home in a squad which included players from all parts of the soccer globe.

The young player who wants to become a pro doesn't have the luxury of waiting for that breakthrough moment when everything clicks into place and he grasps what it means to be a reliable player. He'll be tested quickly and judged on the bad things he does, not just the good, especially if the coach is under pressure. Today, at all levels, only victory earns players trying to prove themselves more time. Even the coaches in a training centre are pressurised to achieve their objectives in one year when normally it should take two or three. Whether the aim is to win a championship or select capable young players to reinforce the first team, the draconian system of judging everything on results generates too much waste because realistic deadlines for developing both players and teams are not honoured.

The slightest slip-up can end a promising career. You don't become a professional footballer in the usual way, by passing exams and getting a degree. If you end up with a coach who doesn't like your style of play and you don't hit it off, everything can go belly-up. A bad coach doesn't try to analyse, or understand, or even adapt to the differences between his players.

I have many positive and unforgettable memories of my first year as a pro at Metz, but I also went through some very tricky patches. I was young and laid back and found myself under the instruction of Mr Joël Muller. He was a good coach, but overly demanding and focused on marathon workouts, which were not for me because I was not a long-distance runner and had asthma which required careful management. So I sweated blood. I had a solid technical foundation and other physical qualities, but under this regime could only occasionally express myself fully on the pitch.

It felt like I was suffocating in a tomb. Not picked for the first team, I missed the rush of the game. Everything felt like an effort. I wanted to have fun, but he wanted me to work like a robot, or a factory worker at PSA Metz, the local company that manufactured gearboxes for Peugeot Citroën. I was a hair's breadth away from quitting football. I felt so small, I got to a point where I'd rest my head on the hot radiator to fake a fever just to avoid seeing Mr Muller for a day or two.

Although I was sure all kinds of opportunities lay ahead and that one day I'd be happy and play with talented footballers, there were times when I wanted to throw in the towel. The fuse of my bomb was burning fast. I was sure I'd eventually manage to extricate my family from their end-of-month stress about making ends meet and paying bills. But I did have my doubts when I heard the coach tell me that I'd never make it to play in Ligue 1. He said: "If you can't run at my pace from the training camp to Cora hypermarket in town, you can forget the professional world and go home to your parents."

It was 30 minutes there and 30 minutes back, at a speed that made conversation impossible. We also did laps of 1,000m which was never my distance. Training in the Lorraine seemed to be all about running for as long as possible. On top of this, I felt like I was being judged on my defensive ability, yet I was an attacking player, albeit one with an aptitude for the defensive side of the game as well. It seemed completely illogical. I wanted to be someone else with interchangeable lungs. I would've done all I could to satisfy them so long as they let me have some fun. I longed for some training to help me improve my attacking skills. This is why it's so hard to break into football. You almost have to pick the team or coach who best fits your qualities; one who functions in a way that agrees with you and the way you play. The problem lies in the imperfections of the bosses and adapting to these. Bite your tongue, sulk in your room and prove yourself on the playing field. In football, the only judge of right from wrong is what happens on the pitch; this is what makes us arrogant or confident, good or bad.

Rigobert Song Bahanag, defensive midfielder for Liverpool, West Ham, Cologne, RC Lens, Galatasaray and Trabzonspor, who started his career in Europe at Metz, would say that Muller was his spiritual father. That he taught him everything and was a coach who understood his qualities and who did everything so he'd become captain courageous – the "Big Chief" – known worldwide for his aggressiveness and his love for Cameroon's national football squad. This despite Rigobert's wild CV, which had been read and binned by Mr Muller. Thanks to Bernard Zénier – a former player with FC Metz who was in charge of the recruitment of players at the club – the CV was retrieved and read in extremis. Rigobert was given a chance in Ligue 1. He was a true competitor. It's from the little details that a great career can snowball.

In France, if an individual is comfortable with the technical side of the game he cannot afford to be too laid back as this can very easily be mistaken for something else. At times, the fate of a player is in the hands of individuals who are competent yet whimsical. The early years of a pro footballer can be perilous to the extreme.

My father returned one day from a meeting at the Concorde Lafayette Hotel in Paris organised by the bosses of FC Metz. The idea behind it had been to get across to the parents of the young French youth international, now 20 years old, that he didn't have a hope in hell of succeeding in the world of professional football. The club's top brass, Messrs Razurel and Zénier were categorical. They backed up their arguments with comments made by other people and even said: "Your son doesn't get the point. He will never get his head round professional football. We'll accept any offer of around one million francs to recoup the investment we have made in your kid."

Strangely enough, that same kid was scoring goals and expressing himself fully out on the pitch when playing for France's Under-21 team. This meeting took place just before the 1999 final of the

League Cup in which Metz took part. I had just returned from a six-month loan at Newcastle United. The club was epic, with legends like Alan Shearer and coach Ruud Gullit – winner of the World Footballer of the Year award in 1987 who'd played in the Dutch team that won Euro 1988. The stadium held 50,000 people. I, who had never been in the first XI with FC Metz, had somehow attracted a bigger club on loan, which seemed illogical. I was thrilled to find myself alongside strike partner Shearer: a legend with over 260 goals in the Premier League alone.

Newcastle's football stars and the spectacular lively town on the river, with its phenomenal and special love of sport, changed me forever. Rugby and football are at the centre of every conversation, even if a pint of Guinness is never far away! At the time, the Geordies' passion made me feel proud and was so infectious I found myself grinning from ear to ear. This happy mood stayed with me ever after because of all the great things that happened to me while there. I was lucky: I hardly remember anyone with an angry face. To hear the Toon Army sing from the terraces: "There's only one Saha" was incredible. What a place to start my British football odyssey! Did my love for the place truly kick-off when I scored that left-foot volley which fired Newcastle United into the FA Cup quarter-finals, and on to Wembley? Destroying the hopes of Blackburn Rovers by netting that 37th-minute goal at Ewood Park certainly must have helped.

This six-month encounter was the catalyst for me to do all I could to leave Metz, this club which was gradually destroying my game and my joie de vivre. I survived thanks to my family, my pride and my faith. I survived thanks to my team-mates, my friends, my trainer Détaddéo Francis, Albert Cartier (assistant coach), and President Molinari, who was like a protective father. I survived thanks to the wonderful city of Metz and most of all, my secret dream: to get my family out of their tower block in Noyers-Crapaud. I hung on. It wasn't all bad. Despite his style of coaching which did not suit me, I will always be grateful to Mr Muller for giving me my first real break in the professional game: not long after returning from Newcastle, I was sent on in the 90th minute of my first match and scored; on my 20th birthday. I cannot say thank you enough. But if Petit Louis grew, it certainly wasn't because of him or the other club officials who shot me down at every opportunity and spread defamatory gossip before I headed off to Newcastle.

When asked that classic question which buzzes from club to club, "What do you think of this player? Is he serious?" they preferred to highlight my shortcomings. They said I was lazy, that I did not like running, that I didn't get the point and was unprofessional . . . Their criticism could easily have branded me and followed me like a shadow for years and years. It's as if there was some kind of confusion between indifference and laziness. I realise that asthma is not an advantage for a marathon runner. I understand that sometimes being late can ruffle a few feathers, but what was said was nasty and uncalled for. They did not want another club to show them up for getting it wrong.

Today, I have learned how to anticipate the interpretations of those who make snap judgements. I know that nine times out of 10 a coach will choose a consistent and hard-working player over a gifted but more relaxed player. I understand that a player who does not give the impression of being serious off the pitch is more than likely to be the same on it. I'm beginning to recognise the signs that do not fool, but appearances can be deceptive.

I felt misunderstood, as though the coaches were talking about someone else when they described me. Unfortunately, some people do not have the intelligence or the ability to take a step back in order to evaluate the all-important criteria of a young player. They stick to a stereotypical image of their ideal prototype; they lack vision. Those who do not fit the desired model go by the wayside. Most coaches know the business inside out and their success rate speaks for itself. Nevertheless, major mistakes are made along the way. I was motivated but only focused on the parts of my game which came naturally. Perhaps I am too Caribbean by nature with dreamy, nonchalant tendencies. I wanted to build on my strengths and experience and work on improving my tactical shortcomings.

I did everything to win my one-way ticket to England because when I was with Newcastle we clicked and I immediately felt free to be me. The game is the same everywhere, but the pace varies. This particular rhythm was made for me: an intense, physical, forward flow underpinned by a winning mentality week in week out, home and away. Same as how Zidane describes being with Jean Fernandez, the ex-footballer who currently trains AS Nancy and is known for moulding players (for some he is their spiritual father).

After the loan with the Magpies, I had to go home to Metz while the logistics of my transfer to Fulham were worked out. Unfortunately, during this time I was given my chance in the first team on my return and I played too well, especially in the UEFA Intertoto Cup. Result: FC Metz changed its mind. From one million French francs plus a bus ticket to return to my neighbourhood the club raised my asking price to 30 million French francs and gave me a permanent place in the first team.

How, from one month to the next, could expert opinions suddenly change so drastically? Who knows: if these two months had gone differently all the good years I've lived would've been the stuff of dreams. These events motivated the people who were looking after my interests even more, so I carried on working despite an immense feeling of bitterness gnawing at me.

I made my choice following my principles and my values. I had persevered, playing the game how I wanted to play it. The day came when I put down my bags on the Eurostar platform at Waterloo Station. Destination Fulham FC and the passion and enthusiasm of English football. I'd arrived, at last! I'd stopped listening to people who said my dream was impossible.

Mikel Arteta, midfielder with Arsenal: "Papi, no one should negotiate their dreams, or ambitions. I used to dream of the Champions League, so I made my choice." It was the same with Edwin van der Sar, who chose to return to the winner's podium and trophies with Manchester United after a stint at Fulham.

It's simple: England is a football paradise. The style of play is "total football" and aggressive. The electric atmosphere inside the stadiums is legendary; each has its own special history. The story of football begins in England. I love the physical commitment and its mad pace.

Xabi Alonso, who played for Liverpool from 2004 to 2009, speaking after he had just joined Real Madrid: "When I look at the Premier League, I cannot believe how the pace was so extreme. I wonder how I did it."

The style of football you find differs according to coach, country and culture. Italy is probably the most tactical and the most defensive. You must concentrate and be fully focused to ensure decisiveness and responsiveness at the right moment, be it to defend, or attack.

Zinédine: "Even today I still tell myself I would never have succeeded in my career if I hadn't gone to Italy. I stepped up a level there, in terms of the rigor and the physicality. I couldn't stop vomiting when training. I went for it and pulled out all the stops. Like everyone else, I wanted to make progress."

In Spain possession football is favoured. Players keep the ball in very small spaces. It's a tactical game, although the key thing is the quality of movement and passing that requires precision and fantastic technique. Barcelona and Real Madrid are among the most feared clubs on the European stage.

In England the style of play is generally very fast and very physical. Players have great all-round athletic ability, combining speed, technique, power and energy. The game is a little less tactical, but so positive and dramatic that a certain level of stamina is needed to endure the intensity. And most young English players have to understand, and fast, that they are not just competing with their neighbours from inner-city Liverpool, Newcastle, Cardiff, or London but also from Paris, Barcelona or Brazil.

England is heaven for young foreign talent attracted by the high wages. This may be one reason why few young English players get the chance to play in the Premier League, although a new rule controls the number of foreigners in a team: clubs are obliged to select a minimum of eight "home-grown" players in 25-man squads, excluding under-21s. This is to encourage coaches to develop more English talent. I remember discussing comments made by Arsène Wenger in the changing room with Phil Neville. The Arsenal manager was quoted in the newspaper, *The Independent*: "In Spain, players can be signed up from around the world and the number of foreigners is the same as in England. How come the Spanish still manage to develop players, while the English criticise the number of foreign players in the Premier League?"

Since 2005, France has been favoured by the big European clubs over other European countries when it comes to recruiting players since they are nearly 50 per cent cheaper than their counterparts bought from a British club. Ligue 1 in France fulfils a springboard-like function, giving young players a chance to catch the eye of the big European clubs who can then buy them for a good price. Players like Samir Nasri and Gaël Clichy at Manchester City, and Emanuel Adebayor at Tottenham, among others, are examples of this.

Arsène Wenger questioned the Premier League's top brass about how the English top flight could remain the best league in the world with this new rule. He sees no need for it to regulate the players on the basis of their nationality. The debate boils on.

In May 2011 it was revealed by news agency Mediapart that the French Football Federation was considering setting up shocking quotas restricting the number of foreign players in its youth programmes. It was just a discussion, not a policy, and the debate could have been sensible. Dual-nationality players produced through this system often decide to play for foreign nations (often in Africa) in which they also hold citizenship. So, under consideration was a plan that players going through the national coaching system would have to make a final choice which country to represent when they turn 21 and qualify for elite squads. The French Federation wanted to guarantee that the best players would end up playing for France. They hoped that confirmed rising stars would play for France, but late-developers or less-gifted players would play for their other country. France has become a victim of its own success, training dual-nationality players to a premier level and then having them line up against the national team in World Cups. The reported conversations that were leaked from a meeting included racial stereotyping: "And who are the predominantly big, beefy, powerful players? Blacks. That's the way it is. It's a matter of fact. God knows, in the training academies and football schools there are lots of them . . . The Spanish say, 'We don't have a problem. We don't have any blacks here'." The whole debate was perverted as tensions flared.

What other pleasures are part of my life in England? The food? Well let's just say that I appreciate my wife's cooking and Italian restaurants . . . although discovering the cuisine of my former club Everton and tasting local products was a real eye-opener! Cheshire smokehouse meat and fish; Jamaican jerk chicken; Bakewell tart and the ritual of tea and shortbread biscuits; Everton Mints . . . These sweets are part of the tradition of Everton Football Club: small children in 19th-century costumes throw them to the crowd before every game kicks-off at Goodison Park. All this has great charm, and "Magic Paula" in the canteen at Everton's training ground challenges the great French chefs. Her fillet steaks and sea bass were my favourites.

The fans in England? They are "The Best". I love their attitude towards players who they seem to accept and respect as normal people. The weather? Let's say that if they can, English families make sure they get a holiday in the sun – places like Ibiza, Tenerife or Nice. Taking vitamin D to make the best of the sun's rays is a recommended dietary supplement. The English, famously, love talking about the weather – maybe it's because they were originally island seafarers. Will there be storms in August? Sunny spells in spring? I love seeing motorists here driving convertibles as early as February with their heaters on full blast – the opposite of sissy. The English are real hard-nuts. Even newborns are kitted out in cute t-shirts despite the chilly breezes.

The language? It's extraordinary. I've had to learn and re-learn, but even if I haven't yet mastered it, I'm proud when my nine-year-old son corrects my pronunciation. I'm proud to be able to travel around the world without needing my own personal translator. At Everton, my Anglo-Parisian-Caribbean accent used to provoke lots of laughter. Communication is a great way of sharing with people I love. To joke in both English and French is just great. When the two get mixed up, it's funny.

Here's an example: When I was playing for Fulham, Mr Al Fayed, who had recently bought the club, used to come and see us in the changing rooms after a match. Today he knows the scene well, but to begin with there were a few hiccups. During a conversation with our coach, Jean Tigana, he asked when we were next playing "inside". Of course he meant "at home". So much for learning the jargon of the game!

It's funny to hear so many Tottenham players swearing in French during training. It means a lot to hear "*Comment ça va?*" or "*Putain, pas de soleil.*"[F*** there's no sun.] It's reassuring and makes you feel at home.

In this environment, wherever he goes, the footballer is welcomed and respected. That is why England is not a stepping stone but the peak of a career. Other European leagues are a mixture of the styles of all three championships (Italy, Spain, England). Looking at the French league, it is the number one producer of players for the other four most powerful leagues (Germany, Italy, Spain, England). These championships submit to market forces since French players inevitably go abroad as soon as they meet the criteria of the big leagues.

Believe it or not, I nearly became British! In 2004, I had just arrived at Manchester United, and was told that it was possible Sven Goran Ericsson would consider me for selection in the England team. I had been playing with Newcastle and Fulham for three and a half years already and had not been selected for the full French squad. I would have ended up with French-British dual nationality. Had I chosen to go ahead, I would never have been able to play for France, which in my heart of hearts did not feel right. And the idea of not playing well for England and having to put up with insults did not appeal: "You French c*** you couldn't hit a cow's bum with a banjo!" or, "You collaborator! We English don't surrender!"

It's a long and wonderful adventure. Some players forge onwards and upwards, while others stagnate and are overtaken. For me, that crucial moment when everything fell into place was when I was between 17 and 22 years old, as for so many other players. My breakout moment when everything clicked happened the day I almost died in a car crash. This incident opened my eyes to how lucky I was, at only 20 years old, and how I hadn't seized my chance or lived to the max. I realised I had to explore life as though it never ends. I became selfish and aggressive. Coaches began to see in me potential as a striker when I had done all my training as a left-winger. I changed without really noticing and matured at the right moment. One car crash in France and everything clicked into place.

My father arrived at the scene of the accident shortly after it happened. I had managed to miss a couple of trucks and cars as my BMW M3 began to drift strangely in slow motion. The early-morning rain did little to help, even though I was not going fast. My old man could not understand how I could get out of the car and still go off to train. I had another car crash in 2011, so who knows . . . softly, softly, perhaps gradually I will change into a formidable goalkeeper.

Patrice Evra: "My breakout moment when it all clicked was during my first derby for Manchester United at home to Manchester City. The match was played at 12 noon. Lunchtime. What kind of time is that to play a high-level game? I was used to playing at 9 o'clock at night in France. I remember wanting to eat pasta with salmon at nine o'clock in the morning, same as Miky [Sylvestre] and you. I was surprised by the intensity and commitment. The game kicked-off at 3,000 miles per hour, and I was taken off at half-time after this poisoned chalice of a Premier League welcome. After that match I realised I knew very little about football despite my best years in Monaco. Bro, it left its mark and enabled me to cross the threshold and go ever higher. I've never stopped wanting to make progress. After that, I wasn't surprised by anything ever again."

William Gallas: "Bro, in England it's explosive. I stayed calm and, because I listened to the old-timers, I managed to adapt quickly despite the language barrier and the rest. Marcel Desailly guided me with great advice at Chelsea and pointed me towards the best contacts in his support network. I've raised my game since I arrived in England."

Thierry: "I landed at Arsenal fresh and new, then went through a slight period of doubt. Now I see that what happened with Arsenal had to happen." Like me, Titi felt at home. Accepted despite his flaws. Loved for his qualities.

Djibril Cissé needs a fanatical public for him to push the envelope: "Bro, I like to feel I'm being geed up; being supported by my fans. Liverpool, Marseille, Sunderland, Panatinaïkos, Lazio . . ." This often comes with problems, but Djib needs to be in the hotpot to catch fire.

I too have always chosen my club according to its history and its vibe. My personal criteria that help me choose which club to play for are: family, stability and ambition. My sporting criteria are: style of play, the coach and the chance to win trophies. My criteria of influence are: salary, location and instinct. I have moved from prioritising sporting criteria to criteria of influence and swung full circle back to personal criteria during my career. Each is important and each should be properly weighed up in order to make the best choice.

6

WHEN THE DREAM BECOMES A NIGHTMARE: MANCHESTER UNITED V CHELSEA, THE 2008 CHAMPIONS LEAGUE FINAL

Destination Moscow: a city steeped in Stalinist history. I picture myself in the Luzhniki Stadium, which looks just like a huge flying saucer. The pitch will be invaded by television cameras from all around the world. I visualise the teams running on to the pitch and hear the distinctive music of the Champions League ring out. More inspirational than the Rocky Balboa theme tune, better than the American national anthem, it's unmistakable. It's like a rallying cry announcing the gladiators' arrival into the fighting arena. It's perfection. When this anthem strikes up, it's hard not to show how much your heart is racing. You feel as if the people in the stands are vibrating to the rhythm of your pulse. I think of the little Chinese boy sitting cross-legged in his home, the good Muslim between his five daily prayers, the old chief of an African tribe stroking his long white beard, the small-time gangster in his Brazilian *favela*, even the triple Olympic gold medallist Usain Bolt, a big Manchester United fan, all lining up in front of their TV sets to watch the match they have looked forward to all year: the Champions League Final. I dream about it standing up, sitting down, awake, asleep, on the bench. I think about it 25 hours a day.

Football is simple at Man United: score goals, put on a good show and above all win for the Red Devils. There is just one problem: my temperamental right knee. It swells and deflates without warning. One day everything is fine and the next it triples in size. It feels like needles are knitting up my ligaments. I'm not able to play the way I like, or to be myself on the pitch. You need mental strength and an intense love for your sport. To carry on playing under these conditions is hellish. When the ball is passed to me on the right, I have to be mindful to avoid putting too much pressure on my right leg. When the ball is in the air and the defender is behind me, I fall back towards him and try by every means possible to control the ball with my chest. But from that position I can't trap the ball. I can't jump or take off like a rocket as I once could. My years at Fulham are far behind me now. I used to run deep, pull up sharp and change direction in a flash. I played without a care and felt indestructible. Now I have to be crafty and concentrate hard, which has never been my strength. The medics tell me it's my synovial joints reacting badly after an operation I had in the United States. Doctor Steadman, the world-renowned specialist knee surgeon who saved the careers of Alan Shearer and Michael Owen among others, had wanted me to have another longer and more complicated operation, but I had chosen the shorter, easier option. My competitive spirit refused to accept that my knee could react badly.

The mythical pitch at Old Trafford is the best place in football to have fun. The 80,000-seater stadium is a field of dreams, with its fantastic atmosphere, avalanches of goals, style of play, highly motivated players, stoppage-time goals, 60-odd trophies, years-old rivalries and jealousies. To wear the same beautiful red jersey as Cantona, Best and Keane did before me is a dream come true. These legendary players have inspired so many football lovers to play for, or support, Manchester United. To survive in this club, you need to work hard to maintain your optimum level. You must be good enough not to be relegated to the subs bench, which is already well garnished with international players. They may be big stars in their country, but the bench at Man U still isn't so bad. There are so many world-class footballers at the club that one below-par performance is enough for a player to get thrown onto tomorrow's transfer scrap heap.

All I want is to train, to play and to take advantage of any opportunity to make further progress. I am surrounded by some of the very best talent there is to work with. I want to reach the brightest of stars. Ever since I was a kid all I ever wanted was to play football. My sport. My passion. I want to play, no matter how badly I perform. I would rather be criticised for a bad performance than not play. Because of my damaged cartilage, vipers' tongues say that I can't be bothered to play and have lost the will to score goals and win matches. They don't even begin to understand the suffering and the despair you feel when you're accused of a crime you haven't committed. I find it hard to believe that people could think a player was crazy enough to say he was injured when he is not and so miss out on the most beautiful moments of his sporting life. Is it a psychological injury? No way, it's purely physical! I search for explanations, answers, new ideas, new treatments, new types of training and the only answer I have is prayer. I've been unlucky, that's all. Why would I not want to experience the best years of my game?

Even Sir Alex Ferguson has a go at me. Despite this mistake on his part, he is the only person I can not allow myself to criticise. Deep down I know why he reacted and acted like that. The thirst for victory. The will to win. The reasoning behind such allusions is certainly one of the many factors that contributes to his phenomenal track record. The disappointment of not being able to satisfy his burning desire for his team to succeed on a collective and individual basis. He wanted so much for me to be a winner and to score goals.

I return from my umpteenth trip to see a specialist, my umpteenth comeback, my umpteenth physical preparation. I feel good. I am inspired and on top form. My dream is still real and my chances of becoming part of club history are possible once more. I can't feel my toes. My boots are often too tight, but my feet do exactly what I ask. Confidence permeates every move I make. Hard work pays off. I've sweated like a dog in the gym. I've followed to the letter all the physiotherapy and co-ordination exercises. I'm completely re-motivated thanks to the help of legendary Ole Gunnar Solskjaer who is retired from football due to serious injury, but always smiling and full of positive energy. Mike Clegg, one of the trainers back then, also helped me hugely with his circuit training. I've proved that everything I've done while waiting to come back from injury was tougher than messing about during training with the coach. I've added broccoli and vegetable soup to my diet. It feels like my blood has turned to firewater. I am truly alive and kicking and more than ready for this global event. I'm ecstatic to be back just in time and to feel so sharp. I am convinced that I will have an important role to play in the final as I have just what it takes to put Chelsea in danger. Your team-mates' confidence when dribbling or making controlled passes to you is inspiring and you have to learn how to make the most of it. You must play your game and contribute to the best of your ability, as well as have the burning desire to win all together as a team. I, in turn, have what it takes to inspire confidence. I'm more than capable of scoring a goal simply by being prepared for one of those sensational Ryan Giggs combinations of chop, step-over, and perfect cross. And then there's Paul Scholes: that little red-headed genie with a whole range of incisive passes. I'm also just as capable of scoring a goal on my own.

The alarm clock blasts me out of my sleep. I'm fresh as a daisy and can't wait for training. The sky is overcast, but the sun makes an effort to shine through the haze. The light dazzles. The players' shirts are drenched in sweat because of their efforts, not the sun's rays. At Carrington, Manchester United's training ground, everything is ready to help us achieve the league and Champions League double. The staff attend to our every need. The training camp is bubbling with excitement. The green grass of the pitch is primped and primed by the groundsmen who are working on it well before the players' alarm clocks wake them up.

After a warm up and some exercises, we play a five-a-side game on a scaled-down pitch. I score two goals in quick succession and the goalies hardly get a chance to touch the ball other than when they retrieve it from the back of the net. Everything's going my way: goals flow one after the other and the coach's feedback reassures me. I feel so good. I'm happy and free. I'm back! I strike, I dribble, I jump, I turn. I'm sharp. The doubt that had been circulating in my veins is replaced by confidence and a hunger for victory. It's unbelievable. *I'm back*. One minute later it's all over. Here I go, off to the infirmary. I'm back alright: back in the medical room.

It's hard to believe that my calf could give out because of such an insignificant move. I'm convinced that it's nothing serious. Just a little twinge. A blocked nerve. An adhesion of the fascia. A spasm. Whether it's serious or not is not the point. It's my dream and I cannot re-live the nightmare of 9 July, 2006. Missing that final was too difficult to get over; to forget. To come close to such a big competition and watch it as a spectator. Again. No, it's impossible. Unthinkable. My body can't let me down. Again. I'm limping, but in five days it will be fine. Everything will work out just as in my dream. I believe it. I believe it so fervently. I pray. I touch every bit of wood I walk past. I want it so bad. I've seen it up close in my mind's eye: the cup with those huge ears which will be my pride and joy. I touch it and lift it up: happy as can be.

When we arrive at the hotel in the centre of Moscow I'm not walking right, but manage to hide it from my team-mates. Rio Ferdinand has faith in me and tells me so. There are others who remind me of the importance of being at the top of my game in this final. There are numerous players like me who dream of these privileged moments. It's the evening before the match and the maestro must compose his match squad; his first team and his subs. Each player is chosen according to their versatility, their experience, their mental capacity, their skills and the ability they have to make the difference at any given moment. There isn't one player at Manchester United who isn't gifted with at least two of these characteristics. The choice is agonising for the manager since the players have been so authoritative throughout the whole competition, yet, despite everything, some will be sacrificed. The group is too well-stocked. There are just 18 players on the team sheet. The squad consists of 30 players of the highest level. I have a major problem. In fact I have a quite a few. I'm injured and it's unlikely I'll recover before the last training session. The one in which the commander chooses his battalion.

This match against Chelsea has a huge element of rivalry, of a battle for supremacy, since the two best English teams will fight to be the best club team in the world. Each play two such different styles and yet are equally effective in getting results. Victory and confidence flow in abundance through the veins of all the players. Chelsea v Manchester United is not the classic battle of David and Goliath. It's Goliath dressed in blue versus Goliath dressed in red. As a Champions League final it's a clash of the titans. There will be duels, opportunities, noble gestures, few mistakes and lots of action.

It's the evening before the match. I work out with Nemanja Vidic on the exercise bike in the hotel gym. The others have gone to training and are giving everything they've got to show that they have what it takes to be in the final group or the first team. Vida has a bad calf too and doesn't look like he's fully fit. A calf strain is a difficult injury to manage. A match at this level demands myriad little twists and turns, jumps and frequent pushing off. I'm still limping after 20 minutes on the bike in the little gym on the top floor of our hotel. I have a searing pain at the top of my calf like an electric shock every time I make an ill-judged move. The scan I had a couple of days before showed up as nothing more than a build up of fluid and some tearing of the tissue. For me, it hurts to jump. Now, I can no longer even walk normally.

On the morning of the match, when I go back to my room after the midday meal, I know that the noose is tightening fast. After our usual 4.30pm snack, I ice my calf yet again. I rest. I pray and ask God for help, one more time. Within a few hours I must prove that I can take my place on the bench. One solution is to do what Nemanja will do: have a steroid injection. I'm ready for anything. My desire to contribute to my club's Champions League victory is at fever pitch.

I call my wife who is staying at another hotel in the Russian capital. I want to hear her comforting voice and ask her advice even though I already know full well what I'm going to say to the coach. She senses straightaway that it's not good news and I'm close to losing the plot. Someone who is normally calm and relaxed, I can't hold it together. I feel a knot twisting in the depths of my stomach. I am tense and pessimistic. I speak fast and loud. I can't breathe properly. How did I get into this situation? If it's not my knee it's something else. Unbelievable. Black magic crosses my mind. This is too much! Who's wishing this harm upon me? Who is playing with a voodoo doll of me? I have never wanted anything but the best for people. I don't understand anything anymore. I've had enough of bad luck.

"Sweetheart what have I done? What should I do? I'll never get back up again after such a disaster. It's just too much."

My wife senses my anguish as droplets of sweat glide down the length of my body, which is in a state of extreme nervous pressure and stress. She tells me to tell the physio that I'm ready to take any risks necessary. That it will be fine. That's what I had already decided to say. As soon as I was injured I could have gone to see him and tell him the same thing.

I call Rob Swire, the physio, to ask him if I can try the anaesthetising shot. I dread going on to the pitch, then having to come off because I can't hold it together. This catastrophic scenario playing through my mind is such proof of my egotism: there are players in the squad who are in full control of their abilities. We're a tight unit and I'm in pieces. Picture this: the substitute who is supposed to come on and make all the difference has to come off after 10 minutes because of an injury that he had before he went on to play. So the team finds itself with 10 men against 11. Ridiculous. A disaster. Vida's situation is less problematic for the manager to deal with. He'll start and if he can't continue, he'll be substituted. Rob and the doctor tell me that I can't use the anaesthetic as it's potentially dangerous for asthmatics. I curse. I rage. It's a living nightmare. It's all over.

In just a few minutes I have to face the manager who I have respected all my life. I would love to say to him: "Coach, I can play." I can play and shoot for goal. I want to lift up the cup by its big ears just like in my dream. The maestro has to know soon, so he can put together his orchestra, his game plan, his tactics, his strategy. A little before the final meeting I have to talk to the manager and the medical staff to let them know my feelings.

I stay a long time in my room praying to God, hoping he could stop the clock to give me a little more time to recover. I never dreamed I'd find myself in this situation. Taking such a decision is horrendous, but it's taken. I'm overwhelmed by a selfish desire. I want to play. I must play.

I'm confronted by a face which is frustrated, despairing and so human, yet so determined to win. The coach tells me I will not be part of the team as he cannot take that kind of risk. He doesn't need me anymore. I understand and I accept his logic completely. The decision is fair, but it feels as though my blood has stopped flowing in my veins. My nostrils flare and my pupils dilate. My breath quickens. My heart races. Nothing. It's too late now for God to stop the clock. As I write these lines I am aware of my suffering and notice how the scar still cuts deep. I didn't realise it immediately, but my career with the Red Devils ended that day.

So today, in Moscow, it's a repeat of my failure in the final of the 2006 World Cup. Once again, I must support my team and cheer them on from way up in the stands of the stadium. It sucks, but there's nothing I can do other than sit there powerless. I'm crushed. I get changed and set off with my team-mates, but I'm not really present. I'm on the bus, but the pre-match tension that normally builds up from then on digs a grave for my footballer's joy.

I hear the Champions League anthem, but it destroys me as I'm not on the pitch. I picture Usain Bolt, the R'n'B singer Justin Timberlake and the other supporters in front of the screen, but *I'm not on the pitch*. I had seen myself score a magnificent goal. I visualise all those who would have supported me, but am not really in the stadium; I'm just a ghost. I sense the excitement and the pressure, but the cameras are not angled towards me. I'm just another face in the crowd. In the changing room before the match my stomach fights a great lump of sadness which rises up inside me, ready to burst. My team-mates offer me consoling looks. I still see myself scoring that magnificent goal, but I'm not wearing my special Champions League boots customised with the number 9. I hear the crowd shout my name, but I'm just in the stands. When I take my place I am crying in my wife's arms. I cry like a little boy who has just seen his favourite Christmas present smashed before his very eyes. A present that he has waited and waited for. It's terrible. My stomach churns.

Strangely, this pain runs deeper than that of the 2006 World Cup. That suspension was stupid, but showed my desire. I wanted to do too well. Two slightly mis-timed tackles, two yellow cards, a great final that passed right under my nose. It was a big lesson to learn from. This time in Moscow, it's unfair. At this Champions League final, I don't want to learn any more lessons. I have learned all I need to know and remember it all well. Why give me something just to take it away again? Why bring me all the way here just to send me home again? Why make it to the final just to sit and watch? It's pure torture.

The beautiful unpredictability of this sport is encapsulated in the fact that John Terry, who should be the hero of the night, is scuppered when Edwin saves his team-mate Nicolas Anelka's penalty. Before that, Terry had had a chance to lead his club to victory in this big final. If his strike in the penalty shoot-out had hit the net, only 11m away from him, he would have given Chelsea their first-ever Champions League title. But he slipped and his kick hit the post.

A blank, or rather a black hole appears after yet another match that has ended in an extraordinary penalty shoot-out, having finished 1-1 in extra-time. Fast, 100 per cent engaged, technically skilled and highly pressured. I'm so happy but . . . it didn't turn out as I'd imagined. Once the twists and turns during this battle for supremacy are over, my club Manchester United are left celebrating. I'm so happy that for a moment I don't realise I haven't even won this trophy personally. My memories intertwine with the good and the not so good. I'm part of that period in time, nothing more. I'm proud, but it's hard. My participation was real enough, but my ego gets in the way of my ability to celebrate the victory in the same way my team-mates are able to.

Paradoxical, unfair and unpredictable. Football is an incredible machine. It is one of those rare sports that can generate a multitude of overwhelming emotions, unexpected moments, suspense and controversy in just a short time frame.

During the 2006 World Cup Final, one of the greatest players of all time, Zinédine Zidane, reminded us of how a dream can appear and vanish in the blink of an eye. A goal from the penalty spot, French joy in the stands, a brief exchange of words, a reaction, a red card, a sending off, a crushing exit when everything had been set to dethrone the Brazilian king Pelé. Had Buffon been a little less attentive he wouldn't have stopped Zizou's header in extra-time. With this goal it would have been a done deal. The Italians would've been screwed and the World Cup would've been French.

Vigilance at all moments is necessary, since we are often our own worst enemy. Often our actions and reactions just seconds after an incident can catch us unawares. Your guard is down. Your concentration and a flash of euphoria make you vulnerable, just like when Zizou gave Materazzi that headbutt.

7
THE WORLD CUP: THE PRIVILEGE OF A LIFETIME

Michel Ebong, an advisor to African players, spoke to me in his Cameroonian-accented English: "*Hau yu dei*! [How you doing?] In Africa, seeing football players spread the pride and joy of their people is all-important. The economy of an African country explodes in direct relation to the exploits of its national football team. African players represent hope, recognition and the riches of a passionate sports culture. Entire streets are crowded with barefoot young people, smiling broadly when they spot their heroes. It's madness. The bus has to find its way through the crowd which loves the show . . . the dream . . . the illusion."

I recently watched the DVD of Didier Drogba, *L'Incroyable Destin* [Incredible Destiny] and it showed me how crazy Africans are for football. It was about the Ivory Coast's qualification for the World Cup in 2006 and Drogba's famous speech after they had done so which helped calm the violent conflicts of a country divided after two or three years of war. Ethnic divisions, religious differences, killings and extreme radicalism have destroyed many African countries; little effort is made to truly understand the people. Money, violence and corruption are effective tools used by those in power. Lack of political stability and an inflexible mindset hamper many of Africa's political leaders. After the team had qualified for their first-ever World Cup finals, Didier was able get more attention than any politician could ever dream of, and his message was as important as all the goals he ever scored for his country. This earned him a well-deserved place in *Time* magazine's "Top 10 Most Influential People of the World" in 2010. He is a shining example for all generations. Here is what a World Cup means to the African people. Where existence is a matter of life and death, football offers a brief but wonderful escape. Looking at the film of the fans on the streets of Abidjan and the expressions on their faces, they seem possessed. The crowd is in a frenzy as if it were high on cocaine. The crowd pays homage to its idols for enabling them to dream once more.

The World Cup provides a financial windfall for its partners, official suppliers and licensees selling sportswear, computer games, official publications, watches, sticker albums and the official music. At least 400 different products are sold through FIFA's national and local agents. In 2006 the big bucks advertising hoardings around the pitch reached an average of 93 million viewers per match and 5.9 billion total viewers for the whole tournament. For a host country, it means an average of around 100,000 jobs created and thousands of consumers coming into the country. The World Cup alone makes profits for FIFA of around US$16 billion.

For me and many supporters, the World Cup is addictive like a drug. Problems at home or at work are temporarily forgotten. It's a chance to indulge in your passion and have a laugh with your mates. Consumers from different countries around the world savour the bittersweet results. Watching athletes play the beautiful game for the pride of their nation seems to make people want to drink. Day and night, everything revolves around the joy and the pain transmitted by the TV screen. Alcohol intensifies emotions and releases inhibitions.

Claudio Ibrahim Vaz Leal, a.k.a. "Branco", winner of the World Cup with Brazil in 1994, is quoted as saying: "Sex and alcohol both played an important role in Brazil's victory."

The Guardian voted the following chant, sung by the supporters of eventual winner Spain, the best of the 2010 World

Cup: "Alcohol, alcohol, alcohol, alcohol; *hemos venido a embor-racharnos, el resultado nos da igual*!" [Alcohol, alcohol, alcohol, alcohol; we've come here to get drunk, we don't care about the result!].

Being selected for a national team for a tournament is an honour. But being a privileged sportsman in this world means experiencing this global event as an actor. The words of a journalist cannot even begin do justice to how a player feels during that month, let alone during the month of preparation preceding it. For me, being selected for the French squad in 2006 was something that had seemed to be an impossible dream a few years previously. But it had become completely logical given my more recent performances.

Although my form towards the end of the 2005/06 season was good, playing for Manchester United, I had only come back from injury in November 2005 which meant I only had a few months to prove myself to the coach. Players will do almost anything to increase their chances of being included in the prestigious list of attackers in a World Cup squad. The five who are selected are the ones in top form, based on the number of goals they are scoring for their club. On 14 May, when I realised that my name was on Raymond Domenech's list, the immense feeling of relief and joy was immediately replaced by a desire to do my best underpinned by a strong sense of responsibility. My happiness and the congratulations of those close to me became secondary.

Of course, France's 1998 triumph, and particularly Lilian Thuram's goals in the semi-final against Croatia, played in a loop in my mind all the time. As did the group of on-pitch leaders in that triumphant team who would become legendary; symbols of French solidarity for a society that is too often divided. They showed how to work together for the success of the team. I remember that brief moment after the 3-0 win over Brazil in the final when racism and issues of colour and social class all but disappeared during and after the victory celebrations. This makes me shiver. Incredible but true: tradesmen offered free drinks, discounts and even gifts to anyone walking around in a blue jersey! Cops joked with small-time hustlers so long as they chanted, "One-two-three-zero." These flashbacks are indelibly printed in my memory and contributed to the realisation of my childhood dream.

In my experience in 2006, each player saw his World Cup through the events as they unfolded and conversations with those around him. As a player locked away in the training camp, it was difficult to grasp the enormity of the event when the priority was to keep focused on the goals and objectives of the team whatever the circumstances. Victory is goal number one. That is why it is impossible to accept defeat, especially when the journey has been so long and eventful.

My experience is hard to describe, despite my happiness to have been able to take part in such an extraordinary human adventure. It is paradoxical and frustrating. When you walk on to the pitch a tidal wave of colour streams before your eyes. You see the stadium, but the fans are blurred. With hindsight, my World Cup went too fast. The pleasure and pride are immense, but it's like puffing on the best Cuban cigar without exhaling properly through your nose and enjoying the bouquet.

The fervour of the French supporters can overwhelm and even paralyse players at times. The pressure sweeps up the backs of the footballers. The hopes and expectations of an entire country are projected on to them.

It was during that semi-final match against Brazil that the World Cup seemed synonymous with the real meaning of putting on a "show". I fully understood its significance. I will never forget those images of the crowd and Zizou's signature "roulette" spin turn. That day I observed the incredible sight of the entire Brazilian team being mesmerised by one player on his own.

In Brazil they were supposedly saying: "Zidane is Brazilian, but he doesn't know it 'cause his parents lied about his background when he was a kid." Yeah right! On the bench, we yelled with our team-mates like we did back in the 'hood: "Whoah! Ahhhhh . . . Man it's kicking-off . . . PoPoPo, see that guy? It's like he's playing in his front room. Piss-taker!"

As we progressed to the final I saw the pride and joy in French fans' eyes and sensed the excitement and stress of each match reflected in my family. There was an insanely staccato rhythm to the whole thing.

It is easier to appreciate the impact of a World Cup after it's all over or, of course, when you're not involved. When you're on the pitch and in the thick of it you're in the eye of the storm. It has a life of its own. From his leather armchair or on the terraces, the spectator picks up on the ebb and flow of the tournament and can see everything clearly. Having an overview means he can zoom in on details. As he follows his team on TV, the viewer also gets commentary from former players, portraits of those taking part, anecdotes, the boos and the cheers and the hooligans. He sees the big picture: the bars and hot dogs, match tickets sold for 10 times their original price, banners and bunting, supporters with their shirts off warmed by alcohol and outdoor big screens capturing some of the live atmosphere of a football stadium as thousands of football fans go nuts in beautiful squares in a whole bunch of countries. There's everything you can imagine. Anything goes. Just follow your imagination, decide how you want to experience the World Cup, then go with the flow. Take time to appreciate, listen and soak up the emotions as well as share them.

But the dedicated players at the peak of their careers have trained hard for months and months to play just a handful of crucial games. They live in a bubble, protected from what is written and reported in the media. Some read and analyse commentaries, others avoid them, preferring not to be unsettled. The player will only face reality for a flash of a second here and there if he and the coach allow it, because each has his way of releasing the pressure. Some listen to music and blow their iTunes accounts sky high, others are gripped by the latest TV series. Very few family visits to the training camp are allowed, so a Skype account for virtual kissing and hugging is all-important.

During the World Cup we adopted a routine which was supposed to put us at ease. We got up every morning like it was a big week building up to a Manchester or north London derby. We trained with team-mates that we had to get to know again; some we had long admired and some we'd only just met. We had to adapt to a system that did not necessarily suit us individually, but was expected to give an extra dimension to the team. Same as with our clubs, we analysed our rivals by watching endless videos. The workouts were a bit different because there was so little time to work on systems and tactics, but the philosophy of the training was the same as throughout the year: we were given tactical benchmarks, techniques and the mindset of world champions. Sometimes we figured out a tactical manoeuvre. Between training sessions each player killed time as best he could because the pressure, expectations and ambitions; and the desire of a nation, were the only things that really mattered. The sensations in all of our minds and bodies remain indescribable.

It is such an exciting tournament. You have to give all you've got for your country, yet how you sense the build up to a match is so very different to the emotional roller coaster felt by a supporter. The player does not go down the long and painful road travelled by a fanatical fan who has saved for months and doesn't take a day off work so he can buy his tickets and travel to the tip of Africa. The player is asked to focus on one objective and to forget the outside world. Yet he has to infect the world with his energy and passion while keeping calm, contained and professional under pressure.

The atmosphere is electric when the coach announces his first team. The tension and the envy are palpable. Those selected furtively glance at each other as they mingle and try not to upset the substitutes. When you are not chosen, it's far from easy to keep up your motivation and spontaneity when you're trained to be a bad loser and to never be satisfied when defeated or left stewing on the bench. Sitting on the bench is especially tough since the moment the whistle blows and the match is underway, the pressure dissipates and is replaced by total concentration and the desire to do well if and when you are called into the action. In the stands, yelling and chanting or snacking on a hot dog acts like a release. On the bench, you have to stay utterly focused, ready to hit the ground running despite the pressure and the stress tingling up your legs. Minutes feel like hours before you go on. In the group of 23 international players, some never have doubts and are brimming with ambitions and dreams, while others are high with the tension of it all, or are just young and therefore happy to be there. Everyone experiences this extraordinary moment according to where he is in his career, his dreams, his mindset and his talent. On the pitch the pressure feeds your desire to do well. Your dreams are no longer yours because the public, your homeland, your origins and your followers who see themselves in you have taken you hostage. And if you pick up on the coach's stress, chances are it will infect you.

Sometimes the desire to do well is so great that your legs and your mind are paralysed. Your pulse rises too fast and does not come down. Sometimes the desire to seem cool, calm and collected interferes with how players and their fans get on. Never forget that the number one objective for the team is to win, not to please the public.

The player's support network will help him to understand how lucky he is to have had an opportunity to give fun and excitement to their country's fans and sports enthusiasts in general. It's as if he were a tiny piece of a huge jigsaw puzzle depicting a beautiful scene. He might see some of the other pieces beside him, but he cannot begin to appreciate the picture in its entirety and does not have enough distance from the whole thing to marvel at the finest details.

In 2006, I was there. I witnessed the aftermath of the Zidane-Materazzi drama. In 2010, I watched the carnival turn sour in South Africa along with the rest of France. French fans are likely to say that their wine had a slight taste of piss and they were forced to spit it out. When the news unfolded that the French team were refusing to get off the team coach to train at the World Cup after Nicolas Anelka was sent home I wanted to call Pat Evra and say, "Listen, the whole world is looking at you. Lots of players and French citizens are with you on that bus," but I couldn't. I look forward to reading what he has to say in his book. His testimony should enlighten all those spectators who find it hard to take a step back in such extraordinary situations. I was so devastated when I watched those disastrous scenes on TV in action replay that it took me several weeks to figure out how and why things had reached such a point. In 2010, the French team was 100 per cent self-sufficient and disconnected from reality. Yet *Les Tricolores*, like all the other teams, were expected to perform on the world stage for one month in front of around 3.2 billion viewers or 46.4 per cent of the global population. The French who stayed home and especially those who had made the long trip to Africa were well and truly vexed.

Sticking to high standards of conduct and good sportsmanship at all times throughout the tournament is fundamental. In 2006 we could not lose face, but were expected to pull our weight and ensure we stood united and proud. For more than a month of intense competition, we were expected to live side by side with a bunch of people, not all of whom we got on with. We almost always brushed against hypocrisy. We had to keep up our team spirit for the good of the group; speak without really saying anything in interviews and look like we were listening. We had to perfect our game of replying to journalists without really giving them any information and not let anything leak out. It was like being enveloped by an invisible shell. The codes of the group had to be followed at all times, whether winning or losing, all the while staying welded together.

What was the catalyst for trouble within the French team at the 2010 World Cup? The codes that play a crucial role in football club and in the national team got muddled up. The players were blind to the consequences of their actions. I longed to call them and tell them about what was being discussed. I know from personal experience how you tend to make better choices with the benefit of hindsight; it's all too easy to judge in the heat of the moment.

The individual may be important, but the group and most of all the number of points and goals scored are paramount. In this world of sporting objectives, without a victory, everything can blow up under pressure from the media and the public. What happened should be positive in the long run because, like a child who has just smashed his nose on the ground, everything will be done to avoid the same thing happening again. A lesson will have been learned.

I do not allow myself to judge anyone. Life has shown us that France loves people in need. Do not distort what I am saying. To be clear: since the South African meltdown, France has hugely supported its young players. A Stade de France draped in *bleu-blanc-rouge* is an extraordinary sight. But it happens more often for rugby. Even in the time of Zinédine Zidane to see such hysteria and hilarity in the stadium was rare. The French Football Federation has improved its PR strategy and image. Flags and bunting along the balconies of the three tiers of stands celebrate the French national football team. It's all eye candy for sports fans.

Football holds a special place in the heart of humankind. Its energy is universal and unique. Try to imagine what it would be like to feel the intense emotions of each player performing on the pitch. Perhaps the players and their fans reflect back to each other the intensity of their feelings, like a mirror of emotions. Brazilian,

French, English, Ivorian and other football nuts around the world go crazy; collectively shouting, screaming and laughing for a month until they are hoarse. Then they talk about it to their kids and mates for years afterwards.

From beginning to end, from errors to exploits, from disappointment to success, from smoke bombs to banners, from a red card to a gold trophy, in just a flash, the essence of football is natural, infinite and contagious. Players understand how important the World Cup is to the world, but it is so big that sometimes the pressure is almost too much for them.

The player is hooked on his sport. He is football crazy – he is mad for it. He respects and worships the game. This global event is the high-water mark of his lifelong career as an elite athlete. He has scaled the Everest of his sport under high voltage and high surveillance.

The tournament has a cumulative audience capacity of 28.8 billion [figures from 2002, for more info see www.fifa.com]. The most unpredictable and potent cocktail of emotions there is, it can cause heart attacks, epileptic seizures, or divorce. It's crazy and it's magic. That's why people pay to watch. Why they cry and slog their guts out. Why fans travel thousands of miles. It can be enjoyed alone without moderation, but there is nothing better than enjoying it with friends.

II
THE DARK SIDE OF *THE SUN*

8
MOVE, AND I'LL SHOOT YOU DOWN!

The beautiful game has become a global soap opera with money and sex as its lynchpin. Players are under pressure to play to the best of their ability and win. Reading headlines about a fellow player like this fantasy in the *Daily Mirror* makes me sick to my stomach: "Ghosts, goats, lady boys and pierced party chickens: the top 10 foreign football sex scandals which make John Terry look tame."

It's hard not to be insulted or destabilised by all the criticism and nonsense written in the press. Whether "constructive" or negative, criticism unsettles players and coaches and impacts on their preparation for upcoming games. At times it can be a motivator, or an extra pressure point, but it is more generally something we have to learn to deal with and endure. Some players use the media to try and boost their reputations, while others will do anything to avoid being interviewed.

Life in the spotlight is like a big game hunt: journalists lie in wait for us – we are their prey. Theirs is a blood sport. If we move they take aim. The pack cares little whether we live or die in their quest for a story. We are watched more closely than by a referee. You can be fouled by the media; they can kick you, trip you up, slide tackle into your lives, but in this game you are given no penalties and only very rarely are you the winner. It's a game where you are built up just to be knocked down. I once read a piece in the *Daily Mirror* referring to footballers as "over-paid, over-pampered thugs" with the headline: "Let's Kick the Footie Gods off their Pedestals."

In each country the scenario is pretty much the same. In France the relationship between footballers and the media is healthier, but the inclination is for the press to trivialise the game or even to mock footballers for being cheesy, whereas in England homage is paid and stars are instantly born when fresh young talent is overexposed. Everything is embellished and the press only really go on the attack when a star gives a lacklustre performance.

The game in each country varies. The French approach is not particularly passionate; the game can even come across as dull. The English approach is much more exciting. Yet all the Brits do is to cherry pick the best of France. Henry, Malouda, Anelka, Vieira, Nasri, Cissé, Diaby and other adopted players like Drogba and Essien, originally discovered in France, now swear by the English system. Oddly, the French did not covet them or value them as the English did. It's a shame and perhaps even detrimental to the French game.

Players who move abroad often struggle when they return home, perhaps for this reason, and also because of the high wages. Nicolas Anelka was hounded by the French media when he returned to PSG from Real Madrid in 2000. It was as if the journalists were waiting for him to mess up, to write reams of copy along the lines of, "He matured at Arsenal and Real Madrid yet cannot get to grips with the French championship." As if this was a way of saying that the French game is tougher and better than all the other European leagues. Despite scoring more than 15 goals in his second spell with PSG between 2000 and 2002, Nicolas could not cope with all the media hype and his bad relationship with the manager, Luis Fernandez. Yet it was important for Nico to return to the club close to his heart, having moved from PSG to Arsenal three years earlier at the age of 18, and to evolve with the other good young players there. But despite the team being strengthened by world stars such as Ronaldinho, Jay Jay Okocha and Mikel Arteta, it just didn't work out for Nico or the team.

I've discussed this with various players. Truth is, the French are more demanding and less admiring of their players. Perhaps this is because of supporters' expectations? Maybe football is not loved in the same way as in Britain? Do French players behave differently at home to abroad?

When I speak badly of French football, I may be exaggerating, but to see cameras being introduced into changing rooms after a game (as has started to happen in my homeland), intruding on the players' privacy and their universe, shows how this world is losing its mystery, its secrets and its class. Thankfully, such practices are not allowed by the French national team. Hero worship is generally rooted in mystery and unquestioning adoration. But in France journalists interview anyone and everyone – players, coaches, substitutes – behind the scenes before, during and after a match, as well as at half-time. After a match in England, you rarely see players in the changing room in their "Pull In" underwear which leaves nothing to the imagination, or hear their triumphant shouts and victory songs.

Training sessions in France are generally open to the public and provide regular access, but having distance between players and supporters is crucial to fostering admiration and mutual respect. In England it is rare for the press to be given permission to attend training sessions. You rarely see players in a context other than the stadium. I think all this has an impact on how fans see players.

Although there are superstar players in France, the press do not make a song and dance about them. I remember Ronaldinho being forced to sit on the bench at PSG when all the public in the stands wanted to watch was him. The raw talent of a phenomenon may be respected, but all too often a more conventional player is preferred. Perhaps the treatment of Ronaldinho was a way of punishing his Brazilian style and flair? Any show of high spirits, singing, dancing the samba or blowing away his fans by performing his trademark "flip-flap" – moving the ball to the outside and quickly flipping it back with the inside of his foot – did not seem to please the coach. French journalists and trainers recognised his great technique, but did they appreciate it? And what about Ben Arfa and Nasri? Two great talents who are stars of the Premier League but are often criticised in the French media for not being "team" players when they play for the national team. I have no idea, but maybe it's the difference between entertainment value and producing a beautiful film. Great long shots, evocative close-ups, plot, pace and good acting make a good movie. But a film with actors lacking the "it" factor and panache can make even the best drama boring to watch.

The English and the French press packs are not that different when it comes to destroying a player. Journalists the world over seem to learn the tricks of their trade in the same school. Over time, accepting criticism becomes a habit, but it's very annoying when the press pack go after the man and his private life. The media defines a player's image whether he likes it or not. When a child hears that his hero is a villain who intimidates the opposition using certain tactics, he will begin to hate him whereas before he liked that footballer's style of play. The media controls public opinion.

Some supporters use football stadiums to insult, scream at and spit on men, yet in the outside world they would be judged and punished for such behaviour. Their out-of-control aggression is like that of some car drivers. Being overtaken or having to brake because of a pedestrian or a slow-moving truck imbues the driver with the aggression of a UFC fighter. Some fans seem to feel that, because they have grown up with certain players and seen them so much on TV, they nearly think they own them because of the expensive annual season ticket they pay to watch their favourite team play. Some fans dress up in a certain way to watch their favourite football team from the stands and show their support while others wear skinhead fashions, high-street designer brands or other vulgar, aggressive gear. They yell at their team, let off steam and vent all the stress that's been building up all week on the players, which no doubt makes them feel better.

A minority seem to think they are playing a video game and see themselves as the owner or trainer of your club, so they show disrespect when you have a momentary loss of form. (A terrible example being the public taunting of world-class player, Fernando Torres, who at one point had only scored one goal in 14 matches for Chelsea.) They'll say, "Hey, Louis! C'mere! *C'mere*! We pay your wages with our hard-earned dosh, so move your arse, sharpish!" Whether you're with your family or not, they don't hold back and can be rude and disrespectful. The fury of some fans can be understood when it comes to players who appear arrogant or disinterested – for example when a group of children ask for an autograph and are turned down. Although I do not attract crowds of autograph hunters, I can still understand that player's discomfort and the fact that they might just not want to spend a quarter of an hour in a shopping centre signing when they're with their kids. We have a duty to respond to these requests, but all too often it's an awkward moment that's hard to describe if you've never experienced it. Sometimes the player adopts an attitude that might appear puzzling. But maybe he has been approached when he is leaving the ground and in a hurry, or when he's on the phone, or refuses to sign an autograph because if he does a whole lot more requests will follow on behind. Others make no excuses and are just unpleasant, but that's just one out of 10 football players. Unfortunately it's from them that the public take their cue and draw their own conclusions, the minority becoming the majority, as is so often the case.

Ji-Sung Park: "To have to go shopping with a bodyguard makes me want to avoid these simple, everyday kinds of things when I return to Korea because I'm afraid of hurting people's feelings. It's great to be recognised, but it's not so easy to please a whole crowd."

Journalists can put on the pressure, and because of them fans sometimes do the same. Some give stories a vicious twist, or spread false rumours to boost sales. Others will focus on a specific player who faces flak from all sides, like Florent Malouda, the subject of repeated and vitriolic attacks from Pierre Ménès, one of the journalists on the French equivalent of *Match of the Day*, during Euro 2008. The journalist is powerful because his voice resonates in people's minds. He influences the coach, the public, the referee and the football federation.

The best way for a footballer to handle criticism is to have an iron will and to answer back by playing decisive, entertaining, exuberant football. The media played a part in what happened in the French squad in South Africa in 2010, but they were not hauled over the coals. The sports paper *L'Equipe* caused serious damage by quoting word for word what they alleged Nicolas Anelka had said to coach Raymond Domenech at half-time during the infamous 2-0 defeat to Mexico. They printed the whole thing on the front page under the headline, "Son of a Bitch". To publish such a shocking headline with no regard for the faint-hearted was a first. Anelka denied that he had used the words quoted in the paper and sued *L'Equipe*, but the newspaper won the case and – surprise, surprise! – it made front-page news.

I have been lucky to spend most of my career in England where the footballer and the man are usually well separated, despite the fans' more often than not fervent, unconditional support. A sweeping statement, perhaps, but that is how it feels. Most English fans are not spectators, but participants in the action, each in their own way. They accompany and support their team during the 90-minute war and wait for the final minutes, firm in their belief that their soldiers will win despite the struggle. They fuel the beautiful locomotive that is football and bring spirit, come rain or shine, into the life of an athlete.

Sport is a wonderful means of escape, freeing the mind and releasing all the pent-up energy a man possesses, but they are not just looking for a good way to unwind after a difficult day. In

Italy, France and many other countries they are not just fans, but fanatics who can be very difficult to control, as is clear from incidents at the Parc des Princes, home of PSG, or the Stadio Olimpico, home of S. S. Lazio when fans beat each other up, smash cars and even try to have a go at players. They show their passion for the game in their own individual manner. In England, as long as the players give the best of themselves they are shown respect. Your car parked outside the stadium won't get smashed up as it might in Europe. Most British fans won't talk to you like a piece of shit on the pretext that you're on TV every weekend, or because they regularly see you up close from the stands. In England that minute of silence in memory of a deceased player really does last 60 seconds.

I remember one particular day of preparation with the French squad just before Euro 2004. Supporters had lined the fence to cheer us on as we trained in the suburbs outside Montpellier. As we ran laps around the training field, we passed quite close to the onlookers. A couple of jokers couldn't resist attracting attention by making loud and insulting comments about certain players – just to show that they considered these so-called stars to be ordinary blokes as if they had known them from the day they were born. They made a point of targeting the most charismatic players. Even I choose my words when I speak to these stunning talents of world football, such is the privilege of having played with them. The fans wanted to get across that they weren't impressed and that, to them, these players were no better than caged zoo animals you throw peanuts to so your kids can have a laugh.

I discussed it with Thierry Henry as we trained. We agreed that this kind of behaviour was one reason why we didn't want to return to France. It was puzzling because I'd imagine these people like everyone else had come a long way to encourage and see in the flesh their heroes who made them dream on TV. Why make that effort just to be unpleasant to players who they admired for their talents? Surely they wouldn't travel a long way to see players they didn't like. Or did they do it to make a mockery of their fame? Were they motivated by envy?

Then I heard one loudmouth say: "Hey Barthez, take your wig off!"

You laugh, but turn around all the same to see who had the nerve to say such a thing. These troublemakers are a minority which makes such incidents especially regrettable. Unfortunately, it's the same guys who wreak havoc in French stadiums. They bash, smash, insult and more. Some have fun throwing coins and bottles. Others indulge in racist comments or violent confrontations between groups of hooligans. They do the worst damage and set a bad example for kids. When I see eight-year-olds accompanied by parents who have a go at the players using all the insults under the sun, I find it hard to believe the same kid is likely to be slapped by his parents for insulting his teacher if he calls her "a bitch." That's why in France it's so difficult to reproduce that minute of silence that is "Made in England".

William Gallas told me about a painful episode which happened during a difficult period with the club Olympique de Marseille (OM). As I have mentioned before, William was forced to accept an amateur contract if he wanted to stay at the club, despite already being an international hopeful.

William: "Bro, I ate dirt. One day I went with the team to play at the *vélodrome*. I headed to the players' car park, but was denied access. I insisted that I was a member of the squad and had a hard time believing what was going on. One man after the other confirmed they would not let me in – it was like they had serious memory loss. When I realised what was happening, the ground gave way under my feet. To show such a lack of respect for the man and the player I was . . . it almost made me cry in front of the stewards. It was one of the ways the club chose to force me to leave."

Imagine if, after two years working in a company, you're asked to make the coffee and get the croissants for a trainee. The stewards had struck him down and almost managed to knock him off his pedestal, dispossessing him of his player's crown.

William: "I had to fight for just a little respect. Only then could I begin to appreciate that amazing club."

I remember this difficult time for William because he went a bit nuts. Marseille rocks because football is the centre of the world. He said: "In Marseille it's all or nothing. One day the fans hate you and the weekend after it's crazy love. The Canebière [the city's historic high street where supporters celebrate when the team wins] in shades of blue is so gorgeous on a victory day."

It's important to show people respect. Whether you're a journalist, coach, player, steward or fan, everyone is worth it whatever the circumstances. Which is why, despite the press and especially the red-tops, England is a footballer's paradise.

A player is nothing special off the pitch. He is a young adult like all the others. But sometimes readers find it comforting to read articles about the imperfect life of stars. The stories in the newspapers are a bit like a soap opera, but starring real people rather than fictional characters. Since the beginning of mankind, from the cave paintings of Lascaux to women chatting over the garden fence, it's the same thing: telling stories. That is why the media is so successful.

Crude gossip is published in the tabloids in the so-called "public interest." Is it in the public interest to destroy a family? To harm the reputation of a great sportsman? Is it in the public interest for a child to be traumatised when he reads that his father is a "love cheat"?

Information and curiosity work together; human nature is rapacious. Movie stars, great artists and now football stars all understand this fact of life. Those who don't soon learn! To sell your wedding for a million pounds to a magazine and then expect to have privacy if you're caught having an affair is asking for trouble. When a player sells his image as being a good loyal family man, and is sponsored for millions on the back of that image, he'd best not slip up.

There is an understanding between the media and celebrities who sell sensationalism. *Move, and I'll shoot you down, 'cos we all want blood* . . .

A top-flight sportsman does not always have the luxury of controlling the extent of his exposure, or his private life, no matter how he behaves. Whether he likes it or not, he is headline news and has the potential to sell more newspapers with a small scoop on his new wife than politics, war, or the latest Hollywood gossip. *A dog barks and the pack follows.*

A living legend as intensely reserved as Zinédine Zidane, despite his desire to live a normal life, is a prisoner of his enormous talent. Yet Mr and Mrs Zidane are the opposite of the Beckhams.

Zinédine: "I try to live a normal life, even though it's not straightforward, especially since I didn't ask to be a celebrity. I just wanted to play football. I have to accept it because there are worse things in life. The important thing is not to play games with the press. For example, using the media when you need exposure for something one minute, then complaining about how you are always in the papers the next will have negative consequences. Always stay in your place. That's what I've always tried to do. Desire and temptation make it hard to stick to your values and not lose your bearings. Inevitably at some point you hear that you're the best, the strongest, the greatest. It's tricky keeping your feet on the ground. The most important thing is to have strong people around you. Family and friends who warn you about getting big-headed are worth their weight in gold. To stay true to yourself is crucial. Goodness me how tempting it is . . . to go out and have a laugh like everyone else, but you have to ask yourself 'why are we here?' To play football and to be the best. You have to put everything else to one side because there'll be time later, after your 35 years have gone by. You're still young at that age."

Diana Law, press officer for Manchester United and the daughter of the legendary Denis Law, who scored the most goals after Bobby Charlton for Manchester United, says: "If you want a private life, you can have it, but you can't also sign contracts with certain types of magazines and newspapers. A choice has to be made because the press is aggressive and when you accept that kind of deal, your private life means nothing in their hands."

In our society, athletes and public figures are a great tool for communication. They are used to launch new fashions and to set new standards. But then there is the danger that this will come back to haunt them because they have to be exemplary at all times. And people say: "What a bunch of attention-seekers those stars are! They don't miss a trick to get into the papers!"

In fact there are only a few big personalities who use the tabloids, fearlessly playing a dangerous game. They are exceptions. When it comes to other players, it's their exceptional talent that the press latches on to, not them.

Diana Law: "Paul Scholes is undoubtedly one of the most gifted players of his generation yet he has never been hassled."

Having played alongside him, I know only too well how Sir Paul Scholes is the most cool, calm and collected of everyone in a changing room. His image is that of a great and talented guy who is totally discreet. His private life remains as mythical as his public one. Many like him get on with life aware of their fame and being recognised in the street for their flair, but consider themselves to be just men who can play with their children in the park like everyone else.

Of all footballers, David Beckham is the most exposed thanks to his talent and his marriage to a famous Spice Girl. His career would have been the same even without her. Less media exposure, perhaps, but still the sex symbol he is today and an ambassador for football throughout the world. He doesn't only have a superb right foot! Married or unmarried, his career wouldn't have been different. I'm not sure that the Beckhams expected to live in a media circus so young. Over the years they've transformed this circus into a paradise which they have mastered perfectly. This was not the case at the beginning of his meteoric rise. To think that you now need a bodyguard for your kids; that you have no control over your schedule; that you can't hide and always have to show yourself in the best light possible, even at a time when there is so much about life that you still have to learn because you are so young and inexperienced. The press is always on the alert. It is constantly on the lookout for scraps of news about football and anything else which can then go viral on the web, to boost sales. The internet makes information available in the blink of an eye so the papers have had to go into hardcore mode to keep ahead of the game.

Admittedly, the level of aggression of certain newspapers depends on each individual country and its customs, as Ji-Sung Park explains: "In South Korea, the press does not look for scandal like a lot of European newspapers do. Culture, values and respect for the immense traditions of my homeland hold an important place in everyday life, so it's not acceptable for stories about adulterous stars to appear as features. Newspapers prefer not to display topless models unlike the West, in the likes of *Nuts* magazine or the English tabloids. It can feel unsettling to buy the *Daily Sport* because half of it is filled with naked women. I can't see this kind of thing happening any time soon in Korea."

The other day on Sky Sports, an Italian journalist explained the philosophy of his cronies with regards to scandals in Italian football. He said that, as personal stories do not influence football, they remain confidential. However, sometimes private information is used as a way of obtaining other scoops. This bargaining seems to me to serve as an insurance policy to protect privacy. I'm all for investigating hot new information which is important for the public interest, but to allow the theft of secrets, confidential anecdotes and to hack into people's telephones is wrong.

When you read about the scandals surrounding former Italian

Prime Minister, Silvio Berlusconi, the prostitutes and all his shenanigans, you can say it was important for Italians to be given this kind of information since they had a right to know about the man who made important decisions affecting their daily lives. Forbes magazine ranks Berlusconi as the 118th richest man in the world with a net worth of US$6.2 billion. His grip on Mediaset television, with an audience share of 45 per cent and 60 per cent of total sales of advertising, is what really matters when it comes to playing the power game. But cronyism, careerism and machismo; corruption, debauchery and the Mafia are nothing new in Italian politics.

The media is to be congratulated for its high-quality probing journalism which uncovers wrongdoing and has nothing to do with celebrity tittle-tattle. The scandal surrounding Dominique Strauss-Kahn – the managing director of the International Monetary Fund and man who might have been president of France – and his alleged sexual assault of a Guinean woman in a Sofitel suite in New York in May 2011; the MP's expenses scandal; the abuse of hospital patients; the exploitation of illegal migrant workers virtually kept prisoner by unscrupulous gangs . . . all these stories are positive examples of good journalistic practice.

Anyone you ask hates being spied on in the street. CCTV cameras are supposed to protect us and deter potential offenders who know they are being monitored, but they are also evidence of the ease with which the state can watch individuals 24/7 and can also serve as a justification for journalists to intrude into our privacy. According to an article I read in *The Guardian*, the UK is the world leader in the surveillance of its people with an estimated 4.8 million cameras installed.

I have nothing to hide from the police or anyone else, but it is normal to want to keep certain things private. Every human being has their own secret garden and has the right to choose whether to disclose information or not. The *News of the World* phone hacking scandal is the ultimate example of how far journalists will go to get exclusive celebrity scoops and has exposed a murky world reminiscent of a *film noir*. From Prince William to Sir Alex Ferguson, 4,000 people were allegedly listened to and tracked over many years.

Julien Laurens, a journalist for *Le Parisien*: "Rupert Murdoch controls most of the leading newspapers of the English-speaking world from Australia and Great Britain to America. This means he is among the top 20 influential people in the world, even politically. The Amaury Group owns top-selling sports newspapers in France – *L'Equipe*, *France Football*, *Velo-mag* and others . . ." The group is also one of the largest promoters of sports events in France, including the Tour de France. Its late founder, Philippe Amaury, dominated the French media world, however he was little known outside France and did not have the power to make or break elections.

The humiliation of News International and the closure of the *News of the World* have done little to shut down the story. The boundaries and techniques of investigative journalism have been called into question. Any recommendations about new laws or regulation made by the Leveson Inquiry are likely to be studied with interest by media groups and law-makers at home and abroad. Limiting freedom of expression is a fine balancing act.

Diana Law: "Courses are given to teach players how to protect themselves. A photo of you in your pool, of your house, or of your children can harm your privacy and even your safety."

It is important to know the tricks used by some journalists to trap players. And to learn how to talk about something without giving any information, a method bordering on hypocrisy. There's no need to be paranoid though. There are a great many good and moral journalists at work, but fewer among their bosses since, after all, they are businessmen.

The question is, am I as important a public figure as Berlusconi? Of course not! Football is fun and provides entertainment for the fans. Politics are a whole other story. A politician has to make important decisions affecting all aspects of people's lives. To what extent is the morality of a public figure relevant to his public life? To understand and balance what the public *needs* to know and what it *wants* to know is not an easy task.

The legal term "super-injunction", meaning a court order that prohibits another party from reporting on something, appears fairly regularly in English newspapers. As is often the case in football, the married sportsman who is hiding adultery requests anonymity and prohibits the press from revealing his name. Journalists use the "public interest" as justification for their articles, as well as the legal disparity which exists between British newspapers and websites or social networking sites based abroad when it comes to privacy injunctions. They don't seem to care about the consequences of their articles on the private lives of the individuals involved.

A newspaper's income comes from advertising sales, although revenues have suffered greatly in recent years. For example, BMW, Sony or Apple will pay up to £850,000 for a single-page advertisement in a national newspaper. The cost of manufacture, delivery and wages are barely covered by actual sales, although the newspaper is likely to sell more copies on the day a scandal breaks out.

Julien Laurens: "English so-called tabloids will sell advertising at any price. The day that Zidane signs his contract as coach for Manchester United is when all the big companies fight tooth-and-nail for their ads to be placed next to the scoop."

Would these journalists be willing to sell a story about their own family to save their newspaper? I can see that a front-page story about a prostitute could pay the salary of employees, but what if it destroys the life of a child? Apparently the French are sensitive to that kind of thing.

Julien Laurens explains: "*Bild* is the equivalent of *The Sun* in Germany and has the highest circulation of any newspaper in Western Europe. It set up a system to produce a special localised edition in France with the intention of launching a tabloid shortly after the under-age prostitution scandal involving Zahia Dehar and a number of French football players. Despite the money already invested, they had to admit that the French were not scandal-seekers and had something of a touch of class in their journalism. The notorious newspaper has had to backtrack and write off huge losses."

In French society, privacy is considered to be a fundamental right. The very concept of an individual's privacy is protected by law in France, whereas English law just condemns certain violations of privacy. So the story of Zahia Dehar and various players in the French squad was recounted with more gritty detail in the British tabloids than back home. In France, the general view is that sex is private between consenting adults, while in England it's a fascinating topic for general discussion by means of sensationalist headlines screaming scandal.

The American actor Sean Penn said that he thought it normal to lash out at the paparazzi when they trespassed on his private life. He said it in a very charming and powerful way: "To lodge a complaint [for assault] against Sean Penn is like lodging a complaint against a lion for biting a wildlife photographer on his territory in the Savannah."

I am not bankable or eccentric enough on the pitch to get caught in a paparazzi frenzy. It can't be much fun having bodyguards for your kids and being constantly spied on, or even having to look out for unwanted company yourself. I'd almost be wary of having a piss in tall grass in case you found yourself face-to-face with a paparazzo taking embarrassing photos!

For my naked torso to be photographed on St Tropez beach, topped off by my Dolce & Gabbana shades, is a no-no. One rule when I'm at a nightclub with my friend, the rapper 50 Cent, is never leave the VIP room together because afterwards it would mean there's too much chat about me, not just him. Lol!

I'd be embarrassed to take off on the latest Falcon private jet for a weekend in Dubai instead of queuing with my luggage like everyone else. I prefer to keep it simple and fly with Easyjet. Admittedly, it's not fun to find yourself next to someone who talks too much or who decides to sit between you and your kids, but you have to make a choice. Lol!

As if Harrods would ever close to the public so me and my family could take our time to go shopping, not during the sales, but when the new collections arrived in store. Each to their own, but that's not me. And I would never play the billionaire diving 40ft off a black yacht with jet skis parked behind. Each to their own, but that's not me. I'm not jealous of that kind of lifestyle, well, maybe just a tiny bit. I suppose being a mega star has a few cool things about it! Lol!

Understanding how the press operates and finding an appropriate strategy that works for you is crucial. William Gallas: "Just doing one article in France which is then misunderstood in England can lead to trouble. That's why, from the beginning to the end of the season, I decided not to speak out. I was hurt by numerous articles that were lies and distortions of the truth and my image. I preferred to protect myself by expressing myself only very rarely."

That's also my tactic. There are those who prefer to answer with great restraint. Otherwise, if you're as frank as Patrice Evra, you're shot down. Pat doesn't know how to waffle. He genuinely says what he thinks, and that's why I feel comfortable with him. You know who you're going to war with.

The life imposed on a player by journalists is monastic. It's actually the opposite of what the press pack wants, but players are almost forced to just play football, stay home and have hours of fun with the Playstation 3. Just like me. Lol! The readers of certain publications must like the idea of seeing all those body-beautiful players who are admired and well-groomed cruising in nice cars and living in paradise being brought back down to earth with a bump.

Anything goes these days. I'm amazed when I hear how papers

can afford to pay high prices for stories supplied by pretty women who entrap players. I use the word "entrap" as women, alcohol, betting and games are the weaknesses of all men – most don't see trouble coming. It's easy to destabilise a sportsman, it doesn't take much effort.

Newspapers are willing to pay a prostitute to let rip about her evening with a celebrity. It's a degrading and unlawful job exercised with obligatory discretion. Times have changed: so many women seem to have lost all self-respect. They don't bat an eyelid as they are given a cheque for £40,000 for their scoop on an English football star, despite their own image also being tarnished as a consequence. They don't seem to realise that it's hard for a woman to repair her damaged reputation.

I've seen journalists infiltrate private parties dressed up as students. For example a reporter from the *Daily Star* had fun exposing the behaviour of married players who she'd flirted with at a party. I do not agree with married men carrying on like this, but it's not journalism. I call it scandal-mongering. Privacy exists for a good reason: to give the family the space to handle a problematic situation without unpleasant articles making headline news. There is nothing more painful to deal with than protecting a child from the turmoil of a break up, or a couple's bitter feuding fuelled by sensationalist stories.

Me and my team-mates from Manchester United were all fined one week's pay because of a grubby incident at a Christmas Party. Rant and rage! I was the first to split, leaving behind my mates, Narcisse and Mike, who'd come over especially from France to enjoy the Christmas festivities. They were having a great time. To this day, all I need to say is: "*Papa Noël*" ["Father Christmas"] and they fall about laughing. We all carried the can because Jonny Evans was falsely accused in a newspaper of attacking a girl. She was attention-seeking. The papers jumped on the story and made the club out to be a sleazy hang out which wasn't the case. I should have asked for a refund of my fine. Johnny had to run the baseline between the coach and his family for some months thanks to this nasty business.

I've seen young players being ridiculed in the press as their exploits are recounted in detail: "He took me like this, he took me like that. He held it for just a minute blah, blah, blah"; "He didn't even pay the cab fare home"; "He has a tattoo here . . ."

These young women are able to describe every detail despite the fact that their nice old dads are going to be as humiliated as them, maybe even more so. Their flagrant ambition knows no bounds. Once again it depends on the country you're in because these cases seem to be specific to England. It's disappointing that it's all become such a media circus because it wasn't like that before.

When I began my career, I thought naïvely that the world of football was simple – the idea being to inspire people and play a beautiful game. I understand much better now that money and success make life difficult for those who are part of the vast universe of football. In some cases, the head swells along with the wallet. Certain players and the media are doing very well out of their little game. An addiction to sensationalism develops. Footballers are a never-ending source of stories of all kinds. This leads to bad press of the kind that some players end up being typecast and are then seen to be representative of all footballers. Others who use the press for self-promotion provide scoops and are then virtually taken hostage. Ultimately the press will spin a story to serve their own purposes, whichever which way they can.

For some of the players who play along with the press, their motivation will be notoriety and a big salary; for others it will be tasty news and a good way of keeping public interest and their name in the headlines. It's a bit like the game played with the tabloids by celebrities like Katie Price and Paris Hilton. The great-grand-daughter of Conrad Hilton, founder of Hilton Hotels, Paris has played the press since her childhood. Heir to a very large fortune, most likely her motivation is notoriety. Whereas Katie

Price used her exposure as a Page 3 Girl in *The Sun* to her advantage to make a fortune and she quickly picked up the tricks of the trade. They are both rich and famous because they have used the media as a platform for their lucrative, well-planned businesses.

Some footballers could behave better; I'm not saying that we are always blameless. Imperfection and being different is part of being human and is the essence of life. For a new player on the scene, to be catapulted into the spotlight is hard to take.

Wayne Rooney has a tattoo on his arm which says: "Just Enough Education to Perform." Wazza is an extraordinary and impulsive player. From my days at Manchester United I remember a boy who would smash his phone on the bus in anger after a call, but also a young guy able to answer the questions in any quiz. We all have our shortcomings, especially at that age. We need evil to appreciate good; ugliness to appreciate beauty; painful moments to enjoy the good times, however short-lived; a Satan to have a God. People would not go to church if they did not fear the death of their loved ones or most of all themselves. People may like the idea of living without worries or fears, without vice or emotional highs and lows, and to have plenty of love and money, but how many people can say they've lived in paradise since the day they were born? Our world is one of contradictions and diversity. Happiness without its opposite would mean living a normal life in a happy medium and nothing more. How boring! That's why I like to focus on the positive and take the best of people; their good energy. Otherwise, I move on. When I analyse football like this I reach the same conclusion; it's the same philosophy.

Picture this: football results are based on pure logic with no surprises, disappointments or setbacks. Goals are only ever conceded to the best teams. No more betting, no more suspense or excitement and no more opponents as they'd get tired of losing every match. It'd make me sick. We'd all be bored after a month. Barcelona had better watch out: if they go on beating the opposition 6-0 again and again soon they won't have anyone to play against!

Picture this: imagine footballers as being well educated, with the same culture and exemplary behaviour and so laid back they do not even celebrate an amazing goal. Without the rebels of football it wouldn't be fun at all!

A successful life for a footballer is one where dreams have come true and a player knows his limits, but never stops trying to exceed them. The best part is getting through to the other side of pain and setbacks. To succeed against the odds makes you proud. The toughest lives are those which lack any kind of meaning or joy. Unpredictability leads to challenges and surprises – good and bad – growth and development. I do not like to be told, "Be like this or that guy," because he comes close to perfection. I am made to be myself, to learn and to have desires. While we should respect society's codes, difference is what allows everyone to enjoy who they are and the choices they make. I feel the need for freedom as often as possible. I love to make my kids or my friends laugh because I have a crazy hair colour which makes me look different and feel happy.

There's a dazzling variety of people on planet Earth: black, white, large, thin, small, tall, Muslim, Jewish, Christian, pacifist, warrior, brave, timorous . . . French, Brazilian, Swedish, German . . . and they all have kids with one another. What a lovely muddle! Football is a cocktail of all that and more; a mixed bag of talents and personalities; a gorgeous and boundless blend.

9

WANNABE, OR NOT TO BE, A WAG?

Written by Aurélie Saha-Gillet

The Sun: "The 22-year-old girl says: 'I will stop at nothing to get a footballer. I don't care what it takes or who I hurt to do it'."

Wow, scary!

I did not think. I just had to go for it or risk losing him. At only 19 years old, when he asked me to live with him, I followed Louis to London. I did not hesitate to choose a new life in a new country at the beginning of a relationship, however fragile. To leave behind family, friends and give up on college . . . who knows? It undermined my dreams, but I was afraid that over there he'd find what he no longer had back home.

A young player, especially one living in a foreign country, needs a strong cocoon around him. Players of this generation are uprooted more frequently and at a younger age so they tend to settle down early. That way they can take their family cocoon with them, wherever they go, which provides the only stability in this destabilising world. The promising career of a player surrounded by the wrong people who give him bad advice can quickly go belly up, even if he is very talented. A coach will always favour a serious player with a good entourage to a habitual party animal.

When Louis asked me to write a chapter about footballers' partners, I decided to do it through my eyes, as well as through the other women I know in the same boat, because it is a perilous undertaking and I do not know everything. Sandra Evra, Anne Sophie Givet, Karen Distin, and Sue Ellen Jager, wife of French striker Jonathan Jager, joined me in my reflections.

There's something for everyone in football. It isn't easy to profile a footballer's partner. The first thing that comes to mind when talking about these women is the concept of the WAG and this negative image. Because, as with her husband, the wife of a footballer is often more envied than loved.

The term WAG (the acronym for Wives and Girlfriends) first appeared in the British tabloids during the 2006 World Cup in Germany when the women accompanying the English team were talked about more than the players themselves. Unfortunately it has become very derogatory, but the bad image of the footballer's partner is nothing new.

Over the last 20 years, meeting girlfriends at school has shifted to meeting top models on TV shows. Soaring salaries, celebrity status, media exposure and the footballer's luxurious lifestyle all fuel women's desire. Many players have swapped their young love for a striking and photogenic bombshell. The sight of certain couples make us raise an eyebrow for a brief moment . . .

Here is a stereotypical description: the archetypal WAG is recognisable by her artificial tan, hair extensions, oversized shades and enormous designer handbag. In other words the popular press generally only focuses on the visual criteria of physical attractiveness. Wayne Rooney's wife, Coleen, has been referred to as a WAG, as have so many others. Coleen and Wayne met when she was 12 years old, which debunks the upstart, gold digger label generally attached to the wives of players. She has built up a successful career as a fashion pundit. The editor of British *Vogue*, Alexandra Shulman, has praised her "brilliant sense of style." Victoria Beckham, described by the *New Yorker* as being "The Queen of the WAGs", was already successful thanks to being a member of the Spice Girls. Others, thanks to their lifestyle and appearance, have attracted attention and have emerged from the shadow of their husbands. The most intelligent and opportunistic ones have been able to capitalise on their husband's fame by becoming well known in the worlds of fashion, pop music and TV, by creating their own clothing line, fragrance or writing a column in a magazine, sometimes becoming as familiar as their player husband. Some resent living in the shadows, although it can motivate a frustrated woman. Some use their free time for charitable work. But the problem of perception is still there. The daughter of a friend of ours who was asked what she wanted to do in her life replied: "Nothing, like Mum."

Maureen Harvey, wife of Colin, former Everton player, coach and manager, says: "I don't envy today's wives at all. I couldn't have dealt with all that publicity and having to dress up every time I went out. We were content with what we had in those days and felt quite lucky, because we did have comfortable lives compared to a lot of people."

So we've ended up with a fashionable phenomenon which is attracting more and more young wannabes, much like modern-day princesses. It's difficult to let a player go off with his team-mates after a game when you picture him surrounded by dozens of girlies desperate to nab him or one of his mates. And it's sometimes hopeless trying not to get paranoid when you read quotes like this one from the *Daily Mirror*: "It's impossible to keep a footballer faithful."

It's a vicious circle of which the footballer must be aware. He should avoid hanging out with bad company and going out too much. It's best to spot and keep away from certain players, such as the type who is easily influenced and who is convinced that as extra-marital affairs are part of the lives of many of his team-mates – whose women forego self-respect and tolerate infidelity as they are the official partner – why not him too? Then there's the type who fears commitment and who refuses to get engaged even after several years together, claiming that he is not ready and asks you to remove your personal belongings from his apartment when you go away for a few days. Also to be avoided is the habitual big spender who chooses to buy his fifth Porsche rather than ensure the future of his family; the gambling addict who loves casinos and all kinds of betting; the player who is so self-satisfied and shallow that any attempt to bring him back to earth is impossible; and finally the self-centred macho and the navel-gazer who are both incapable of leading a normal, balanced family life. If a player has been told since he was a child that he is the most handsome and the best, he'll always believe it. But hey, there's someone for everyone. Familiarity breeds contempt.

Karen Distin: "It's alarming the way young girls get into debt, hoping to reach the status of being a footballer's wife, as if it were a goal in life."

Certain unscrupulous websites advise so-called "wagabees" on how to snare a footballer (places to go, attitudes to have, what to wear, or even the appropriate plastic surgery to have!) so long as you can pay for it. Even worse is the English site offering young girls the opportunity to meet professional players in exchange for registering with them . . . a kind of dating website for the Premier League! Many of these girls would be disappointed to know what daily life is really like for the majority of envied WAGs. Many believe that we lead an extraordinary fairytale existence, glittering with rhinestones and sequins, laden with benefits of all kinds and that thanks to the money earned by our other halves, we avoid everyday pressures. If only!

Where does the negative image of the WAG come from? She arouses jealousy and is despised. She is beautiful, young and rich, always well dressed and married to a sportsman with an athlete's body who gives her a great lifestyle and pseudo-celebrity. The WAG has a bad reputation for being extravagant, superficial, scatterbrained, profiteering, calculating and haughty. She supposedly spends her time fussing over herself and squandering her footballer's money. Defying such prejudice is hard, thanks in no small part to the TV series *Footballers' Wives* based on the shenanigans of three couples in absurd situations.

After consulting my friends, we concluded that there are largely two groups. We all know a couple of WAGs who are haughty and never say hello when we bump into them; who arrive at the stadium ready for a stroll down Cavalli's catwalk; who spend time with their girlfriends in paradise while their husbands sweat blood all season training and in matches; who go out with the girls only to come home drunk in the small hours leaving the task of educating the kids in the hands of various nannies; or else there are those who hope their husbands don't get picked for the next World Cup so they can have a longer holiday. Ultimately, we put down on paper just five or six names even though we have all had a different journey, some by way of the big clubs, others the smaller ones.

Ultimately, the stereotypical WAG with all these shortcomings and sense of entitlement is a little princess. There is a touch of WAG in all of us, of course, but those who are a blend of all these negative attributes are rare. A woman's self worth and who she is have little to do with money or the celebrity of her significant other! Véronique Zidane, who I hung out with during Euro 2004, was one of the most down-to-earth and modest of the group, never setting herself apart or snubbing newcomers, never leaving her children but shielding them from her husband's fame and participating enthusiastically in different activities. We'd all assumed she'd be surrounded by a bunch of staff! What a humbling experience for pretentious young women! Her daily priority, as for all of us, was to protect her family cocoon, a task made complicated by the family name.

The second group is not generally represented by the tabloids. A genuine player's wife is discreet, devotes herself to her children, her family life and preserving her marriage. She invests herself entirely in her relationship to ensure that her man plays well every weekend; she supports him through difficult times and when he is upset or injured; stands by him when he is under fire and sometimes has to bring him back to the fold. She has to motivate him when he is burnt out and sometimes serves as a scapegoat . . . Louis has often been unlucky and I remember some of the difficult episodes he describes in this book. His ongoing disappointments and struggle and periodic desire to throw in the towel were mine also.

What is a player looking for in his wife? What is her role? Axel Lablatinière, the agent of around 30 players, writes: "If she can put the needs of her partner before her own and turn a blind eye, then she will be a good player's wife."

As a whole, although some might refute this, a player prefers his wife to stay home and care for him and the children rather than pursue a personal career. Being a footballer's wife is incompatible with having a professional line of work. A player's career is unpredictable, with last-minute transfers, irregular holidays, days off at the 11th hour and unexpected injuries . . . a player's wife must be available 24/7. If you do work, problems can become disruptive. Frequent moves and the language barrier block you from flourishing or being promoted. Employers can't resist making inappropriate comments about your having no real need to work, or else transfer rumours about your significant other can raise doubts among your colleagues and bosses.

Karen, the wife of Sylvain Distin, worked for several years: "As a footballer's wife doing a 'normal' job you are not taken seriously, and it would have to be something you can do wherever you go. My real job and my role are to organise everything and keep my family together."

The twice-yearly transfer periods are stressful because football moves fast, in a good or bad direction. You never know where you'll be at the end of each transfer window. If the player is good, he will have an opportunity to move on and do even better, if he is ill, injured or laid-off because a new player in his position has been bought, he will have to consider other options. Uprooted on average four to five times in a 10-year career, moved from city to city or from country to country, his wife will have a hard time pursuing long-term studies, a career or anything else. She has to put her life on hold in favour of her husband's career, which is short, intense and decisive. The player will be focused on his needs in order to stay sharp and to provide his family with a comfortable retirement. He will at times be a selfish athlete obsessed with competition. I recently read an interview with a footballer: "In this profession we make sacrifices every day and are constantly called into question, so a player expects unfaltering support from his wife."

Whether she likes football or not, she always supports her man. She feels the pressure of the big tournaments and resonates with him when the ball hits the back of the net. She tingles with pride at the sound of the national anthem when he is chosen to represent his country, or when she hears the rousing opening of Tony Britten's anthem for the Champions League, adapted from George Frideric Handel's *Zadok the Priest*. She watches with joy as the kids do a lap of victory in his jersey at the end of the season and feels agonising suspense when he stays on the ground after a tackle, until he gets up. Defeat brings tears to her eyes, especially when her player is the one who is held responsible. She has a hard time not slapping the fan in the stands who, from kick-off, bad mouths and curses her man.

She needs to learn to adapt fast to a new environment, country or culture as she's the one who deals with not only the player's daily life, but their kids and the day-to-day admin. The player tends to live in a "football bubble". Everything revolves around him and the game, whether it's going out for a meal or when to have a nap, and he is often the one who is most disorganised. Some wait for the bailiff to come knocking or for the power to be cut off before paying the bill. This negligence could be due to the fact that playing professional football is so addictive and physically demanding that the player has neither the time nor the inclination to look after himself. It could also be because he has got used to everyone doing everything for him since his early days at a training centre. Most likely it's a bit of both.

Sue-Ellen Jager: "The player tends to forget what it means to be a husband and a father, so us women have to take matters in hand." In some cases agents do this, only to become an intrusive presence. Axel Lablatinière confirms that some players also let their wives manage their careers and their finances.

In addition to being a wife and a mother, marriage to a footballer is a full time, 24/7 job which is generally undervalued and unappreciated, as Karen points out. When I ask everyone what they find hardest, the unanimous response is: the lack of recognition. This is largely due to the huge financial imbalance within the couple. The woman has to cope with outsiders, their families and sometimes even the players themselves seeing her as a gold digger. She's the one who has the difficult role of bringing the player back down to earth to face the reality and constraints of everyday life – as well as dealing with domestic squabbles when the rest of his entourage proclaim that he is the best! She also has to veto his acquaintances since, as Sue-Ellen says, "A player must be protected from the 'predators' lurking in the undergrowth," or from all the financial requests that arrive daily in every shape or form – from charities to friends and family. Managing to meet all these demands is a headache – although making priorities comes naturally – such as when a new friend wants a new car while your grandparents are still living in a shoebox! Making priorities begins to come naturally.

Money can quickly become a poisoned chalice. The way the salaries of players are made public is the root cause of numerous problems. Those so-called friends who are in fact motivated by self interest, or those false friends who have no qualms about soliciting you, will often come up with a supposedly fantastic deal which is of zero benefit to you. Of course, the moment you turn them down, they're gone. It's as though you're some kind of free banking service. The woman in the background often sees them coming from miles away, whereas the player is fooled and only detects the scam as it happens or once it's too late. The footballer's wife must be independent and autonomous as she is often alone without the support of family and friends in a new environment where everything has to be rebuilt from scratch – schools, a social network. She often has to multi-task because if he is playing in one of the more gruelling championships, the player will be on the pitch every three days so just won't be around. This can be very frustrating for the woman who waits all day for him in the hope of spending some time together and then he goes off for a nap! Preserving the unity and the balance of a family on the move is not an easy task.

We've been lucky with Louis. Despite his many physical problems, he has stayed for a long while in the same country. So our children have been able to do most of their schooling in one place. Stability is important, especially for those children who react badly to being uprooted often. They lose their bearings and their school friends. The choice of a player's club at the end of his career is sometimes made prioritising the well-being of his family over his footballing and financial interests.

Some who have WAG status experience more problems than other wives. As the saying goes, a good man is hard to find. Some couples struggle from one small contract to another, with no real guarantees or savings, or opportunities to advance like everyone else. You become a WAG from when the player is a semi-pro, but that does not mean swanning around in sequins and rhinestones.

Despite the drawbacks, we wives of footballers consider ourselves to be very fortunate, even though our lives are more ordinary than you might think from reading the tabloids, or watching TV. Us lucky ones live without financial problems, in beautiful houses. We can visit our families whenever we like and

send our children to the best schools. Our kids are often cultur-
ally enriched by learning another language. We can offer beautiful
gifts to family and friends as well as travel to gorgeous destinations. We experience extraordinary and intense moments and are
caught up in the rhythm of an exciting sport because of our
player's successes. So it's crucial to know how to enjoy it all if
you are lucky enough to have the opportunity.

Ultimately, we all dream of simple things. Most of us are
impatient for our man's career to end so we can enjoy having
him all to ourselves . . .

10
MR BIGSHOT

*L*ibération: "We take them to be role models for kids who have lost their way in life, but in reality they are just bling-bling traders."

Once upon a time, Barbie was the iconic creature of a young girl's dreams. The ultimate role model, she had made it in life and had it all. Everything changed when Page 3 girl Katie Price revolutionised the crude and vulgar business of glamour modelling. The brassy sex-kitten in killer stilettos who uses her body as a business concern is the new hot girl in town. How does a passionate young player looking for romance avoid getting trapped?

Diana Law: "Football attracts lots of young women because it's exciting. As the saying goes, 'If you can't beat them, join them.' If the boyfriend is addicted to football it's better to go to a match with him than never seeing him. She gets hooked and is powerless to fight it, a bit like me. I was born into the world of football and bathed in it as I grew up. I love the game, even though none of my girlfriends like the image the game now has, and all that surrounds footballers."

Laura Doyle at global sports management agency, Stellar Group: "Nowadays, there are websites, blogs and even books giving advice about how to become a WAG. They give instructions about where to go, what personal investments to make, how to make the most of opportunities and eventually seduce a top-flight player. I've heard there are even parents who push their daughters to find one. It seems over the top but it's a reality."

This kind of woman will do anything to trigger a couple of scandals then write a few books because it generates easy money and celebrity status. If she gets married then divorces, even better, as her family will get a good slice of the pie.

Diana Law: 'The media is guilty of promoting the image of all footballers having an easy and glamorous lifestyle while simultaneously doing all it can to sabotage players' private lives by publishing 'Kiss 'n' Tell' stories. Every Sunday morning, if you look at the bottom of the page of certain newspapers you'll see ads asking for girls to reveal their stories in exchange for quick money. This attitude is detrimental."

These young women do not seem to realise that they should be trying to represent beauty and a touch of class. They are muddling up love and sex. It's a tricky business.

Recently, my wife was sent a link via spam on Facebook. A French 18-year-old whose face was barely concealed rattled off a litany of sexual adventures. She even seemed proud of having been treated like a "bitch" already more than 40 times. She described a scene which was pretty embarrassing for everyone concerned. I say everyone because there were five or six of them. One here, one there and another over there, taking her every which way . . . bent over doggy style . . . stand and carry. They were almost falling over each other while screwing her. I'm not vulgar, but that's what she said, word for word. She looked like any other girl her age and, despite the crude mask, seemed cute and smart. A young teenage girl who was totally aware of what she was doing had decided by herself to take matters into her own hands. She happily goes to university and is from a good family. Her dream is to marry and have kids. But in the meantime, she screws. It's hardcore! To think that the guy who eventually falls for her won't have any idea! Chances are she'll agree to marry blindfolded if he happens to be a young footballer.

I did everything I could to ensure that our first child was a boy because I was anxious about having to cope with a young girl having adolescent crises. I have two little soldiers, and now a girl, but at the time I was up for creating a small football team. For our first two children, I ate huge amounts of salt, prayed a lot and researched granny's best recipes for conceiving a boy. It worked. My wife doesn't know it yet, but I plan to have our daughter chipped with the latest human microchip. My little angel; the idea tickles me pink. I have two boys I'm training up as paratroopers to protect their little sister – although they won't be like those Arab big brothers in the neighbourhoods who are so overprotective of their kid sister that they sometimes lose the plot. But there is a high probability that I'll get paranoid, father that I am.

A girl likes to be protected by her old man, even if he's a little crazy. It's better than falling into bad company and regretting it later. Even smart girls can succumb to peer pressure. But if you're too strict, she's sure to do the opposite of what you want. The trick is to find a balance. Choose your battles. Figure out what is most important. Be reasonable. Only argue about major mistakes. A girl has to mess up so she can learn from life itself. It's an art which, a few years back, I did not feel capable of mastering.

The idea of having a daughter freaked me out, although in reality it was what I always dreamed of. Just to have had a little sister makes me feel proud in a way that will always stay with me. But it means you have to erase any memories you might have of how a young teenage boy can behave with a girl. It's far from easy to convince yourself that that big black bloke is just a nice guy who loves your sister or your daughter. It's a tough call, so I'll delegate to my boys, a.k.a. the paras. *Ha ha ha.*

However legitimate and powerful it is, the feminist movement hardens girls and they seem to forget what they represent to men. The media interferes with their innocence and I would even venture to say pushes them towards bad ways. Today, when you speak to young people about sex, most think they have to be a stallion in bed like Rocco Sifredi or that they should reproduce what they see on TV or on the internet. Whether it's the guys or the girls, there are fewer taboos and the sky's the limit.

One statistic says that most boys picture their ideal woman to be like Pamela Anderson or some other babe with silicone breasts. Gone are the days of Catherine Deneuve and Vanessa Paradis. Now it's *Basic Instinct* and *Desperate Housewives*. Today's woman is tough and protects herself from appearing vulnerable. TV and magazines play an important guiding role. Sometimes they are like funfair mirrors, distorting the reflection of our women as they look at themselves.

Back in the day, the ideal woman was curvier. Her body was truly her own, no implants or botox, just exercise and massage. Victoria Beckham, Lindsay Lohan and Angelina Jolie are beautiful, but each is as thin as the other. Celebrities such as these serve as role models for young girls. They have access to the best doctors, dieticians, designers, photographers and fitness coaches in the world. Their photos in magazines are retouched and do not always reflect reality, and not all readers realise this. In Britain, the number of girls admitted to hospital with anorexia has increased by 80 per cent in a decade. Gone are the days when a woman looked for a strong man as her protector. Women's rights are enshrined in law in the West, which is a good thing, but as an alternative to having a career some use marriage as a means of protecting themselves and their future financially. It may be a gross generalisation, but perhaps that is why there are more divorces and independent women who prefer to live alone. There are a lot of men who are cowards and idiots of course. We have become so demanding that some prefer to stay alone.

The perception of female beauty has been distorted over the years. Has the concept of the ideal woman for a footballer experienced a similar change? I took the time to talk to some of my mates about it since the WAGs phenomenon kicked off in England.

Phil Neville: "The word is an insult. WAG shows disrespect to my wife and many others because it means a person who is only there for the fame and is a gold-digger. I think most players' partners would not agree to being called a WAG, which calls into question their feelings. The majority consider themselves to be quite normal and not at all on the make. They are often talented, intelligent women who find themselves in somebody's shadow."

Phil is right. You have to be tough to be a footballer's partner, or at any rate, to be my wife. Insecurity, fear, invasion of privacy, the pressure and the highs and lows of a player's career are hard to bear. The fashion for WAGs began tentatively five or six years ago. Now the ambition of a generation of young women is to bag a footballer and to go even further if they can.

Diana Law: "In my parents' day it was the same. Women in the 1960s also dreamed of meeting a handsome footballer because it was glamorous to be a player's wife. Nothing has really changed, it's just the press which goes on about it so much more than before. Now with Twitter, Facebook and instant messaging, news travels much faster. Nothing stays unreported as it did 40 years ago."

How can a talented young player know if it's genuine attraction which landed him in bed with the hottest sex bomb in town? Would this pretty girl be under the sheets if he was in a worker's overalls and had to go off to his job on the assembly line?

Some young stars who are bachelors are so fearful of all this that they prefer to hire female escorts to satisfy their lust. Nobody, certainly not the players who are married, will confirm my words, but what would make them feel ashamed – more than using a prostitute – is the horror of being seen in the papers with a woman who claims to be willing, but has an eye on the envelope bulging with cash from a tabloid in exchange for her revelations. Among young rising stars serious relationships do exist. The type that ends well when the girlfriend who, despite feeling unloved, does not seek revenge and does nothing more than think, "He's all over the shop, what a dickhead!" Broadcasting compromising information might cross her mind, but it goes no further. She would be described in football circles as being the "right kind of girl". To find her, a player has to believe in his lucky star, even if there are still plenty of great girls out there.

Some of the press around the French edition of this book focused on footballers using the services of female escorts and misrepresented what I was trying to say which is a serious point, with the aim of showing the potential pitfalls. The fear and paranoia of young players about falling into a honey trap needs to be tackled. Nowadays, players come into the game barely out of their teens. They are vulnerable, insecure and often very lonely, away from family and friends. Like all young people they often make mistakes, but do not go through the usual rites of passage in a "normal" way, because they are under constant scrutiny and hugely pressurised. Perhaps clubs could play a pastoral role here and introduce a buddy system – older players could steer youngsters away from trouble.

Just the two of us

Life as a couple has its problematic moments, and you need to be philosophical enough to overcome them. In fact, a source of fragility in a couple can be the failure to nurture a healthy level of friendship. A special couple like that of the footballer and his wife can be even more fragile and difficult to manage than a so-called "normal" one, where they both work and bring in equal amounts of money.

The meeting and the first kiss are memorable milestones and are as important as they are for other couples. What differs is that furtive little question trotting through the player's head, "Yeah! Hot stuff! But hey . . . wait a minute . . . why me?"

It doesn't last long, but if you're already a little known, this sneaky thought is there. Clear, positive signs are needed before it fades.

Some football players admit to being with a woman who is above their expectations. No need to name names, or mine, but frankly to be married to a Toyota vehicle body-fitter doesn't sound nearly as good as being the wife of a footballer who plays for a top-rate club. Similarly, a small number of WAGs are with a pro for the gold credit card and the good life.

I am suspicious by nature, but strongly believe in the true love I found. Most players believe in what is not overrated or calculated.

I mean what I think and am simply decrypting the Morse code in my chest. I'm not into fads and am not a relationship guru. I just believe that over time I have managed to understand the feelings I have for other people and those I need in return.

Women are gorgeous, innocent, tender, caring and intelligent. But what a pain they can be at times, and complicated too! I have an extraordinary wife who is an exceptional mother to our children but, as I have observed in others, she is capable of behaving in a way that is puzzling to a man. When I talked to other players, we all felt as though we were all living with the same person who has the same behaviours, offers the same criticisms and often follows the same routine, even though all our stories are slightly different.

Even though I know she will read this book, I do not mince my words when I tease my wife. I am easy-going, but hard to understand. I sometimes struggle with how women express themselves and their reactions. It took me a while to understand, but now I laugh.

Here's a nice example: when a woman particularly wants her partner to please her, she goes into double-touch mode; a kind of verbal dribbling technique from Venus that Mars has a hard time fending off. Picture this: we are sitting comfortably in the living room ready to watch a good movie. It's cold. She sees the special blanket for home movie nights, but it's on the other side of the room. She does not want to get up and would like proof that her feelings matter to me. Through almost chattering teeth she utters a long drawn out: "I'm soooo coooooold . . ."

She will not say that, of course, she's spotted the blanket and would like me to fetch it. She waits for me to guess what she wants and then, with a little kiss on the forehead, cover her tenderly. Woe betide you if you react in the wrong way! You do something for her and so show your love. She asks you without asking – her equivalent of the "Tiki-taka."

Sounding almost surprised she says, "Oh! You're a love."

We aren't all cuddly by nature. But we make an effort because we love our wives. Quite frankly there are times when it's a pain in the neck and I'll pretend I haven't heard her, or I'll suddenly pay serious attention to the Evian ad. There's no point in me giving worse examples here as it would be putting petrol on the fire for nothing.

All couples go through cycles of tension. When my wife has her period it's chaos in the house. And a rise in testosterone or adrenaline levels turns Prince Charming into a ball of nerves and he behaves like a total dufus.

William Gallas: "It's the kind of conflict which comes up regularly. Nadège does not always understand when I come home tired from training. So I have to remind her that I haven't been off having a coffee for three hours with my team-mates and I suggest she comes to watch a training session or some pre-season sessions so she can see the intensity for herself. I remind her that when she has something she's obliged to do, she will often ask me to help, but when I'm on the pitch even if I'm not enjoying it she cannot help me and probably wouldn't offer anyway. If she doesn't want to do the housework, I will find someone to do it. If she wants to go out and I'm not home, she can still find someone to help with the kids. So I ask her to understand my need to recuperate and to be supportive when there's something I don't particularly want to do. Fortunately, she gets the point in the end, but I have to remind her."

It's the same for me back home. There's often a row as I try to get across that it isn't easy for me either and having a nap is not something I want to do, but is a necessity imposed on us by the intensity of the game. It's not laziness – if we could, we'd all much rather play tennis or go karting. But we owe it to ourselves to recuperate so we can maintain our high levels of play and try to do even better the next time. I have no choice in the matter.

Sylvain Distin: "Even though they are on the frontline and are in a position to appreciate that some days of the week are harder for us physically than others, players' wives still struggle to understand. They have trouble fully realising what training drills to improve our running and breathing like 15-15, 30-30, VO2max involve, or how it feels to do hundreds of press-ups, because all they see with their eyes is what they remember . . . a husband playing with his team-mates in a stadium where the crowd chants his name. When our wives say they are tired because it's been such a busy day, they don't seem to get their heads round the intensity of physical training we are sometimes forced to do. They love to say their days are more tiring than ours, particularly from a psychological point of view.

Sylvain Distin concludes: "Playing football is definitely the most fun job there is. 15 hours of training per week is the opposite of a living death, even though some 15-minute blocks are way less fun than others. Being a mum in a footballer's home is no bad thing either."

When I come home after we've gone jogging in the forest, run relay races, done some backwards runs and sprinting, it seems madame wants to take over as physical trainer. She has a 90-minute shopping spree planned or would like me to stack up large, heavy boxes in the double garage. I sometimes have to remind her that if she's tired, it's because of the decisions she made, not mine.

I often tease my wife, who is a horse riding enthusiast. She makes me laugh when she comes homes exhausted, having battled to stay on the back of her horse, Emisario. I smile and say to her: "My love, it's the horse that did most of the exercise. This beautiful, muscular creature is sweating and should be complaining about backache, not you. You're not the one who actually trots and gallops, *ha ha ha*."

I do not consider myself selfish or macho, but as the primary provider of income it's normal that I should come first, or in any case certainly not last. This is something which some women find difficult to accept. If I'm tired, I sleep, because recuperation is important.

Some football pros live in a kind of bubble that shields them from the realities of our society. For a couple, it's a daily challenge to fight the temptation to get everything done by paid helpers. The combination of money, fame and youth do not favour being a good philosopher.

The player's schedule is as unsettling a subject for him as it is for her. Each tends to denigrate what the other is doing. I don't get it when I'm told she has no time or is stressed, because from 9am when she drops off the kids 'til 2pm when I get home, she's had all that time to herself. No one's been on her case; she has had no one to support, listen to, or reprimand. She can do nothing if she likes, even if I know she is the active type. I'm certainly not going to say anything. So, I must admit that when I get home, I'm puzzled by her complaints or reprimands, even though I know that keeping everything in order is not easy. It's simple, nobody is forcing her to do anything. And she has the control of her schedule, which is not the case for me.

She finds it hard to understand what a guy like me finds interesting about Playstation. It's a great tool for releasing tension, as well as a way of being left alone, since I occasionally need to escape, solo.

My wife and I may grumble about who does what in the house, or what we get up to out in the world, but since my transfer to Tottenham, living in a hotel or an apartment away from the cosy intimacy of my little family makes me long to have them with me. I can hear my kids shouting and having a laugh as I speak with their mother on the phone, and I miss them. It's not fun to hear that my lil' princess has started crawling and that her second tooth came through, without me having a say! I miss our domestic scuffles and mutual support. But this is a choice my wife and I made together and I have to accept the downside of a fantastic opportunity.

As a couple, the flow of life is subject to the same recurring problems. It takes experience and the ability to step back to handle them well without losing too much energy or dignity in the process. Rich or not, these situations have to be dealt with, same as everyone. Not all players are well paid and money is not always the solution. Life is not about living without problems, it is about finding solutions to problems.

The family is often a sensitive issue. You need to be resilient to keep everyone happy because of changing finances. You have to deal with all kinds of scenarios. "I don't want to see so and so because of what he did to Uncle Jacquot." Or, "I heard you gave Damien €3,000 so why are you having a go at me, your old mate, for two pairs of shoes?!" Or, "Don't invite so-and-so to the wedding . . . you know very well why." To receive bank details in an envelope from a friend or family member because they've moved apartment or want a new car can give you an unpleasant headache.

Another sensitive issue is that of mates and girlfriends. Childhood friends you hook up with in nightclubs or on holiday are fine. But it can be tense with people you've only known for six months, especially when they are women. Players' partners are obsessively fearful of nightlife. Their ears prick up when you say you're going out. It's as though you've announced a trial separation. She almost notes down in a little notebook the number of mini-divorces she's had to put up with in recent months.

The subject of children is more complicated because, wonderful and joyful as they are, they also create stress and tension. An interrupted nap is not everyone's idea of recuperation. A certain amount of freedom and independence disappear in spite of all the time-saving gadgets at home and it's easy to forget other people's problems. Never think a kid strengthens a relationship because, to have a child, the couple needs to be mature and ready to make sacrifices. A young footballer tends to become a father when he's young, largely because of the immediate financial comfort. But young couples do not always think through all the responsibilities involved.

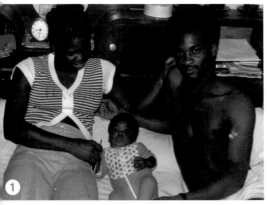

❶ I don't know if this boy will be a star.

❷ My parents got me used to being capped at an early age!

❸ With my first team mates at Soisy-Andilly-Margency.

❹ I was honoured to represent my country with the under-21s in a team including Nicolas Anelka.

❺ Fresh out of INF Clairefontaine, I'm proud to play for the Garnets.

❻ Testing my mettle against West Ham in the Intertoto Cup.

DIVISION 1

① Welcome to England! On loan at Newcastle.

② Celebrating promotion to the Premier League with Fulham.

③ I've had some crazy hairstyles.

④ Celebrating my first goal for France, created by guess who!

⑤ "Titi, isn't life sweet in England?"

⑥ Zidane is Brazilian, but he doesn't know it!

⑦ Receiving the yellow card that ruled me out of the World Cup final.

1. From the neighbourhood to the stars!
2. The best feeling in the world!
3. You've got to be hard and firm on any form or shape of racism.
4. The three Frenchies of Man Utd: me with Patrice Evra and Mikaël Silvestre.
5. Winning the Carling Cup with Cristiano in 2006.
6. I wanted to participate a bit more as we booked our place in the 2008 Champions League final.
7. Aurélie is in the background even though she played such a major role.
8. Destination Moscow.
9. It's a privilege to share such a special moment with those one loves.
10. Two legends.

16/3/2006

16/3/2006

1 Family time is priceless.

2 Family time in Guadeloupe is vital.

3 My grandparents and cousins.

4 We all love homemade sorbet!

5 I like to pass it on.

6 A long way has been travelled.

7 I have been on the ground a lot, but the important thing is to get back up again.

8 I was not a big fan of the pink shirt.

9 Trying to achieve the impossible.

10 My record-breaking FA Cup goal, which meant nothing because we lost.

❶ My first goal for Spurs on a special night.

❷ You see me old, but I'm smiling like a kid.

❸ Adebayor and I both started at Metz

As fathers we try to support the mother of our children doing the chores, but always end up having the best role with the kids. She gets annoyed when you stay calm and are the one who is easily listened to even though she is the one who spends most time with them.

Men often say to their wives: "I'm not your child," because sometimes she forgets she's not our mother, although some players do behave like great big babies! All because our wives think they can educate us, change how we are and apply the same rules to us as they do to our kids. It doesn't always work, especially when she's a housewife! Players are already ordered about by our coach in training: "Do this . . . faster . . . over there . . . that's no good . . . start again," and so on. So it's not great to face the same thing at home. If our wives do not work, we are often the only ones who stand up to them.

During an argument she might say: "You only think about yourself . . . you're always out . . . I've had enough . . ." The kids will sometimes break the ice with a smile, or they'll have an accident in the middle of the whinge. So it ends abruptly: "You're lucky this time! We'll deal with it later." We cry and laugh and a few hours later we've forgotten why we quarrelled.

The disastrous subject is adultery. The jealousy and anxiety engendered by this subject are destructive. As a professional foot-baller, there are times when you are in a no-win situation. Regardless of whether or not you've done something stupid, you're dead meat. Our women won't leave it alone. When you smile and remark that you just have one go left to tap in the PIN of your mobile phone she'll say: "Why do you need a code, what've you got to hide?" I totally understand and feel for her. Truth is, men have a very bad reputation because the temptation is aggressive.

It's a catch 22, but I reply: "Losing a mobile is easy and I don't want my mates' numbers to go walkabout and end up on the street." It isn't healthy to attempt to control someone else's actions and gestures to appease fear. Doubt is one thing, but for such feelings to invade and suffocate your partner is another. Trust builds over time. Your actions define who you are. As is often the case, finding the right balance is the answer.

I have noticed that the more honest you are, the more trouble there is. So to give her all or nothing is a mistake. I say to her, "You can't believe for a second that when I pass a woman in the street, I close my eyes not to see them because I love you. To close my eyes would be to lie to both of us."

Best avoid being too honest because what you say goes in one ear and comes out through her mouth, with added ammo. It's a no-win situation, so best to say nothing, or the barest minimum. A woman's innermost feeling is that she does not want you to come home with a smile on your face saying: "What a night out, I had a great laugh!" Do that, and you're asking for trouble. If I find myself in a shop buying her a beautiful dress, more than likely my wife will remark that I only did it because of the pretty salesgirl.

Yet I am not handsome, as some are. Even when I am home for 24 hours on the trot, the female brain will always multiply by 10 the number of nights out, or dig up old stories. Her mind will minimise the time spent with her, the loving declarations made or the number of bouquets and gifts given to her, or will overlook the fact that she is the chosen one. The confusion between sex and a genuine, loving relationship is terrible.

Recent scandals in France involving footballers and prostitutes don't help. I empathise with the terrible insecurity in which a footballer's wife lives. It's tough. In the world of football today it's hard to ignore all the available temptations. A player is a man like any other and he likes to know he is attractive. He likes to be acknowledged for what he does right and to be reassured that he is a great guy who is appreciated. Men and women have the same needs, but express them differently. It is certainly easier for a woman who knows what she wants to get an answer. Men tend to go looking for more than just information, it's their nature. A woman will keep a secret misdemeanour hidden in her black box while a man will boast about it in all the nightclubs.

Sex is an intimate and private subject and it all depends on the couple. Suffice it to say, on the day of a match, it can affect how a footballer plays. Some argue they need sex before or after a game. Certain women wait long weeks for their partner to get in the mood. Some football managers say that sex decreases aggressiveness and ban their players from sex the night before games. George Best was up for it the night before, but not an hour before a game!

I wonder how men would behave if women's earnings in the workplace doubled over theirs. Would they avoid one-night stands and aim for a lasting relationship? I wonder if that is the solution, so that society stops seeing women as objects of desire. Although I'm convinced that for a man to have all the money in the world is pointless unless his loved one benefits from it. My wife is the most beautiful discovery I made on this planet. A gorgeous creature who I try to make happy, despite my flaws.

If you sweat blood at work, it's so you can go away for the weekend – but who with? When you drive nice cars – who are you trying to impress? When you buy the best clothes – who's it to attract? If we go to war, it's to offer gold ingots and diamonds – who to?

Because of our flaws, our women require continual reassurance; frequent hugs, attention, flowers, gifts, kids, income and all the rest. That's why the best thing for each individual to flourish and grow is for madame to have an activity that gives her a measure of autonomy; a protection in the event of a setback. It's a great way for her to get out of the shadows and become someone other than the wife of so and so.

Who knows? Once the football career is over the roles could reverse, with madame taking the reins while the player becomes the partner of the star.

III
MAY THE
BEST MAN
WIN

11
DREAMS AND HEROES

Christopher Reeve, the actor famous for his role as "Superman," once said: "So many of our dreams at first seem impossible, then they seem improbable, and then, when we summon the will, they soon become inevitable." Like many kids, I loved Superman when I was little. He was one of my favourite heroes.

Back in the day, becoming a professional footballer was a real yet seemingly unrealisable dream. As a kid, I would look at the stadiums without believing for a minute that as a young man I'd end up enjoying the meticulous work of the groundsmen of Old Trafford, Goodison Park or White Hart Lane. I dreamed alright, but didn't have all the role models kids get today of all these young guys succeeding in making a living from the sport they loved. Back then TV coverage of football was minimal. Whether in the inner-city or the countryside, today's young people have before them this image of stars who have struck it rich at a very young age. The likes of George Best were a rarity, not the norm. Today, the dream of playing high-level football has become amplified; it is almost too tangible, even misinterpreted. Nowadays, over and above wanting to be a professional footballer, kids want the money, the cars; everything. They want it fast, they want it *now*.

Every young player dreams of playing at a professional level, signing for a big club, taking part in a tournament and winning. To get to the final of the World Cup is the ultimate dream come true. Suddenly you are a potential hero carrying the dreams of an entire nation. It's the privilege of a lifetime.

In an interview with *The Guardian* when he was playing for

Real Madrid, Zidane said: "I don't know if we are the best team in the world, but I know that I am lucky to be playing alongside some of the best players around. It's a dream."

To dream and have objectives is crucial, even if they are buried deep inside you. To get a new football, play in a big tournament, get a convertible, own a house, play for a big club in a big competition . . . these are just some of the holy grails every young player goes for and wants to achieve. To dream of scoring a goal or winning a match is a common dream yet remains the lifeblood of a true competitor who really believes it can happen and sets targets for himself in order to attain his objectives.

Each player's goal must be to exploit his talent to the max. He should wake up every morning with last night's dreams in mind and give himself a good kick up the arse. This is an effective way of aligning reality with his dreams.

I have an indelible memory of a real event which, when I experienced it, felt like a waking dream. I could not believe I was actually living it. During this happy illusion of reality, I see myself scoring goals in the best league in the world. In 2004, wearing a red jersey customised with a large number 9, I score my first goal with Manchester United. It is a free-kick from the right which luckily deflects into the back of the net. Free-kick takers like Giggs and Fortune were not playing, or were on the bench, and I, the newcomer, didn't hesitate to put myself forward and have a go. As a courtesy, they left me to it and I seized my chance. And it wasn't a dream: it really was me who scored a free-kick at Old Trafford.

The following weekend, it took the famous "hair dryer" treatment to wake me up to the very real ambitions, demands, pressures and dreams of a coach hungry for victories. I was reminded that winning is all that matters. I played my second Premiership game at Goodison Park against that little prodigy, Wayne Rooney. I was dreaming still. I scored two fine goals in the first half. Perhaps I was floating in the clouds, as after that I missed two more easy chances.

As I headed for the changing room at half-time, we were 3-0 up and my shoulders were almost swollen with pride. It would have been enough to just stay in my place and enjoy the moment, but my wake-up call was violent. Sir Alex Ferguson deafened me. I was taken aback. It was definitely me he was yelling at, again and again. He was unhinged, but I quickly understood why. He was unhappy because we had not come in with a four-goal lead from the first half which would have wrapped up the game. He was infuriated that I had missed several opportunities and reminded me that this was top-flight football. Wow. I woke up even more scorched 45 minutes later when we were knocked back by the spirit of Everton as the Toffees brought the score back to 3-3. Goodison Park was on fire: that explosive atmosphere feared by all Premiership teams. It was a clash with twists and turns, commitment and self-sacrifice until the referee blew the final whistle. Everton were a team possessed by the rhythm of the crowd which assailed its opponents like Spartans. Duncan Ferguson pounded everything that moved; Gravesen was like an illegal pitbull biting through to the bone; Tony Hibbert sliced up anyone who ventured into his path. Sir Alex was right to be wary of the soul of Goodison Park. It would take the instinct of striker Ruud van Nistelrooy to get me out of this nightmare with a header in stoppage time to give us a 4-3 victory. Despite scoring a double and with the match over, I woke up and realised that my dream was in fact a reality, and it was no longer exclusively mine.

Various elements have to come together at the right time to make your dream come true. It is important because players need to have a goal; a target; a challenge. A player can be satisfied with his success, but will want more of it. Some would call it perfectionism, but it's how you move on from good and bad situations. If he's been selected then he wants to go higher. It's not enough to get to the World Cup, once there his dream is to score; once that is achieved his vision is to score in the final; then to win it, pulling off the ultimate aerial move – a bicycle kick.

The sky's the limit *ad infinitum*, or as Spain's World Cup-winning captain Iker Casillas said, "When the World Cup ended and I had to go back to training, I said right away that I wanted another World Cup to kick-off, *rápido*."

Non-connoisseurs of the game might think that players are merely posers obsessed with their image and that, muscular like Greek gods, they will happily show off their six packs at the first opportunity. Detractors do not see the point of a bunch of men running in all directions after a round object for 90 minutes, while both goalies look on and get shot at. "Pathetic," they conclude.

Sitting on his couch and watching the game on TV, often even a player is convinced he can do better. But the amateur often forgets those small details which contribute to the bigger picture: the fatigue; the sweat which sometimes forces you to shut your eyes for half a second, just enough to distract you; the pressure of the coach and the public screaming in the stands; the pitch and its bad bounce; the rain or the searing heat; and your immense desire to do well.

It's easy to criticise a player. Fatigue is a primary reason for lack of concentration. Fans seem to have memory failure when it comes to that 30m sprint which allowed him to evade his marker and propelled him into the six-yard box. Despite having legs like lead because of this, he's juggling and dribbling and has enough spleen to get him where he's supposed to be. From the sofa it looks like all the player needs to do is push the ball into the goal, and that's what most of the pundits will say. But they have amnesia. How do they think he managed to get into this position in the first place? Thanks to his burning commitment and above all, a desire to score more than anyone else. But this effort can drain him of his powers at the moment of truth.

A player's efforts during training are reproduced and re-assessed every three days for upcoming matches during 11 long months. Only players in Britain play on through the festive season; in the rest of Europe everyone takes a break.

Football allows us all to let off steam and to share experience. It is a universal passion passed down from one generation to the next. The game is always changing and continues to take us all by surprise. It's normal for enthusiasts to dish out harsh criticism, and taking it is one of the things they believe players are paid for. But to hear journalists criticise, sometimes to the point of total disrespect, is distressing, especially when you know that they understand how difficult it can be. Some are in no position to take such a stand or are simply paid to be an agent provocateur like French journalist Eric Zemmour who enjoys stirring things up. In 2011 he was convicted of "provocation to racial discrimination" for claiming on Canal Plus TV that "the majority of drug dealers are blacks and Arabs" and that employers are entitled to discriminate against them. Fortunately, the majority of pundits are excellent professionals and know what football is all about. They understand that mistakes happen, especially given the electric pace at which the game is played, but they need to chat to make sure they and their show are talked about to help keep up audience ratings. I used to particularly like Gary Lineker, Andy Gray and Richard Keys. I've since moved on to Gary Neville and Jamie Redknapp, who are like a breath of fresh air; they are real specialists and generally what they say is spot on.

The ball is what everyone on the pitch wants to master. Everyone wants to get to grips with it, to express themselves through technical moves, freestyle tricks or precision tackles. They all somehow want to be at the end of a cross. Everyone feels the pressure. Everyone is going for the goal. The ball moves faster than any player – even though at full speed he can run at around 22 miles per hour – and never gets tired. Thanks to his team-mates and his opponents, a great player has the opportunity to make fancy or signature moves that make the fans happy. To win a match, a side has to do everything it can to make fewer serious mistakes than its opponents. Managers can still dream of the perfect match. The ultimate dream of all young footballers is to shoot into the top corner of the goal of the world's best goalkeeper in the final of the World Cup, bringing victory to his country.

Wayne Rooney's spectacular overhead kick goal against Manchester City in the 78th minute to seal a 2-1 win on 12 February 2011 was sheer brilliance. After the match, he humbly said: "I think it was my best goal."

This complicated technical move allows you to score from the centre of the box from a ball that is flying right over the players' heads and requires the striker to turn his back to the goal before launching himself into the air. Even some of the most agile players still have to master the famous move inspired by the American athlete Dick Fosbury, who revolutionised the high jump with his "Fosbury Flop", netting him an Olympic gold medal in 1968.

Executing an overhead kick sounds simple enough: throw yourself backwards into the air without the reassurance of that thick mattress provided in high jump competitions, time the scissor-like movement of your legs so that you kick the ball when it is directly over your head. But this aerial move is football fantasy. To pull off this acrobatic masterpiece requires incredible agility, balance, timing and power.

Picture this: during a match, a high-level player can run anything up to a half-marathon, including 1,000m of high-speed sprints – the equivalent of more than two laps around a full running track. Should he have the opportunity to do a 100m sprint with the ball, he'll be tackled as he runs. It's all stop and start, with a pull of the shirt, going down with a challenge, getting up to keep possession of the ball. He will make contact with the ball 20 to 80 times in a match depending on his position and his team's style of play. There are few opportunities for him to catch his breath during an intense game. Performing the bicycle kick requires courage and deadly focus at the right moment. The player needs to be in the right place at the right time and to make good use of that floating cross which triggers the tilt in his head – the so-called "striker's instinct". He must just trust it.

What runs through his mind? "Mate, it's now or never . . . So what if I banana slide on to my back and smash my coccyx in front of three billion football fans watching the World Cup final? So what if they all laugh at me if I miss the ball? Go on, go for it 'cause they'll respect you for trying!"

The striker's supporting foot is firmly planted in the manicured grass of the magnificent stadium that has been especially chosen for this grand finale, while the other foot is trying to get the right balance. This supporting foot, which is crucial to determining the course of a powerful shot, is facing in the opposite direction to the goal. It will soon propel him into the air and guide the other foot to kick the perfectly designed ball, which is the product of hours of scientific research and "Grip 'n' Groove" technology. The manufacturer's employees are proud of their work on this spherical object which has contributed to such a major world event.

The striker's kicking foot is enveloped in a red-and-gold football boot with light metal studs. Already valuable, it will be worth 500 times more on eBay after a goal is scored with its help. It is now ready for action as the player flips himself backwards to briefly face the sky for a quick face-to-face with God and the fans in a state of electrified expectation, although he never takes his eyes off the ball.

Zoom! The red-and-gold boot is in the air, ready to catapult the ball towards the net at brutal speed and with a powerful thrust of his athlete's body. All the stress of the tournament and a season of about 60 games have accumulated in his legs. His body is honed to perfection but very fragile. Will it support such a display of strength and flexibility?

Boom! As soon as his foot makes contact, the fans in the front rows of the stands are poised to leap up. They will be the first to shout, "Woaahhh!" and "Unbelievable!"

After this perfect kick, he then has to beat the best goalkeeper in the world who is the holder of the Golden Glove Award. He is known for his lightning reflexes and breathtaking saves, his impressive vertical and horizontal dives. He is adept at stopping shots and collecting crosses and long passes in flight.

For the 'keeper, it is as though the ball has slowed right down. As it flies towards the goal, the goalie has to make an instinctive decision about how to position his hands which are enveloped in gloves specifically designed to stick to the ball, giving him an automatic advantage. When wet, these gloves are so effective they can even pull off body hair.

For most players and spectators, the official match ball has all but disappeared. From the moment it made contact with the red-and-gold football boot, it vanished in a blur of speed and power. The player's acrobatic skill is so tremendous that all eyes are riveted to the execution of the move and his landing on his back, or arse. It's like watching the swing of Tiger Woods and losing track of the little, white, spinning golf ball.

For the striker who pulls off this exceptional move the ball also disappears. Strong vibrations from the shock of landing travel from his tailbone up the spine into his neck, which is sore from twisting to try to keep an eye on the ball. Only a second later will he find out where it ended up when he hears the roar of the crowd.

By happy coincidence, a defender looms in front of the goalie blocking his view, but he still dives full length. He only skim-touches the ball because the striker's shot was so powerful and the ball is whirling through the air at such speed. The ball lodges in the furthest and hardest place for a goalie to reach that is most coveted by all lovers of spectacular goals: the top corner.

"Gooooaaaaaaal!" The stadium is full to bursting, the fans are hysterical, the clamour is deafening. The striker, the fans and the whole world watching are high on adrenaline.

The bicycle kick came out of nowhere and the whole world marvels at the fantastic sight. The stamping feet of the supporters of the triumphant team make the stadium and its 120,000 seats vibrate. To lift the cup with pride, having given the victory to all your team-mates and a jubilant nation, is the privilege of a life-time. Such is the stuff that dreams are made of . . .

Scoring after a sharp turn and finish at a World Cup would be more than enough to satisfy me. It's every footballer's dream. Not only does everything have to come together for it to happen, but the player has to be in a national team strong enough to get through the three-year qualification phase through which around 200 highly competitive national teams are filtered. He has to get through the tournament to the final and has to be good enough to at least come off the bench. To score the winning goal is beyond most people's wildest dreams.

Over the 90 minutes, mistakes dictate the key events of a game at all levels. But at the World Cup an added criteria is needed: the flair for creating the unexpected at the most crucial moment which brings a touch of magic. It could be that the defenders of both teams have played beautifully and a player's brazen cheek takes everyone by surprise.

International football has come a long way since the first international game played in 1872 when Scotland hosted England, watched by 4,000 people. The drama of the World Cup, with its highs and lows, twists and turns, penalties and exploits, makes for such compelling viewing, it takes precedence over all other tournaments. The World Cup is played every four years for a month. So a world-class player who has a 15-year career only has four chances. He doesn't have much time to get deeply involved in the competition and if he reaches the final, only to lose, it really isn't cool as it's another four years before he can have another go. With all due respect, I really don't think the Faroe Islands will ever make it to the final. So if you are Faroese why not move to Rio de Janeiro long enough to get your papers and marry a gorgeous, kind Brazilian woman who looks good in a bikini? Otherwise your dream won't even get off the ground. That way, Brasilenho, your chance of winning a world cup is 100 times greater.

Truth is, this all-time dream of scoring that overhead kick does not happen to just anyone, despite all the talent in world football. Dreams and objectives are powerful motivators which spur you on after periods of doubt and failure. Throughout your life they are an invisible force pushing you to go as far as you can.

We only stop dreaming when we are called Zidane. He says to me: "Since I retired, I no longer dream, but I still have exciting goals. Today, I want to help others and pass on all I can because football gave me so much."

Zidane's dreams have all come true. He made sacrifices to bring alive his vision of what he wanted to achieve. As for me, I still dream. When you become a professional, your dream does not belong to you anymore. You share it with your fans, as I often like to say.

12
MUSIC TO MOVE YOUR SOUL

Music is a perfect and essential means of relaxation and escape for a footballer. And it's a great way to get you buzzing before kick-off. For some it's good old rock 'n' roll like Survivor's *Eye of the Tiger* from the *Rocky* movie. For others it's a good rap – 50 Cent's latest single and you're ready to go. The playlists of team DJs like Phil Neville at Everton or Patrice Evra at Man United are generally a reflection of the team's vibe. To pump up the bass in the changing rooms of clubs in the English football league is normal, whereas in other countries there is total silence.

Alan Shearer is the all-time top scorer for the Premier League with Blackburn and Newcastle. I was amazed to hear his voice before one of my first games in the Premier League when I arrived at Newcastle on loan. We were treated to loud music and our captain in full karaoke mode before we went out on to the pitch. I'm pretty sure it was the Rolling Stones's *(I Can't Get No) Satisfaction*. It was fantastic, especially as I had only ever known the stiff, stressed out atmosphere of the FC Metz changing room, although that now might have changed. It was great to see our captain relaxed, and more like he was ready to face Simon Cowell and the *X Factor* jury for an audition. Alan's change of personality when the referee blew the whistle was striking. He transformed himself into a machine set to destroy the defenders and the goal nets.

Today, every time I go into the changing room, I generally need to see my team-mates with smiles on their faces and a desire to transmit their enthusiasm to their team-mates. It's a reminder that this green space which we play on serves as a stage on which to perform our show for the fans whilst we have fun along the way. Football and music are a fulfilling combination which, coupled with a healthy family, makes me feel like I'm in paradise.

I see myself back home not so long ago with my firstborn son. The little man was the master of the house even though he wasn't talking yet. We often play music in the house. Suddenly 50 Cent's summer hit *In Da Club* started playing on MTV Base. Everyone started to nod their heads as a reflex and I let rip. *Turn it up and shake the house.* Then I noticed my six-month-old gyrating his hips so rushed to check him. After a few seconds my heart swelled with pride as I realised that my little angel had been trying to get into the groove. He had realised he had to do a horizontal movement of the head to dance. The innate nature of humans who choose rhythm as a form of self-expression has always amazed me. I had not yet had a chance to show my little man Michael Jackson's "moonwalk", or take him to see Usher and Chris Brown in concert together. Movement is part of life, and the law of motion is rhythm. A child is calmed by the rocking of the cradle, as an adult enjoys his favourite sport or music. Dancing to music produces ecstasy the same as playing beautiful football in harmony with your team.

It's enough to place a black-and-white football on the ground or to play good music for people to start moving their feet. In neighbourhoods, *favelas*, ghettos or slums there are great sounds and enough footballs to create a unique atmosphere. Good football comes from the street with all its imperfections. It is rooted both in its constraints and carefree spirit; the inner rage to get out; the ambition fuelled by a desire to live better.

Sniper, a French rap group originally from Deuil-la-Barre in the northern *banlieu* of Paris, describe the journey of a young inner-city kid to stardom in their track *Carved in Rock* which also links the worlds of music and football. The objective of the singer or artist is to be recognised by his peers and to feel that he has illuminated the lives of others, leaving a lasting impression on their minds; the footballer is the same.

It is often said that the worlds of music and creativity are linked to drugs. For some lead singers and members of rock and reggae groups in particular, it's all about inspiration and chilling out. Drugs are banned in all sports of course, but music is a real shot in the arm for me. I'm not one for stress, but am definitely up for inspiration. You should see me in a club with my friends, making a fool of myself trying out new steps on the dance floor! But I only go clubbing to enjoy the DJ spinning tunes, to be with friends and dance – that's it.

Music can move me to tears or cries of joy when I'm in sync with what is playing. Football can provoke the same reaction. I often ask myself, "Louis, if you had the choice between being the star in a legendary band or an anonymous winner of the World Cup, which would you choose?" My answer is a question mark!

Football is a symphony; coaches are the conductors; players are the artists and the pitch is the concert hall. Sport comes naturally in a young athlete. It is instinctive for many boys, like nodding the head to the bass when a good tune comes on. A boy needs to express himself physically. If he wants to expend energy and sweat, to defy others or himself, he is more than likely to play football before choosing another sport which suits him better. Tennis pros, rugby, basketball or volleyball players, even Formula One drivers, often started off messing about with friends on a football field. As did many great writers and artists.

My youngest boy, who had just started to walk, didn't like using his hands when he saw something on the ground. Round, oval or triangular, he'd kick it with impressive precision. I believe this reflex showed that he had a strong innate sense, a natural ability, despite the fact that he saw his father regularly kicking a ball.

Why doesn't my little one pick up the ball in his hands, take a few steps forward and toss it behind him like a rugby player? Or just pick it up and try to kick it as high as he can? Football requires pace, fast feet with the ball and loads of energy. And only a ball is needed. You don't have to pass backwards to move the ball forwards; you don't need a net, or a hoop and backboard. The rules of garden football are simple: kick the ball to see how strong you are and how far it will go. You can kick it towards a wall then, step by step, you improve at passing to friends. It is this simplicity that makes football so enjoyable to watch, making it the number one most popular sport worldwide with 300 million practitioners, closely followed by volleyball. Third, it's basketball. The 2009 Champions League final was watched by more people around the world than the American Superbowl.

Genetics is nature's way of passing on information through the generations, continually combining traits, which is why every human is different. The genome is like a hard disk containing a blend of dreams, trauma, gifts, faults and all the great stories inherited from our ancestors which go to create what we are like; how we behave and survive in our environment.

I was in the *crèche* organised for the families of players on the French team just before Euro 2004 in Portugal. All the kid's toys were gleaming in the sunshine. My eye was drawn to a little boy who was full of life, doing impressive dribbles and nutmegs in the tiny playground. I did not know whose son he was. Later, I described what I'd seen to Olivier Dacourt, the former French international whose club career included playing for Inter Milan and AS Roma. He cut me short.

Olivier Dacourt: "Ask yourself who his Dad is? Think about it . . ." I realised in a flash. Smarten up, it's obvious! It was Zidane junior.

Heredity has always fascinated humans. DNA, metabolic pathways, self-renewing, self-reproducing cells . . . the tremendous complexity of it all is beyond comprehension to most people. Yannick Noah, a superb tennis player and now a fantastic singer, produced a son, Joakim, 6ft 11in tall, who now plays basketball for the Chicago Bulls. Paul Ince's son, Thomas, who moved from Liverpool to play for Blackburn and then went on to Blackpool, looks set for a brilliant career. With luck, you inherit Dad's technique, Grandad's staying power and your mum's beautiful face. Add to this the "it" factor which gives you competitive edge and you end up being a good player, not just a good guy. Some are born with "good genes", but that is not enough. The great Pelé said: "Success is no accident. It is hard work, perseverance, learning, studying, sacrifice and, most of all, love of what you are doing or learning to do."

Football is full of uncertainties because the results are unpredictable, despite the clever tactics of the best Italian coaches like Marcello Lippi and Fabio Capello who are known for their rigour and their obsession with creating an impermeable defence. However hard you train and are coached, one day you're on top form and the next you're called "biscuits" because you go to pieces in the box. The best way forward is to just get out there and try to enjoy yourself.

Music generates lots of money which generally does not overly concern people. The impact of musical icons lives on well after they have died – Michael Jackson, Bob Marley and 2Pac will always be hugely influential. Guitarists are like great footballers: skill, patience and perseverance are needed to rehearse for countless hours so that they can perform and make people dream. Jimi Hendrix, BB King and Keith Richards: their passion fuelled them to follow their dreams with courage.

A voice. A style. When it's truly unique it's instantly recognisable: worldwide. To be able to move people and take them on a journey through the power of melody and lyrics is a great gift. The power of some lead singers over their record company is similar to the power of some world-class players over their club presidents. Football and music are like two slot machines which continue to pay out prizes – the one major difference being piracy. Until recently, around one in three CDs sold worldwide was a rip off and in the digital world around 95 per cent of music downloads online are unlicensed and illegal, so only a small percentage of the income generated goes back to the producers and artists. Because of piracy and illegal downloading, record companies are not taking risks like before, so bands have to go on the road and play live to bring in extra income.

The football industry managed by FIFA in Zurich continues to rake it in thanks to sponsorship deals and multiple tax breaks. But it won't be long before a big fish brings out a new kind of audiovisual piracy. That way, people will be able to watch games easily without paying.

Footballers listening to music on their headphones is the latest bug-bear. Detractors say that it erodes team spirit and puts up a barrier between players who used to bond on the team bus, but now journey in a solitary bubble. For me, it shows the importance of music in sport.

Is it unsettling to see young players go to a match with the latest "Bose" headphones clamped on their heads? Admittedly, it's not as good for team morale as a good game of poker, or brag, or blackjack, but journalists like to amplify and distort an image or a personality. It's like a reality TV show where candidates are chosen for their differences, which are then exaggerated and played on. A candidate with a noticeable pimple on their nose who touches it nervously will be filmed almost exclusively as though the producer has decided he wants him to make him look like Gargamel, the evil wizard from the Smurfs.

A player doesn't go into town, work out, go shopping, to a nightclub, to church or to pick up his kids wearing his headphones. He has them on when he gets off the team bus because he is listening to his favourite tracks to chill out and motivate him before a match. It's not easy to step into the arena in the right frame of mind. From the moment he leaves his hotel room to when he enters the changing room, he just wants to relax and only thinks about the game when the manager gives his instructions to the team.

I read in the *Daily Mail*: "Stoke City striker Dave Kitson says iPods make players 'miserable' and crush morale during the crucial period before matches when team-mates should be bonding." And in the *Daily Mirror*: "Dowie criticises the iPod generation of footballers." To caricature the footballer in big headphones is all too easy when he is in them only for a short ride. Some managers have banned them because of public opinion and not because of a genuine belief that they are detrimental.

Picture yourself in a footballer's shoes, entering Real Madrid's Bernabeu Stadium or Celtic Park in the Parkhead area of Glasgow. Immerse yourself in a bewitching atmosphere with the fans vibrating to the rhythm of their collective heartbeat. Now imagine you played an excellent game the previous week having listened to a selection of artists on your Mp3 like . . . 2Pac, Admiral T, Booba, 50 Cent, Bob Marley, Michael Jackson, Gipsy Kings, Rihanna, Jay Z, Black Eyed Peas, Kassav, Stromae, Notorious Big, Diam's, Eminem, Balavoine, Nirvana, Sinatra and others . . . so what would your playlist be? Do you think you should stop listening to music because headphones upset public opinion, even if they have been helpful to you?

Music has always been everywhere in football. Imagine Brazilian players without the samba, the Spanish without merengue, Africans and Afro-Caribbeans without zouk or the coupé-décalé dance. We wouldn't have much fun. Thanks to Roger Milla, Cameroon was the first African country to reach the quarter-finals of a World Cup: his dance, inspired by Makossa music and improvised around the corner flag to celebrate his goal, is a musico-football symbol.

Camaraderie is the bedrock of team sport, and music is a tool to motivate success in this era of high-pressure sport. Money and the need to get results increasingly require intense focus. Some believe that failing to entertain the public is a sin; music is a relaxant and it plays an important part in the whole spectacle of football. Terrace chants are the main way groups of supporters communicate their joy and passion and share it with others. Fans' songs encourage the home team and destabilise their opponents. Here are some examples.

Paris St Germain:
Allez Paris S.G.! [Go for it, Paris S.G.!]
Vous êtes notre fierté, [You're our pride,]
Vous allez enflammer, [You'll set fire,]
Ce stade de légende, et du virage Auteuil,
[To this historic stadium, and from the Auteuil end,]
S'élèvera en chœur d'une voix phénoménale,
[A chorus of epic voices will roar,]
Cette chanson capitale. [This, our capital's song.]
Lala la la lala . . .

Marseille:
Aux Armes, aux Armes, [Call to Arms, to Arms,]
Aux Armes, aux Armes, [Call to Arms, to Arms,]
Nous sommes les marseillais, [We are Les Marseillais,]
Nous sommes les marseillais, [We are Les Marseillais,]
Et nous allons gagner, [And we will win,]
Et nous allons gagner, [And we will win,]
Allez l'OM, allez l'OM, [C'mon OM, c'mon OM!]
Allez l'OM, allez l'OM. [C'mon OM, c'mon OM!]
Hohohohohhohoho . . .

Manchester United:
Take me home, United road,
To the place that I belong,
To Old Trafford, to see United,
Take me home, United road.

Tottenham Hotspur:
We are Tottenham,
We are Tottenham,

Super Tottenham,
From the Lane,
We are Tottenham,
Super Tottenham,
We are Tottenham,
From the Lane . . .

For France in 1998, the team anthem was Gloria Gaynor's *I Will Survive*. For Tim Howard's United States team in 2010 it was Stromae's *Alors on danse*. These two hymns to glory were a hit in the changing room and on the team bus. Music gives an impetus to the matches.

So here I am with my iPod getting ready for kick-off. I listen to the songs which sound good down my earphones, like Craig David's *Rise and Fall* or Cypress Hill's *Superstar*. When I'm looking to fuel my confidence and my pride, I listen to *Champion* by Chipmunk feat. Chris Brown. This song gives you a great ego boost and renews your confidence which is so easily eroded in just a week. His words, 'I'm always pushing myself to the limit, Making sure I stay ahead,' and the tag line, 'Some people wait their turn, Some people but not me, I was born a Champion,' say it all.

13
SUPERSTITIONS AND LUCKY CHARMS

*D*aily Mail, 1 September 2010: "What a sucker! Everton striker Louis Saha turns to leech treatment in bid to get fit for France."

Tips and strategies to boost a player's confidence, spiritual beliefs, voodoo fetishes and "juju", lucky mascots, the symbolism of colours and clothing, tattoos, lucky dates, songs and invocations – fate and the superstitious beliefs of sportsmen are a fascinating subject!

Most players do specific things before a match so that they have sound reference points in their psychological preparation. Some play all year in the same boots, others wear their underwear inside out. One will be obsessed with how he puts on his shorts, another with how he ties his shoelaces. One will pray, another will listen to a special playlist on their iPod. Sometimes hairstyles are inspired more by superstition than by fashion. I like to think I am successful with my different styles. Sometimes kids laugh when they see what I have done which makes me smile; their laughter brings me luck. Lol!

In an interview with Robinho, he remarks that after he has argued with his wife he usually plays a good game. This superstitious belief makes me chuckle. It's not great from madame's point of view, admittedly, although some might say success by any means is good. John Terry is well known for having numerous superstitions, which range from where he parks his car, to how he puts on his boots, or listening to the same Usher CD.

When I signed for Tottenham, I went to celebrate with my mate in a restaurant in Ilford. I was so happy I offered two glasses of champagne to the waitress and the owner, who didn't know much about football, but we got on well. As a gesture of appreciation, he gave me a lucky charm memento: the champagne cork with 50p stuck in to it. I took it with me in my kit bag to the Newcastle game the following weekend. We won 5-0.

Sometimes paranormal practices will be undertaken to benefit a team or to adversely influence the opposition. In 2002, the psychic Uri Geller claimed he had used his psychic powers to help the English team win against Argentina. On his website he says: "If you believe in the law of attraction, and you understand the power that one person's emotionally charged thoughts and feelings have, can you imagine how powerful the combined energy, thoughts and emotions of millions of people, would be?"

Certain Africans will go for miles through the bush to see the village *marabout* (a north African spiritual leader and teacher). Sitting on his stony land, he will pronounce in his strong African accent: "Little one, I see you have a great future in the spotlight if you give me an offering. I will utter incantations to the forest God to inspire you in your career. I will protect you with my charms and will help your wounds heal fast if you trust me."

Many become hooked and swear by their guru. They are willing to pay big bucks for protection and to be given special energy to play better. A national technical director in Cameroon is fighting the use of superstition in football, saying that the witch doctor does not control the ball. He wants to give every man his due. It's the player who makes his own luck. He pointed out that lucky charms have not yet helped an African country win the World Cup.

You hear stories about the use of lucky charms on the pitch or in the shoes of the competing players. Marabouts wear pendants around their hips and have a whole arsenal of rituals on hand to help their team win: prayers, holy water, amulets, totems, cures, consulting djinns, sacrifice, curses and so on. Their preparations usually end with a ritual bath to protect the players – strikers in particular. There was a clash of witch doctors before and during Côte d'Ivoire v Nigeria during the qualifying match for the World Cup in 1998. The whole stadium could see the Ivorian miracle-worker in the away stand with a large vessel on his head. The score went in favour of the Ivory Coast . . . Didier Drogba believes that the more people who are praying for you, the stronger you feel. He believes in blessings and prays for God's protection.

In July 2010 it was rumoured that Jose Mourinho had visited a famous witch doctor in Africa. The soon-to-be coach of Real Madrid was unfazed and swiftly denied the Kenyan witch doctor's story. For nine years, Mr Mourinho held an unbeaten home league record (150 matches, 125 wins, 25 draws, 342 goals, 87 conceded). From 2002 he did not lose a home game for any of the teams of the top four championships (Porto, Chelsea, Inter and Real Madrid) under him. It was only on 2 April 2011 that he relived the bitter taste of defeat, when Real Madrid were beaten at home by Sporting Gijon. When you play away against Mr Mourinho's team, it's better to stay at home! All this had nothing to do with spells except for his magical ability to galvanise his players and intimidate, in fact terrify, the opposition. Chelsea players radiated a strong sense of invulnerability during his reign which evaporated after his departure for Italy. His aura was magic.

Many players believe in God and make the sign of the cross as they walk on to the pitch. Like Steven Pienaar and Kaka, they will also make this gesture after scoring or missing a shot on goal. Brazilians often look up at the sky and thank the Virgin Mary. Whether they do this because times are hard or not, they believe in their God or their lucky star which gives them their courage and their talent.

France's former national coach, Raymond Domenech, was apparently a proficient follower of astrology, although it did not serve him very well. The former international Johan Micoud teased him gently about it when he wasn't selected for the 2006 World Cup: "Maybe I wasn't chosen because I'm a Leo, and there were already too many in the French team."

A few years ago, I stumbled across a website called astrotheme. com. I was amazed by my accurate character description simply from the date and time of my birth. I recognised myself in almost every sentence. So I began to believe in astrology, but I still prefer to assume that I am the one who controls what happens to me. I have had a go with power balance bracelets, leeches, yoga, acupuncture, spiritual healers and I even tried to be freed from a spell. I have done everything to try and overcome my injuries. Let's say I believe in all that players cling to in order to boost their confidence or their luck. The power of believing is what makes you strong. Although not much has worked for me.

Some believe that certain numbers carry a dynamic energy. The German team refused to sleep on the 13th floor of a chic hotel in Lisbon, fearing that it would bring them bad luck at Euro 2004. Zidane made legendary the number 10 and David Beckham the number 23. Thierry Henry chose the number 14 in honour of Johan Cruyff. At Everton, I went from number 9 to number 8 because I was born on the eighth day of the eighth month in the year 1978, so it felt good to me. At Tottenham I am number 15 because that shirt was free.

Nicklas Bendtner reimbursed Arsenal fans who had bought shirts with his old number 26 on them when he changed his number during the summer before a new season. He was determined to play wearing his favourite number, 52, hoping it would bring him luck. He commented: "It means a lot to see supporters wearing your name and number, and I want to ensure people aren't inconvenienced by the change."

Sylvain Distin believes in body-building; in the support of those around him; in the kisses he blows towards his wife, Karen, before a match. He believes in the intense effort he puts into his tactical work to practice his craft even better; and in his team.

When I ask Thierry Henry what it is that gives him a helping hand, he answers in an assertive voice: "I've always worked hard. I know it's a cliché and everyone goes on about it being the reason why you do well. Petit Louis, for one thing, my father always pushed me to work harder than anyone else, and secondly, I realised that my only gift, which comes naturally, is my speed, and I fully exploited it. At first I was no good at free kicks so I worked hard at them, and started scoring. Bro, I had problems controlling the ball with my weaker foot, so I worked hard at it, and started scoring with it. Putting in extra hours in training was my strength."

Chance coupled with confidence give an important boost to the efforts and talent a player tries to express on the pitch. You have to give yourself the means to be successful and anything goes, so long as your opponents are not hurt in any way.

I read somewhere that the Moroccan Football Federation asked Puma to change the colour of their players' jersey. They switched from green to red to invoke fiery Mars and bring them vitality, power, strength and passion.

In sport there are many great associations with the Irish symbol of good luck, the four-leaf clover. Legend has it that the first leaf represents faith, the second hope, the third love and the fourth luck. This magical green leaf can be found on the Celtic FC badge. One of the club's fans' favourite chants resonates with pride: "With a four leaf clover on my breast, And the green and white upon my chest, It's such a joy for us to see, For they play football the Celtic way . . ."

The 2005 Champions League final, AC Milan v Liverpool, is seen by many as one of the competition's greatest finals. From being 3-0 up at half-time the tide turned against Milan. Liverpool scored three goals in six minutes in the second half and the final was eventually decided by penalty kicks. All of Europe was talking about that crazy game. Rafael Benítez, Liverpool's manager, admitted that he was surprised by the way in which his team won their fifth European Cup for the club. Liverpool's victory was so incredible that people said it was because of outside intervention. Since then, whenever Liverpool plays, thousands of fans say they must wear the same "lucky underwear" or go to the same "lucky pub", and that they have to do everything the same way as they did on the day of that miraculous win which remains engraved in the memories of all their supporters.

AC Milan got their revenge in the 2007 rematch when they won their seventh European title with a score of 2-1, some said by a stroke of luck. The Italians' first goal was a combination of determination and fate. The trajectory of Andrea Pirlo's free-kick was perfectly judged by Pepe Reina who dived and had it covered – just as Pippo Inzaghi rushed at the goal. The ball hit Inzaghi's chest which unwittingly deflected it past a wrong-footed Reina. This surprise goal in first-half injury time was not just luck as Inzaghi was a prolific scorer in European club competitions with 70 goals to his credit and more than 300 goals in all competitions. A winner's aura is infectious; it can lift his team and bring it luck. This opening goal gave his team-mates a confidence boost, spurring them on to victory. Inzaghi was not in position to deflect the ball by chance. He had made his own luck. You need to learn how to create luck and maximise it and not wait for it to come and save the day.

Whether by prayer or psychology, and hard work, if you are going to win a football match you need a certain amount of luck and, at the very least, the referee to not be against you. Referees play a crucial role in the game and must be respected by the players. But when you get back to the changing room there are times when you feel so frustrated with them that you could tear your hair out. It is almost impossible for a referee to keep perfect concentration or to manage to see and interpret everything correctly because of the fast pace and high intensity of the game. To keep their eyes simultaneously on the players in blue, the players in red, as well as the ball, is a feat in itself. To know all the rules and apply them correctly at the right tempo; to recognise if a player is faking; if the ball has gone over or just touched the line, if a foul was committed while the ball was at the other end of the pitch . . . the correct making of tough decisions depends on the vigilance of the referee and the linesmen. It could also depend on a small camera that could quickly validate a decision. But the debate about the use of instant replay video footage is still stuck at square one in part because of how impractical it would be to equip every championship pitch – amateur and professional – with identical technology. But the world of professional football should have a more reliable system of adjudication because such massive amounts of money are involved. Without the need for controversy it could also, possibly, greatly limit the scourge of match fixing.

During the 2010/11 season I discussed this with Chris Foy who officiates in the Premier League. He said: "We feel that the intensity of the game has increased by as much as 20 per cent this season, putting more pressure on the players." I saw him running long laps during his training, requiring a great deal of effort. The physical stamina required of a referee is not far off that of a pro player. And his attitude during the 90 minutes of a match has to be as good as his decisions if he is to keep his cool in the heat of the moment and not offend or annoy a player under pressure to get good results. Some referees, with their arrogant style of decision-making, seem to want to be seen as infallible robots as though their powers are those of an all-seeing, all-knowing God. Football is the most difficult sport to referee as the ball travels so fast and in just a matter of seconds something can happen 15m away from your line of vision. It can be hard to uncover wrongdoing as there are so many potential points of contact on the field of play and so much is going on in different directions. Frankly, there are times when players and managers have to play a very subtle psychological game with referees before a match because if you blank them, or even go too far the other way and try to get them in your pocket, you could end up encouraging them even more to slightly disadvantage your side. Increasingly they seem to become a kind of 23rd player on the pitch who is either with or against you.

Naturally, good referees are barely noticed or famous because they are almost invisible. A red card was given to Jack Rodwell, the Toffees midfielder, by Martin Atkinson for a tackle on Luis Suarez during the Merseyside derby on 1 October 2011. As this was a bad decision the Football Association cancelled the suspension, but the damage was done. The match still ended up as a victory for Liverpool, but the result was unfair because Everton were unjustly forced to play with 10 men for 67 minutes. To have so much inconsistency is damaging even if to make a mistake is human, which everyone understands. It's not easy.

Superstition is like music: it's good for stress relief. Before a game, as well as listening to good music, sometimes I listen to a recording of myself that I have made in which I affirm my qualities and past exploits. This helps me once I'm on the pitch, to hold my head up high and to influence fate. I repeat phrases like: "You're an actor in your game. Your destiny is not how you respond, it's how you act," or, "Inside the box, trust your instincts and remember that a defender can't touch you, so keep your cool." Sometimes I'm too laid back and a reminder of things which have worked for me in the past is good.

Maicon, the Brazilian defender, tells the story of how his ex-footballer father took his and his twin's umbilical cords and buried them under the grass of his former club, praying that one of his sons would become a footballer. Maicon, who plays for Inter and Brazil's national team, was named the 2009/2010 UEFA Club Defender of the Year and was nominated for the Ballon d'Or trophy as Europe's top player. Magic? Well, who knows, but it's a great story.

A team in Zimbabwe were ordered by their superstitious coach to ritually cleanse themselves in a river infested with crocodiles and hippos. Seventeen players bathed, but only 16 got back out. The worst part of this story is that they then lost the match. Black magic? Well, who knows, but what a tragedy.

In his autobiography, Robbie Savage describes how his father made him drink a glass of Guinness every night when he was a kid to build him up. So the idea that he had to have a drink before a match became a superstitious belief. He'd take a bottle of white wine in his kit bag to away matches to drink in his hotel room. It went from a glass of wine the night before the game, to a half a bottle, then a bottle. Then he was voted Derby County's Player of the Year in 2010.

Sportsmen, coaches and fans have always believed in the weird and the wonderful. From Europe to Africa and Asia through to Samoa, superstition and the beliefs of nations are infinite when we speak the language of the offside, nutmeg and sombrero. Football thrives on passion, tribalism and the irrational, all of which are inscribed in man's genes.

IV

BLING, BLING, THE TIMES THEY ARE A-CHANGIN'

14
THE TROUBLE WITH
MONEY

*D*aily Mail: "Named and shamed: The Premiership clubs which pay backroom staff 'poverty wages' as players pocket millions."

Who gets what?

For clubs, football is big business. Emotions and loyalty don't get much of a look in when it comes to decision-making within the boardroom. The public pays for a good performance, so the spectators have rights. But the conflict between market forces and the demands of supporters can cause disgust and dissent on the terraces. For fans, football is essentially driven by emotions, loyalty, love and passion, all of which are being replaced by merchandising and broadcasting rights, and the transfer window.

Most fans put up with paying high season ticket prices. In exchange for their vocal support and a season ticket, all they ask of the club close to their heart is for the team to go for it, and win. A season ticket at Everton costs around £400 a year, Liverpool around £600 and Manchester United around £800, but to get one fans may have to spend years on the waiting list. It can take up to 20 years to reach the top for Old Trafford. Season ticket prices for Arsenal currently range from £950 to £2,000. So it would be fair to say that you need passion, contacts, persistence or money to gain regular access to certain stadiums. Holding an annual season ticket is a privilege and is passed on by inheritance. Let's not even talk about the £120,000 per year cost for a premium box at Old Trafford. At PSG's Parc des Princes stadium the most expensive box costs £8,000. At a time when the cost of living is soaring and people are losing their jobs, the cost of season tickets is still increasing. In return for his ticket, all the supporter who pays will gain is a feeling of pride if the team wins or, in the event of a bad defeat, a sense of disgust. Is he getting the experience he really wants?

Club chairmen are the ones who invest and players are the ones who train and perform regularly to entertain the public watching from the stands or on TV. The big bosses are paid on the same criteria that govern all businesses today, but the stakes are much higher. Everyone involved in a player's transfer negotiations plays a part and profits from it one way or another. Sponsors pay huge sums to a club for their logo to be displayed on the players' shirts and all kinds of rights are part of the deal, sometimes going as far as the naming of the stadium. The whole sponsorship package often constitutes one of the club's main sources of revenue. TV companies pay billions for the right to screen the big matches. Even the transfer of an average player from one big club to another is counted in millions of pounds. So football is very big business, even though it is only sport. But for supporters, the fact that their team can sell their best players or the way some club owners sell out their club can be infuriating and creates conflict between the two parties.

Very few football players talk openly about their wages. Whether with one another, with the family or the media, wages are a taboo subject that unsettles everyone, yet no one can avoid the issue. At this point I prefer not to divulge my salary. Suffice it to say that strikers are generally better paid than midfielders and defenders. A healthy bank account is one of the key privileges of my golden life. However, I will try to outline the key elements of a transfer and clarify a seemingly straightforward transaction, even though to fully grasp the context you really need to live the experience.

In 1957, the world of football was revolutionised by Sir Matt

Busby, then manager of Manchester United. TV was catapulting football to even higher levels of popularity. Fans could watch the game's greatest stars and hold on to those images forever. Sir Matt decided to go to war against the media, specifically broadcasting, and asked that all players be paid according to their value: "No reward, no TV." In other words, he said that if TV would not share its profits, it would not be allowed to broadcast football matches. However, league football only gradually gained a nationwide audience as cameras were given limited access to certain stadiums. Some, not all, world football games were screened. In the 1960s, the BBC launched *Match of the Day* and ITV *Match of the Week*. In the 1980s, league matches were screened live for the first time. In 1992, when Rupert Murdoch and English football joined forces through the creation of the Premier League and the satellite TV deal struck with BSkyB. The game was transformed. More matches were shown live than ever before, and clubs could now afford top-flight foreign players. Top division footballers now earn 46 times as much as they did in 1984/85.

The first symbol of the star system and of the word "icon" was certainly George Best, who played for Manchester United from 1963 to 1974. He had a great gift for inspiring people to talk about him on and off the pitch. He was a phenomenal player – the Cristiano Ronaldo of his day. He was handsome, charismatic, endearing and a fantastic player. His friend, Michael Parkinson, wrote: "He could hit long and short passes with equal precision, was swift and fearless in the tackle and he reintroduced the verb 'to dribble'. He was as imaginative and whimsical in midfield as he was economical and deadly given a chance at goal." This pioneer of football changed the image of the sport and its potential to galvanise television ratings. He paved the way for players to reap the fruits of their talent.

In England today Sky and ESPN fight to pay £600 million for exclusive rights to broadcast the Premier League in a single season. This means viewers can see unforgettable one-on-ones such as

Didier Drogba v Rio Ferdinand. In the 1990s, Sky only spent £60 million a season. Now, in France, millions of euros are invested per season by TF1, Canal + or Al Jazeera for rights to broadcast Ligue 1 so fans can watch clashes like PSG v Marseille. Huge amounts of money are paid to leagues or federations for redistribution to their member clubs.

For the mainstream media it is a business that works well, yet the intensive coverage traps players on the front-line as they can't avoid being written about in the press, or being caught in the spotlight of criticism. Players take the rap while everyone takes the cash, even though we all make a living from this glorious game. The tabloids take advantage of the demand for football news to sensationalise events and unhesitatingly tarnish the players' image and that of their world. This is troubling because TV bosses would not invest so much money just to advertise or make players famous; they seem to want to boost ratings in a contrived way since salacious gossip has little do with the game itself. When you see these broadcasting companies making profits of £600 million it brings home the extent to which football is an important part of their revenue stream.

Today, according to the official figures, only 20 per cent of FIFA's total income is redistributed to the 208 national federations across the world. I don't know much about it, but I am surprised that 80 per cent of its turnover is needed to run the organisation. A footballer's earnings are not as disproportionate as that.

FIFA does not hide the power it holds over the whole business of the sport. The recent process to select the hosts of the 2018 and 2022 World Cups showed the world the extent of the power wielded by just 20 or so men in this massive global industry. In the media, suspicions are rife about under-the-table bribes and kickbacks.

At the time of writing, the effects of extreme temperatures in Qatar are being studied as if the committee did not know that the World Cup is hosted in the summer and not in midwinter. The promise of air-conditioned stadiums to cool the 50-degree desert heat in June underpinned Qatar's winning bid for 2022, but now the feasibility of this is being questioned on the grounds of expense and sustainability. Without such stadiums, the heat will endanger the players, who will have to get re-hydrated at every throw-in; maybe they will be allowed to carry a small bottle and a towel around their hips? The public could pass out in the heat, or get sunburned in their seats. As for the fans who enjoy getting drunk, they'll be desperate to find a shady corner, or a portable water cooler mist spray. Maybe FIFA will organise fun battles with plastic bags of fresh water for kids to help prevent dehydration and hallucinations. Expensive and potentially environmentally unfriendly solutions are likely to be implemented to meet the criteria of a hundred or so powerful men adept at pulling strings.

Following an agreement, FIFA compensates clubs whose players are involved in the World Cup, which was not previously the case. The total funds allocated for each tournament is close to US$40 million. Clubs have long campaigned for this, since they are the ones who pay the players who bring in the revenue to FIFA's tournament; and when players return injured their clubs felt cheated and powerless. Now things are more balanced.

To think that the first meeting of the Football Association was held in 1863 and that FIFA was founded in 1904. The principles of football back then had nothing to do with money and every-thing to do with encouraging fair play and competitiveness. The turnover of FIFA in December 2009 was US$1 billion from spon-sors, broadcast rights, World Cups, games and all derivatives. It is one of the richest organisations in the world. The Champions League generated 73 per cent of UEFA's income in 2010, in other words £917 million in total. Of that, £622 million were allocated to the 32 teams that participated in the 2010 Champions League. The winners, Inter Milan, received just under £41 million of this in "prize money" and broadcast rights. The financial revolution that has taken place in football over the last 20 years means that more responsibility and greater transparency are needed, as for any business. The integrity of the sport is in danger. Football may be at its peak right now, but everything could change very fast. The burst of the internet bubble in the 1990s and the more recent global stock market crash are proof of this.

John McBeth, former president of the Scottish Football Association, said in an interview: "If we take care of the game the money will follow, but if we take care of the money the game will die." A massive club like Rangers entering into administration shows how any club which does not control its finances correctly can destroy the very thing that the fans love, day and night.

It's all too easy to target footballers. So the question remains: Are the wages earned by top players well-deserved, or indecent? There is often talk about footballers' salaries, but rarely about the profits that go to those who own and run football clubs. There is an ongoing debate about a salary cap to block wage inflation which is steadily increasing and posing a threat to smaller clubs. The disproportionate gap between footballers' wages and those of, say, doctors and teachers mirrors the economies of the developed world where the gap between rich and poor is widening.

The fact remains that when we compare the wages of a single professional athlete to those of an office worker, or a fire-fighter, a tremendous sense of injustice is aroused. But would reducing the salary of a bunch of footballers change things that much? The wallets of ordinary citizens would remain the same, regardless. Footballers are soft targets compared to top executives, high-flying bankers and internet billionaires and are more in the public eye due to intensive media exposure. The example of Bill and Melinda Gates leading the way supporting good causes around the world with around 90 per cent of their immense fortune is, unfortunately, unusual.

Sport is not and will never be, completely, considered a job. Do not think that I am biting the hand that feeds me. I understand jealousy, but craftsmen that we are, we just do the same as anyone else in the same position of power over their wage-paying boss: we ask for a piece of the pie. The sale of the Premier League's overseas broadcasting rights for 2010-13 will raise around £1.4 billion, more than double the previous level of £625 million. All this is thanks to the enthusiasm of football fans and how the top level of the game in this country is presented. The same goes for Germany, with its stadia full to the max, as are the coffers of its clubs. As fans often like to say, they are the ones who pay our salaries. But a fan will rarely ever say that he pays our bosses, who are our employers.

If employees had the power in a McDonald's, in Microsoft, on the railways or in any other industry they would do the same if they could. We do not always fight for similar things, but it's human to take advantage of a favourable situation. Footballers do not hold anyone up at gunpoint and are not doing anything illegal, unlike groups of Argentine fans who have taken almost every major club side hostage so they get their share. They are the powerful and feared *barras bravas* (organised supporter groups) who are well remunerated by way of tickets and parking rackets and a share of the proceeds from merchandising and refreshments sold inside stadia. These mafia-style, violent fans have even received commissions on player transfers. Wow!

Unlike top-flight footballers, most employees are replaceable and are therefore likely to be paid a derisory wage, despite the lucrative profits of the companies they work for. The terrible example would be that of employees of large corporate or well-known clothing brands operating in Asia. There are numerous cases reported of kids working hard for very long hours and being paid a pittance, yet there is a counter-argument which says that they are so much better off than others; and that arguably they should consider themselves lucky. In India, Nepal and Pakistan where the majority of the population lives in poverty, making barely enough to put food on the table, these kids get out from under, but are brutally exploited. Children who come from impoverished families have no means of defending themselves.

Powerful multinationals may think they pay a good salary, but will make swift use of their great sword of Damocles. In Asia there are no trades unions and there is no risk of companies being tried before industrial tribunals. This example goes some way to show that a salary is determined by the value of a person and how hard it is to replace them.

The power held by some players over their boss is that they are irreplaceable. Their boss, therefore, has to respect their value.

Effort or sacrifice?

To talk about effort and sacrifice in the context of a well-paid hobby is not possible. The nurse, the fire-fighter or the soldier would not understand if a guy who kicks a ball about complains about the slightest thing, given the salary he pockets for doing a non life-threatening job. Comparing these jobs is not feasible. Suffice it to say, only some major European clubs and PLCs can offer very high wages. Comparing salaries is not a way to start the debate, neither is comparing effort and sacrifice a way to conclude it.

For years to come, from the most to the least talented, no one escapes the daily tests of endurance and tough training schedules. Whether you end up playing professional football or in the Marines, it comes down to passion and following your dream. For one guy it's all about serving his country, for another it's all about playing for the team that is the European champion. A Marine or any soldier has to leave his family and adapt to a tough lifestyle. A player is expected to play consistently high-quality games, which is not as simple as it might seem as you settle into your sofa to watch your favourite team on Sky Sports. A player might be exhausted from the endless round of intensive training and matches, even if he has just has a month's holiday

to relax mind and body. He'd better not return from his break several pounds heavier for pre-season fitness training as it is physically and mentally demanding and often lasts twice as long as his holiday. I am comparing the incomparable because to play football professionally is primarily a vocation, a choice, a desired – albeit well-paid – sacrifice.

Pre-season training is dreaded and disliked by most footballers. Playing is fun, but preparing for it is hard work. Big games where there is a lot at stake are major tests. And before considering negotiating a good contract, you need at least two seasons and 80 games under your belt. Some would say I am exaggerating, like Patrice Evra: "For me, football is not hard, and to run after the ball is only natural. I have so much energy I have no idea how I will channel it later."

When our two wives talk to each other about pre-season preparations it's as though Pat and I are in a different line of work. If I call my wife, Aurélie, to tell her that I'm wiped out after three sessions a day, Sandra will say that Patrice is loving their tour of the United States especially because they went to the White House. He rarely complains of being tired. Sir Alex Ferguson did not let Patrice play a Champions League group match against Rangers in 2010 when they were all but qualified. I told him it was so he could rest, but Pat replied drily, "I'm upset because I want to play every game and I'll have time to rest when I retire. For me football is anything but work."

Every man on earth is made up of a certain number vital organs, but Pat has twice as many as the rest of us! I should call him $E = mc^4$. The normal laws of physics don't seem to apply to this guy.

The guy is such a machine that I remember once, during a match for Man Utd, Pat fell and rolled on the ground, screaming and clutching his calf. He seemed in such agony that Rio Ferdinand, the physio and I rushed to see what was up. It turned out to be just cramp. As he had never had cramp before and is never injured, Pat thought he had pulled a muscle, or had snapped something like his achilles tendon. This was his first experience of a painful injury because he never has any! Later, when Pat was messing with our heads in the changing rooms, for weeks the only joke we needed to shut him up was to yell the same way he had for a single cramp. Ha ha ha!

The comments made by Carlos Tevez some time ago saying he was exhausted by football did not just come from the fact that he needs time to recover. The sport which he loves and which has given him so much has already demanded a great deal of him. At 26, he talks about his retirement. Carlos is a player with incredible energy and he proves it in every game, making him one of the very best in the world. But his small size does not spare him the knocks. He has to compensate a lot mentally to keep hold of the ball and protect his body. Beginning as a professional aged 17, and never having taken his foot off the pedal, he realised that being far from his family and his country complicated life and was a strain. Wages are unequal from one footballer to another as they are from one country to another. You seize the chance when it presents itself, even though money cannot buy everything.

Carlos was suspended by Manchester City in September 2011 for not entering the pitch as a substitute during their Champions League match against Bayern Munich. The entire sports world fiercely condemned his reaction and could not get their heads round it. People struggling to make ends meet were horrified by what seemed to be a selfish act; a gesture for which Carlos alone knows the explanation and the root cause. Nevertheless, his behaviour was endlessly chewed over and the impact of the ensuing furore on the footballer's image was devastating. Was he the only one at fault, or was he used? What other factors were at play? The coach and his man-management; the player and his strong character; his agent and his desire for a high commission; the club and its almost surreal finances; other clubs offering him millions; family status; or simply the system in which we all live.

People who don't know him are bound to say, "Sure, he can react like that because money isn't a problem for him now. If he were in a tight spot chances are he'd have thought twice."

Having hung out with him, I know that once Carlos's mind is made up, it's made up. Carlito is a genuine guy and when something goes wrong, he will say so. Soon after the attacks on him, numerous journalists, ex-players and coaches had to swallow their poisonous words as they realised they had been too harsh in their judgements. He had not refused to play. He had only refused to warm up, because he felt he was ready to go on to the pitch. The moral of the story being, don't judge if you don't know the whys and the hows. To think you get the point does not give you the right to criticise.

My career first began 15 years ago with a professional contract at a salary rate of £1,000 a month. It was a real fortune for someone of my age. Thanks to my first pay-cheque, various debts and family problems magically disappeared, although, since there is a difference between gross and net pay after tax, there wasn't much left over. The money came and went. Of course, journalists do not bother to specify this kind of thing, and consistently give out the highest figure to fuel tittle-tattle.

When you turn professional and become financially viable, your parents' problems inevitably become yours too, considering all the time and energy they have sacrificed to support you and make you laugh; all the money invested in education, clothes, food, Christmas, birthdays, nappies . . . everyday life. Every son's dream is to be a good return on his parents' investment. He'd like to extricate his parents from their daily grind and give them what they cannot afford. He'd like them to understand how grateful he is for their love and encouragement. Football enabled me to do this. The frugal years of my youth made me what I am. If you are used to having it all easily, especially in a material sense, it is hard to motivate yourself to excel, to accept suffering and to realise that you cannot always get your way.

I had to go easy on my parents when I was growing up as we could not afford excesses. Having enough money to make ends meet at the end of the month was always tough. Back then, the days had a strange way of lengthening as each month progressed, as if each one stretched to 41 days, like a special calendar for people who work night and day. For people in difficult situations, the calendar should be shortened to 25 days. My parents slogged their guts out to give me the chance to live my dreams.

According to some people, being a top-flight athlete is not a real job. But making a living from your favourite sport does not lessen the workload. Not all the players in the world get paid as well as those at Manchester City. Footballers slog their guts out like everyone else. Hard work is an unavoidable daily challenge and you have to show up, even when you feel physically tired and mentally drained. For 365 days a year, without exception, you are required to go for it, because rest days are as important as training days. We have to recover, heal, eat, drink and motivate ourselves. These little details are what being professional is all about. A pro can't say to himself: "You know what, you ran like the wind this month and your head is a bit scrambled, because of all these upsetting problems. So you deserve a week off." You could only get away with that if football was a game practised purely for pleasure.

Now it's all over

Unfortunately, the pro's coach will put together a long session of aerobics to make him work just that little bit more. All he wanted to do was practice strikes in front of goal, or have fun with a tennis-ball, but he will have to sweat and find the energy to prove to his coach that he deserves to play in place of another. He curses the coach:

"*Foda-se, pff bacalhau, puta que pariu!* F**k, you f***er, f***ing hell!"

I often complained about the intensity of the training at Everton, which I found long and arduous, compared to what I had experienced at other clubs. But when I think about it, I am more than happy to admit that my sport provides its protaganists with the most pleasant life. A footballer has the opportunity to shine, have fun on the pitch and put on a show through a whole a season that is enjoyed by countless thousands. It's enough to play a great pass, or to score a goal and that's it, he's a winner. To earn a living doing what you love is a great privilege.

I read these lines from the Indian yogi and mystic Sadhguru's book, *Flowers On The Path*: "A player begins to forget the youthful spirit of play when he does it to meet the expectations of others. The game becomes work." A player must continue to express the joy of being a footballer, but the pressure to get results makes that very difficult.

At one point, I had a leftfield theory that a public that is too demanding or strict with its players could, despite the quality of the team, completely undermine it, such as has sometimes happened at West Ham, Newcastle United, PSG, Marseille, Middlesbrough and other clubs with high potential and a great fan base. The team could be undermined to the point that they end up fighting against relegation, rather than fighting for the Championship. I'm not sure if the fault lies with the players or the managers in not preparing their players to cope with the pressure of playing in front of a large and expectant crowd, but it's not the fault of the public who want victory so badly. The fans are the 12th man.

The soul of the stadium can galvanise, or oppress. You need to learn how to humour and comfort the audience, and sometimes listen, but most of all to bring satisfaction. It's a bit like the actor-audience relationship in a theatre. Achieving this takes know-how since an audience wants to see a perfect hat-trick and other skilful moves, as much as it expects results. This is not an impression, a vague idea, or even an excuse, it's the difference between playing at home and away. It's the difference between making a good tackle, or a corner, and sensing how the opposition is overwhelmed by the tension and the pressure as it feels the longing permeating the stadium.

In a football crowd there are the happy people and there are the angry nutters who want to trash the place. Such are the powerful emotions which flow through the veins of football. Some get the point while others insist on vomiting their venom as a form of release. It is understandable that people project their frustrations on those who earn high salaries.

Once, a guy sat next to me on a plane and said: "Mario! Mario Balotelli!" I answered, "No," from behind the visor of my cap which I had pulled down to help me fall asleep. But the guy banged on anyway: "Footballers are arrogant and overpaid. How can young guys be given so much money?!" I allowed him to go on at me like this, almost nodding in agreement. Then I raised my cap to give my point of view. This guy had no idea of the life risks taken by young hopefuls, barely aged 16. He wasn't there when they seized the opportunity to make their future. It's like having a go at the winners of the lottery when you've never even bought a ticket.

A player must be able to control his emotions and understand those of others as best he can. The topic of footballers' salaries is one that everyone loves to discuss and critique; but players' sacrifices are indiscernible. I have spoken many times with various fans on Twitter who never miss the chance to compare their salary with mine, the hours they work and mine. Twitter enables me to better understand them as well as to explain my point of view. This has helped break down the wall which protects us players from criticism and occasionally threatening comments. I managed to get across that we are, for the most part, straightforward guys who are all too aware of our situation. I tried to show them a side rarely seen in a conventional press interview. It's easy to forget how, why and where it all begins. There are those who

occasionally come to watch us train and then, on the day of the match, when they see that some of us are tired or not in the game, they are critical saying it is not normal to be unfit. But the human body is not straightforward like a car, which just needs fuel to move forwards at full speed. To achieve a perfect action that eventually leads to a goal, you don't get 20 takes like in the movies. In the stadium you get both a player's imperfections and his brilliance, live and direct.

Cristiano Ronaldo is invaluable on a football field because what he does is virtually superhuman. In terms of marketing, his value is phenomenal. A footballing superstar will generate astronomical worldwide sales of his team's jerseys and kit; his sponsors' jeans, boxers, shades, gels and computer games. All this may earn the player a huge income, but only a small number reach such dizzy heights. Players are not all rated the same, and club chairmen do not treat them equally. If you are too easily replaceable, you are transferred at the earliest opportunity like a piece of meat. In football, to get a salary rise is like being promoted to a more important position in a company. It's going up a level with added guarantees for the club in order to justify a certain value if the player moves on before their contract has expired.

Other sports

I visualise elite swimmers doing super-intensive hours of training. Even if they love swimming, they must get sick of the smell of chlorine and climbing out of the water with reddened eyes, after three hours of swimming largely underwater holding their breath. Swimming interminable lengths of a pool would make me want to avoid H_2O and never wash ever again. The championship swimmer has to work consistently to maintain high levels of endurance. How terrible to do all that training just for a few special dates in the year. I'm sure that like all of us, on some days they'd rather be on the beach catching some rays.

My friend Bob Tahri, runner of the 3,000m and 1,500m steeple-chase, was the French star of the World Athletics Championships held in 2009. His performance in the 3,000m was worthy of the greatest that made me cry, like I do, when supporting Manchester United or the French national team. He needed so much self-confidence; rage, drive and courage; intensive training and of course setbacks; to fuel his last big push on the last lap of the race. Incredibly, the first four in this race beat the world record. Bob took the bronze medal.

On that triumphant day in Berlin, Bob Tahri became a legend. He did not get there by doing the usual endurance training and technical exercises. This guy prepared himself to weave his way through the Kenyan demigods of the track. He followed a training programme at high altitudes on the peaks of East Africa to transform his metabolism. He endured the worst conditions so he could compete realistically with the sacred giants of his sport, and beat even more records. You really need a burning desire to win a medal which usually belongs to the Kenyans. Hats off, bro!

The size of their salary contributes greatly to the motivation of some individuals. The American sportsman tackles the question of money without hang ups and with great pride because his homeland has the right attitude towards it. Americans have a tendency to show off in their sport. Whether it's basketball or baseball, it's their way of expressing self-confidence and impressing the opposition. This means the issue of money is demystified and becomes a tool in their little game. Nothing bad about that, it's just a different state of mind.

Shaquille O'Neal, the NBA star, made this wonderful comment about money: "I'm tired of people going on about money, money, money all day long. I just want to wear my Reeboks, drink my Pepsi and play basketball."

This is said with humour and subtlety when you realise that all the companies he mentions are his sponsors. European, and

especially French, sportsmen constantly have to justify themselves. The French resent the rich, especially those who pass down their wealth from one generation to the next. This dates back to the French Revolution. In America, amassing a large fortune is something to be proud of.

Patrice Evra: "The footballer's wages are not those of a golfer or a Formula One driver. Those sports are generally for rich kids. And yet there is no feeling of unease. Football is popular. It is the people's sport – the sense of unease is rooted in that."

The wages of Formula One drivers, golfers and tennis players – who are generally middle class and do not come from the inner city – are not so hotly debated. Are class prejudice and snobbery mixed in? Could someone from a humble background afford golf equipment and membership to a club? How many people have driven a Formula One car, the cost of which could buy a penthouse apartment in one of the Western World's first cities? Whereas everyone has kicked a ball, or at least has been hit by one!

To participate in a class of racing inferior to Formula One, like Karting or Formula 3000, you're still obliged to pay a minimum of around £8,000 for a season. From that moment on, you have to find a sponsor. If you want to try your luck you'll need large amounts of credit and parents like those of Jenson Button or Kimi Raikkonen. My father would have had to do 10 jobs all at the same time to raise the money for me to take part in just one race. Unlike many other walks of life, having a rich or famous father in football only gets you so far. A footballer is judged only on his ability with the ball.

Most people have enjoyed a kickabout so they think they understand the world of football enough to make criticisms. I was sure I was well-informed about motorsport, having followed a few Grand Prix. How I'd love a sports TV junkie who thinks he knows all about Formula One to have a discussion with my mate David or Oliver Webb, a racing pro. It was enough to watch one of their driver mates on YouTube and see his hands positioned on the wheel to realise that there was nothing professional about my analysis. Watching the racing driver take the corner, David spoke with ease about adhesion, mass and aerodynamics all in one sentence. Best let the professionals do their job and explain it to us.

Would people who are jealous of footballers be less annoyed if the salaries of rugby players were on the same scale? The intensity of that sport and the build of its commanding athletes inspire respect. Their monster tackles and torn ears are impressive. It's easy to see how their game is so demanding, which is why there is a minimum of six days rest between matches. To see these giants show outstanding respect towards their opponents and the referee right through to the end of play is remarkable. They have a similar aura to Japanese sumo wrestlers. To see fit, well-groomed players diving and feigning injury, or rolling about on the ground claiming a foul, must irritate the fans of fearsome rugby players like French rugby's cult hero, Sébastien Chabal, a.k.a. "Attila" and "Rasputin".

Of course, I respect all sports. The difficulty of each discipline has its own value: the sweat on the brow of an athlete. The common objective of sports like volleyball, rugby, handball and basketball may be to score goals or points, but there is one detail worth mentioning which sets footballers apart from other sportsmen. Football is special because it is played primarily with the feet as opposed to the hands. Therein lies the great challenge of the game, as it feels more natural and easier for most people to grip, catch and throw a ball. But despite appearances, football is not so easy to play well. The brain is the powerhouse which sends the right signals down to the feet at the right time to perform the desired actions. The messages sent to the hands in order to grab, for example, a basketball with its rough surface no doubt travel faster than those sent to the feet. Of all team sports, football is unique in this.

35 years soon come . . .

Given the number of professional players there are out there, long careers of 15 years which consolidate the fruit of a player's hard work are extremely rare. And any such career would contain an undercurrent of anxiety about coaching changes, competition, injury or poor form. There are more than 100,000 professional footballers in the world who are desperate to keep their dream alive, and if the chance of a move to a better club or a higher salary comes their way they go for it. Taking another player's place is part of a competitor's daily life. A salary which seems huge at first glance needs to provide a cushion for when the player retires. After their careers have ended, only a small percentage of players manage to reinvent themselves as a coach, the manager of a club or a sports journalist.

For a footballer, the accumulation of capital is effectively a race to a comfort zone. The sooner you get out of the woods, the better it is psychologically to enable you to let rip on the pitch. Once you have security for yourself and your family, you can then play without that added crushing pressure.

Some do not use their time and money wisely. They fail to keep an eye on their expenditure, spending money like water, living from one day to the next. Some might argue that you only live once, to which my answer would be, sure, and you could end up just having one career in a long life. Managing your assets is a difficult game to play, balancing a secure future against today's whims and desires.

A lifestyle which requires you to enjoy everything to an almost unlimited and excessive degree needs serious handling. Some will go for the ultimate privilege of renting a yacht for the holidays. But just because you can afford a private jet does not mean you should book it when there's a scheduled flight which leaves and arrives at the same time. Like everyone, footballers dream of living in a nice house, or for the younger ones a penthouse with a panoramic view where they can impress their conquests.

A player is almost obliged to eat with his friends in the best restaurants, although they rarely ask to pay the bill. It feels strange when I shell out £100 to fill the belly of my Ferrari which needs a drink every four days or so. Ten years ago, at today's prices, it would have cost £500 a month just for petrol for a similar car. This may sound ridiculous, but I feel almost compelled to pay it if I want to please myself.

The same goes for all of us when it comes to home, travel, security, comfort . . . We buy the new iPhone or the latest iPad, while Apple is already figuring out the best marketing strategy for their upcoming models which are ready to go and will make what we own obsolete. Large companies play their game with the competitive spirit of footballers.

To live better and avoid being accused of one-upmanship with a neighbour, who is less well off, you move house. You pay extra for peace and security. This new lifestyle may not be absolutely necessary, but it is hard to refuse in this consumer society we live in.

You have to watch out for debts, otherwise they could leech a career weighed down by too many financial obligations. The risk of ending up with no savings in the twilight of your career is high.

Be wary also of the Stock Market. Risky investments and bank loans with variable interest rates could, a few years later in retirement, mean you go from a monthly income of £40,000 to a deficit of £8,000. The repayment of loans or investments can tighten the noose, especially if a separation is on the cards. Statistically, football relationships only survive in 30 per cent of cases once the player's career is over. Divorce is the worst-case scenario. The average salary of £25,000 per month net in the top division in France will not provide indefinitely for the years to come without any income, especially with alimony to pay. Money and children

are often good ways for an unhappy wife to hurt her player. He is often guilty of not having clearly expressed his feelings for her or his appreciation as she stood by his side. Amicable divorces are rare. A strong desire for revenge, with lawyers fanning the flames of the fight to ensure they are handsomely paid, finishes off any chances there might be of the young couple reuniting. I may be generalising, but this isn't so far from the truth in many cases that I am aware of.

A player must try to manage his vices. He should only go into a casino accompanied by luck and common sense, and leave before this supposedly sophisticated form of entertainment becomes an addiction. If it isn't poker, then it's betting on the horses. Too many talented young players become trapped and cannot recover without help.

I've always remembered what Gerald Baticle, my team-mate at FC Metz, said to me: "Louis, you must learn to manage your money. You will need at least ten million francs [£1 million] at the end of your career. Be watchful, Petit Louis, because time passes and the money goes fast."

I've tried to keep this in mind. He was very right, although certain stars have other concerns. To return to the question of comfort, some have a great many people dependent on them. There are numerous African players who help not one or two families, but whole villages, and so are unlikely to experience great luxury. There are too many people around them needing help.

Patrice Evra: "I have a big family. In Africa, even if you're the youngest, there is a tendency to nominate you as leader if you are earning a good salary. I always refused this position because in everyone's eyes you become a kind of bank. I have even missed the days when I had no money. Only with experience and time have I managed to say no. It's complicated. I had to get out of tough situations inside and outside of my family circle."

By this Pat means that people need to experience what we do, so that they can understand. The wages are not always indecent, because some players have the opportunity to help numerous people who would not have been helped otherwise. Charitable works are a good way of putting some back into society, and ensuring that money goes where it is really needed; it's like becoming a Robin Hood of modern times who does not steal anything. To act on the principle of the movie *Pay it Forward*, starring Kevin Spacey, is a good move. The idea is to help three random people truly in need, without asking for anything in return, and for those three people then do the same in turn.

Handling large sums of money is not at all easy for a young player, let alone if he's extravagant. The hit of famous American rapper, Notorious B.I.G., *Mo money, Mo problems*, describes the dilemma: "I don't know what they want from me / It's like the more money we come across / The more problems we see."

To feel contented with your career, there are two criteria that must be met. First off: correctly judge your potential and objectives by constantly reviewing your limitations. It's important to retire with good memories of strongly emotional events. Second: be satisfied that you have accumulated enough for a fairly comfortable retirement, including a nice house, one or two flats for family and kids, a few small investments and savings in case of hard times. It's important to think about life after football and not be taken unawares by a sudden change of activity. Learning to cope with the lack of adrenaline and, for some, the lack of recognition is essential. The public complains about footballers' wages, but easily forgets all those who end up with nothing, because time goes by in a flash. I'm only 33 years old, but it feels weird for me to say that some of my team-mates were only eight when I started to score goals at Fulham.

Zinédine: "You know, as I do, that it all stops fast. You can be called Zidane, or something else, but when it's over you're left

to yourself. Out of my generation, of the years 1980-90, there are players out on the streets. I'm lucky, but it isn't like that for the majority. Of those former players and those who failed, you hear nothing. Nobody cares."

For various reasons, many top-flight players can suddenly find themselves without a club, and so cannot pursue their careers. Less serious players can be left with nothing, or worse, find themselves drowning in debt, while others are simply forced to stop. Emmanuel Petit, world champion in 1998, ended his career in 2005 without a club because of his damaged knee. The injuries that I have come to know only too well during my career are the reason why many players are wary of the future and cocoon themselves in the present. Who will offer support and fetch you when you leave hospital after a serious injury that ends your dream? The most wonderful letters of encouragement from fans and the support of relatives can never relieve the pain of no longer being able to play. In such moments, only a loyal entourage and insurance can help a player to recover. The shock is terrible and the problems you had anticipated mean you will gradually slip back into the real world.

I discussed all this with Sylvain Wiltord, who played for Arsenal and at the time of writing is at FC Nantes. We rubbed shoulders during the 2006 World Cup. Aged 36, he cannot imagine life without football. Sylvain, a.k.a. Nino Brown, is a serious pro and loves all sport. He is one of the most impressive players during training with a formidable striker's instinct and an incredible work-rate. Despite his nonchalant joker's air, I have come across few players who showed such intense motivation on a training ground. He is a great example of dedication for young guys coming up. Don't be fooled by appearances.

Sylvain: "Hey, Bro, it's tough getting up every morning and saying to myself that one day I won't play any more or share the fun of it with friends and team-mates. The atmosphere in the changing room, the pressure of games, travelling in a group, the adrenaline and everything else. It's massive. It's an essential need."

Edwin van der Sar, who played his last game at Old Trafford on 22 May, 2011: "Wow, it feels strange not to have to do something, not to feel the joy of victory and receiving praise, not to have adrenaline in my veins. I must admit I tell myself that I could still be there with my team-mates. When I watched Manchester United beat Chelsea 3-1 at the start of the new season, I felt like it would still have been possible and fun to play, but I am aware of the tremendous effort and pain endured to play at this level. Louis, it's tough, but at 40 I want to enjoy my hobbies, my retirement, without too many injuries. I ended up having quite a few injections in my arms and shoulders to enable me to play, something you know all about."

Edwin has not only won numerous honours during his extraordinary goalkeeping career, but its longevity means he is the oldest player to win the Premier League, at 40 years old. At 39 years, Ryan Giggs defies the laws of nature. After more than 900 appearances he still has more of an appetite than most 20-year-old guys. For most people to pull off such a feat would be unachievable and unrealistic.

Growing uncertainties in working life and the need to make off-the-cuff emergency decisions affect employees in different ways. For example, the atmosphere in an office turns sour when news breaks that the company is not meeting its expected earnings so hundreds of jobs are on the line. For a footballer it's not easy to continue studying alongside his professional training. So after 15 years, he will try to rebuild his life with no qualifications. To be seriously injured at the start of the first professional contract can cut short a promising career.

Opportunities can't be missed or else they will be regretted later. Before turning professional, these young players lived in a way that meant all too often they had to tap on the minus key of a calculator because going broke was a fact of life. Best not mess up or they'll be back where they started.

Football agents

Discussing the controversy about wages inevitably brings up the word "agent". The role of players' agents is to maximise their client's salary, trouble-shoot problems and give advice about sponsorship and image rights. More than anything, they are there to make money based on the performance of players, or clubs. They are often paid by way of a commission of around 6-10 per cent of the player's deal. What's new? An important point to bear in mind is that the higher the salary and severance and transfer fees when signing the contract, the greater the agent's cut. They will negotiate the best they can for the player, and reward themselves afterwards. If you sign, for example, for five years at a salary of £150,000 per month with an annual sign-on, or loyalty, or other bonuses on top, the agent could come out of the transaction with a cheque of around £450,000 for the player's five-year deal. For this the agent will have negotiated contractual terms, made around 20 phone calls in one year when they mentioned you to various club chairmen as one of their players under contract, asked for an appropriate salary, checked the ins and outs of the contract.

With the help of Bruno Satin, authorised agent for the FFF (French Football Federation) and director of IMG (International Management Group) and with my limited experience, we will now attempt to describe the process of buying and selling a player for those readers who are not clear about how it works.

When Real Madrid bought Cristiano Ronaldo for £80 million in the summer of 2009, the transfer from Manchester United was based on the market principle of supply and demand. One club has a need, the other club has the product, and the player has a market value. Cristiano did not receive that sum of money – it went to the club that sold him. Licensed agents and other intermediaries such as a lawyer or other powerful individuals take their share just like Wall Street traders who are involved in a major transaction. The agent will negotiate the best contract for his client with the new club, its equipment supplier and sponsors for good guarantees and financial returns on the player's image rights, his contract, his individual bonuses and its other obligations.

In this case, as the vendor Manchester United had a chance to make a huge gain on a player purchased for £12 million six years earlier. The balance sheet in two years: more than £68 million of profit for United, over 80 goals for his new club for Cristiano, record sales of Real Madrid jerseys. It's damn good business for everyone.

What goes on during the transfer window is basically a huge talent market. During these periods before the season resumes and during the month after Christmas football players can be transferred from one club to another. It is thoroughly exploited by the agents. Outside this period a player cannot be transferred. When it opens, agents both good and bad get busy, on the prowl for opportunities. The wheeling and dealing generates a great deal of pressure and stress for the player and his family. It is a pivotal time that can destabilise the coolest and wisest of heads. Lives are on the line every six months. The actions of a player's agent can be devastating. The advice of the agent is always listened to very carefully.

Supporters complain bitterly about the player's lack of loyalty to their club. Big stars like Steven Gerrard have suffered from this pressure. When he was approached about a transfer to Chelsea, a group of Liverpool fans made it clear they were desperate to keep him on the banks of the Mersey. Rumours were going around that they had even threatened his family, so Liverpool's star player was obliged to backtrack. Fans are powerful, vocal and respected. During the transfer window, fans make it clear who they want their club to keep and who they want them to sell. Spend a couple of minutes reading a club forum on the web and you will see how supporters give advice and leave comments. In this atmosphere, the player soon realises that if he

is good, fine, but if he's crap, he'd best clear off, sharpish. Today, loyalty means nothing. Players under contract can request a transfer by means of a letter. On the other side, a chairman will sign a two-year extension for the soon-to-be-released star player so he can sell him behind his back for a good price during the next transfer window.

On the morning of 31 January 2012 a series of phone calls with my agent confirmed that Spurs' interest in me had become a concrete reality. My world was turned upside down. Should I bring my family with me and take the kids out of school, or leave them behind? They would have to make new friends and re-adapt, yet they are so happy where they are. When I discussed my options with David Moyes . . . When I spoke to my agent, Jonathan Barnet, to clarify the conditions . . . When I assessed the challenge and made my mind up . . . it all felt as though the thinking and questions happened in just one hour. It's 10 am: my phone battery is already on 60 per cent. I was supposed to join my team-mates to prepare for an evening game against Man City, but instead a quick meeting was arranged with the manager. Noon: I'm home, packing what I can and heading for London by Smart car. Lol! My phone battery is down to 40 per cent. The fine voices of Lenny Kravitz, Rihanna, Admiral T and others keep me company during the three-and-a-half hour drive. First stop: an all-important meeting at a hospital with Wayne Diesel – one of the physiothera-pists for Tottenham – for my medical. My phone battery is on red and I wish I had the car charger as I hit the M25. When I finally find the street and park, a black hole has swallowed up the gorgeous picture of my kids on the phone screen. Battery: 0 per cent. Dead. I look for Wayne in the large hospital entrance and ask for him. I nearly shout in frustration as I have no phone. Aaargh! Has he gone to the game v Wigan and forgotten about me? Wow. It's nearly 8pm. I ask again. Could there be two hospi-tals in the same street?

A lady says: "Oh yes, it's just 300 yards away . . ." I ask a taxi for directions. I'm lost and can't even call anyone. I could end up with no time left to sign for my new team. When I finally find the hospital, it's a huge relief. I had forgotten how long a medical can take, especially with my record. Papers signed and medical done in three hours, but it felt longer as time stretched out like a rubber band. It had been a bittersweet 16 hours of tension, stress, relief, scans, check-ups, phone calls, excitement and uncertainty just inside the transfer window deadline. What a crazy day!

As is the case in most professions, there are the good, the bad and the ugly. A rogue agent will negotiate behind the back of a player with the club's board and persuade his client to sign for a lower fee, or will pressurise the player to move to a specific club where he knows he will get a higher commission, regardless of the implications for his client's career. Some agents will use false club names, flash internet sites and documents to justify their so-called mandate to impress a newcomer, who then signs a contract which is not genuine as the agent is fraudulent yet because of the piece of paper he has signed the player still has to pay him a cut of the deal when he is transferred to a club. These rogue operators are not easily traceable because they use rechargeable phone cards, or work from cyber cafés.

Players' agents have not been licensed by FIFA since 2001 – they are licensed directly by the member association for each country. Nowadays there is no such thing as a FIFA players' agent, so it's important to check the agent obtained their license from the relevant member association of FIFA. Agents contribute to the inflation of the market, but are an important support for all those young *nouveaux riches* of the beautiful game who are the ultimate shark bait. Agents take a big piece of the pie so the player should check any contract with them very carefully. A couple of years ago, Manchester City paid nearly £13 million on agents' fees in just two transfer windows. I read on the BBC Sport website that as few as 30 per cent of international transfers are

concluded using licensed agents, so it now seems that FIFA is going to ditch the system for regulating football agents in favour of "broader control over individuals who represent players and or clubs".

If he likes, a player can negotiate and manage his affairs with the help of a lawyer. To do this the lawyer needs to be well informed about the market as well as about the tips and tricks to pull off a good sale. He also needs to be sufficiently well known to get through the door of the guy whose sister is the secretary of the club coach's friend. Good contacts are crucial: they increase your chances a hundredfold.

A player like Thierry Henry has not needed an agent since he won the World Cup 12 years ago. The French football star, who now plays for the New York Red Bulls, had wanted to live in the Big Apple since his first visit aged 19. Titi well and truly reached his chosen destination.

Politics and football

Politicians talk of setting a cap on players' salaries. They say this would help the smaller clubs survive better against the big. It's not so simple: there are many different, clashing interests. Politicians would be better off tending to their own business and cleaning up their back yard before preaching from the soap box. First off, why don't they oblige the banks to repay taxpayers who shelled out large sums of money to save a crippled banking system? Why not cap the bonuses paid to the top dogs in finance? Why not try to find a solution for unemployment and debt? Reading the quality press shows how some politicians are up to their necks in transactions involving billions of pounds while their activities with big business are unquestioned. Yet all a taxpayer has to do is miss paying what they owe for a month or two and they receive letters threatening to sue. Couldn't politicians make reforms that genuinely ease the strain on the wallets of their citizens? These kinds of questions run through the minds of most people, judging by radio phone-ins.

Couldn't governments stop investing billions in nuclear power and the arms industry and focus instead on debt repayment? To dream of a world without weapons or war may be idealistic, given Man's nature, but it's good to dream. There is much work to be done before turning on what happens in football stadiums. The question of footballer salaries is important, but so is the question of arrangements and special favours exchanged between the all-powerful businessmen of the planet who enjoy meeting at the World Economic Forum held every year in Davos.

The Premier League is opposed to a salary cap. Speculation on the value of players has reached such heights that it is unlikely that the major clubs and bosses would agree to imposing one. A cap would lead to a significant decrease in the number of large transfers and the world's greatest footballers would have less incentive to change clubs, or come to England in the first place. The sale of jerseys and other merchandise would fall, along with the enthusiasm of the fans. Finding a solution to prevent the increase of wages without compromising the quality of the players and therefore the game is important, firstly, because a player will switch clubs if he is offered three times his salary. Secondly, even if he is living in the lap of luxury, if the cash keeps on rolling in over his head and the football fat cats are getting fatter, but he is not given a decent slice of the pie, he will not agree to make sacrifices.

Ultimately, football is useful for a government hoping to distract the media and the public from bad news. Although sometimes it's the opposite. The scandal surrounding Dominique Strauss-Kahn, Head of the International Monetary Fund, and his arrest in New York erupted at the same time as news about the controversial plan for racial quotas in French football clubs. The idea that quotas would be introduced for young players, aged 12 and 13, based on their racial background rocked the world of French football, but was effectively pushed into the background.

One incident made me realise how the worlds of football and politics do not speak the same language and are ignorant of each other's ways. During the last World Cup, in Knysna, South Africa, players from the French squad went on strike during a training session in protest against the exclusion of Nicolas Anelka after his heated exchange with the coach, Raymond Domenech. Anelka was eventually sent home. Politicians united behind the demand that the French players should not be paid their salaries. To picture the minister announcing this to the French team made me laugh. Why? Because it revealed how, in judging this major crisis facing French football, certain politicians were not even informed. No one had told them that footballers are paid for the 12 months by their club. They don't get paid to play for their national team. The French Football Federation pays bonuses, but nothing else. It was not a problem of terminology, because the words, "bonuses" and "wages" are used across the board in the business world. Politicians don't have to love the sport, but they could at least get to grips with the basics before debating in front of millions of TV viewers. Many do a good job, and of course it's hard to push for change: whenever you please one, you upset another.

Politicians frequently fail to mention the billions of pounds generated for the economy by players by way of taxes. Football brings a lot of money into a country. The English league alone has a cumulative worldwide audience of nearly 4.8 billion. In 2009/10 the revenue for the 92 top professional clubs amounted to more than £2.5 billion, according to the Annual Review of Football Finance from the Sport Business Group at Deloitte. Yet all people can come up with is a salary cap. Why not try out the concept by capping the bonuses of top corporate executives, indexed to their company's performance?

Employees, doctors, teachers and countless others resent disproportionate wages, and how young players like to splash out on big cars and Franck Muller watches encrusted with diamonds.

But everybody loves beautiful cars, and advertisements are based on living the dream. We are part of a consumer society that produces more and more, so to make the economy function people have to consume more and more and work even harder . . . and products are increasingly taxed.

Having a salary cap would make sense to bolster small clubs, to raise money for better training facilities, or to free up cash to help out players in need. Reform is necessary, but a salary scheme agreeable to everyone would be hard to work out. Greater transparency is needed to better identify different approaches – who pays what, who benefits, who loses out and how to help small clubs in difficulty. Although well-run clubs only pay players the maximum they can afford, others exceed their means in a bid to become successful and so get into debt. Self-regulation is not the solution. In France, the DNCG (National Directorate for Control and Management), monitors the finances of professional clubs; if a club goes over what they can afford there is a ban on recruitment of new players, or limits are imposed on the number of player transfers. An independent organisation such as this could see to it that a club sets a salary cap for a specified period with the consent of its players; calculated by ranking European clubs, African clubs, and so on. Salaries would be based on the current financial situation of the club; if in debt the club would have to accept a lower ceiling. So a small club would have no real argument for exceeding its budget.

Tim Howard, goalie for Everton and for the United States national team, told me he favours the idea of a salary cap to prevent a club spending more than 80 per cent of their revenue in wages. Some want a study of the American sports system to be carried out, although it functions at another speed. The NFL's 32 teams are worth an average US$1 billion, and each and every one of them is profitable.

Tim Howard: "Before the start of the 2011 season, players

of the National Football League went on strike because they had no insurance and no guaranteed contracts. So a team could transfer a contracted player as it saw fit. Players were not entitled to compensation and did not have the right to turn down a club. Picture this: a player's contract with his team has ended, one reason being the team no longer wants him, so he is free to go. Well, Louis, you'll be surprised to hear that the team with whom he is no longer contracted has the right to claim compensation from the team that decides to give him a job."

The American draft system ensures that the strongest and weakest teams are shuffled like a pack of cards every year because no one team can sign up all the best young players. It is coherent to the extent that it seeks to make the championships of all elite sports competitive and exciting. The system allows the worst teams in the NFL the previous season to have first pick of the best up and coming players from the College teams for the new season. It means that the competition is driven more by tactics and talent than the finances of a handful of billionaire backers taking all the best players to a single team.

Alternatively, there is the National Basketball Association's salary cap, which is calculated as a percentage of the League's revenue from the previous season, so it varies from year to year. It limits high salaries in order to safeguard the profitability of all the teams. There are certain significant exceptions that allow teams to exceed the salary cap in order to sign players and also to help teams keep their current players. Basketball players are treated like commodities, though. Ronny Turiaf, the French basketball player who plays for the New York Knicks, told me that one of his former team-mates in the NBA had to pack his bags without being able to say a word in protest, after receiving a phone call telling him to leave fast. He was part of a swap deal and had to leave with his wife and kids and head for a new club.

Trouble is . . .

Sylvain Distin, who, at the time of writing, plays for Everton: "I understand how astonishing it must be to the public when a greedy player demands an increase just a year after signing an already juicy contract, under the pretext of having received offers from other big clubs. Back in the day love of a club, not its money, was the wealth that mattered. A player wanted to play for the club close to his heart where he made his debut, for his entire career."

There is a big gap between what the average footballer earns compared to the salaries of the game's superstars. The fact is that great players like Ronaldo, Beckham and Saha command mega salaries. *Ha, ha very funny*! Believe me, if you only had players like Louis Saha on the pitch viewing figures would plummet! Man does not choose his passion, it chooses him. Managers, journalists and fans create the constellations that connect the stars, producing different groupings. I often like to say that most players of the French amateur league (CFA) could easily play a couple of good matches in Ligue 1, but that does not mean they could hold the level. To play well in a match or for a season is not the same thing as being a good player. Professional football is all about consistency.

At every level it's the same. I, Louis Saha, today, with all my experience, training and determination and with the best coach in the world, could not reproduce the magic of Cristiano Ronaldo or Lionel Messi. I just cannot reach such a high level of technical quality, reliability and endurance, because for all our qualities and gifts we also have limitations and handicaps. Both those living legends are capable of elegant blistering pace and powerful jaw-dropping moves. Above all, they have few bad patches of form. With all the will in the world, I could not do what they do, even if I were less injury-prone. I do not think I'm such a bad student and I believe in my qualities, but those two are exceptional. If I

wanted, whatever the cost, to become the new Messi with his trademark style and salary to match, forget it. Impossible. I respect and admire those kings of football. That is also why they are so highly paid, and I really have no problem with that, because it is right that such footballing superstars be paid more than most.

Sylvain Distin: "Bro, it's a tough call when a player is paid 10 times more than another, 'cause in the end he's a man just like you and me."

It's a good point. But Lionel, Cristiano, Zizou and other footballing prodigies, I say to you: "Total respect."

People often expect footballers to set an example for young people, especially when they are very well paid. Yet players are young, so-called adults, who never asked to be exemplary of anything. They might try not to be rude, but often fail because they are impulsive firebrands as are so many others at their age. Some want to win trophies and to make history, others just want to have fun and enjoy women and music, or their money. Most want to have it all, and they want it now, which is only natural.

At Manchester United, Gary Neville and I often chewed over the question of values, money, the need for agents and what really mattered. He had strong views about everything. Some scenarios make the idea of imposing salary caps a non-starter. How could a club be banned from paying a player a salary that was over the cap, if the board thought they had a priceless gem on their hands and wanted to do everything to keep him? Would a young player going from strength to strength and attracting interest from top-flight clubs and the possibility of big salaries have to accept the same salary from the club which had developed and supported him since he was a boy? It's hard to envisage an identical salary cap across the board unless it was limited to the highest current salary.

Negotiating a contract paying in excess of £80,000 per week may be indecent, but it is a feat that should be celebrated in any profession. That does not mean that I would have gone the way of Sunderland striker, Asamoah Gyan. Aged 26, he couldn't pass up the opportunity of getting a salary almost as good as Lionel Messi's when he was offered the chance to play for Al Ain in the United Arab Emirates. Extreme perhaps, but there you go.

Let's say that from the age of 30, I would not have hesitated to take such a chance had I been sure that I would not have the opportunity to play again for a big club and win the Champions League. A decade or so ago, my current salary would have made me the highest paid player in England. There lies the trouble, that feeling of unease . . . inflation.

Zinédine: "I admire people who succeed, especially when they do it without a balaclava and a gun. The footballer has not committed a robbery."

Footballers' wages rise along with the profits of Russian billionaires, Indian, American and Arab businessmen. It isn't just to please us that a club evaluates a performance and pays so highly for it. The problem arises when a salary is not linked to performance. Nobody in the world would refuse a good salary. How are you to know that your kid will not end up with a serious illness requiring expensive medical care, as was the case for Jean-Pierre Papin, the France and Olympique Marseille star whose daughter was born with a brain condition – from which happily she has now made very strong progress. Money can be a saviour when luck turns bad.

Back in the day, money was less important because we bartered for things. We created the hunger for cash. Money is the one true parasite in our lives if we allow ourselves to be dominated by its power, and by the greed and jealousy it creates. It is an important tool, but that's all: gold bricks providing a foundation on which to build a beautiful life. Managing money in full sight of people who have little of it is a dilemma. Only people with a totally pure heart know how to resist the lure. But to relish what God has given you to enjoy is purely human.

15
BLING BLING: BIG BOYS' TOYS

*T*he *Times*: "Footballers' Drives: The Top Ten Premier League Runabouts. Despite the almost limitless choice, the wealthy young men of the football world keep choosing the same cars: We round up the soccer elite's 10 most popular drives."

In our consumer society everything has a price and everything can be bought or sold. Players love their objects of desire: supercars, gadgets, designer gear, jewellery or a large villa. Material culture is fuelled by competitive displays of one-upmanship; its driving force is the desire to impress or be impressed. As most players come from poor neighbourhoods, showing off their new "toys" is a way of displaying their success. Players are under pressure to be voguish, to look good, to drive the latest models from car showrooms and wear the season's cutting-edge designer fashions right off the catwalks of Paris, New York, Milan and London. If you're not looking good, you'll be criticised. Everything has changed: values, money, the pace of life and the intensity of the game. Sound management of footballers' egos and status anxiety is essential. The football world is loaded with bling, although traditional values still count for something. Even the young guys who play at the top of the Premier League for one of the world's number one clubs, Manchester United, have immense respect for Sir Alex Ferguson. The Boss, "the Master", and Sir does right by them.

The Boss

The master at managing the clash of generations is Sir Alex Ferguson. With 37 years experience as a football manager and

10 years as a professional player, he and he alone is able to appraise and handle the differences in culture and atmosphere that football has experienced since the inauguration of the Premier League in 1992 which modernised football, giving it a new glitz and glamour, and which critics blame for stealing its soul. He is one of the rare happy few who has sat in the same manager's chair and the same dugout for many years. He has seen new fashions come and go, along with a slew of good and bad players and their families, every winter and summer. He has always trusted in his young hopefuls. He commands his kingdom to perfection and copes with crises and capriciousness, strong emotions and the myriad of personality traits. He knows details about all his players' lives, whether significant or insignificant; and he stands by them. It is a privilege to interview such a living legend on social issues and the glorious game.

I ask him how it is that his players have always managed to make progress, despite the changes of the last 20 years. He replies in his usual wise way, in warm Scottish tones: "I realised very quickly that my team had to adapt. For 26 years, I constantly made sure that my staff and I kept up to speed because the pressure of the public's expectations and its opinions became increasingly important for players, coaches and chairmen. It's now got to the point of each player having to have multiple blood tests, dieticians and a personal training programme. Whereas when I first began in the game, players drinking beer before a match or enjoying a burger and coke, was tolerated."

"In my early years at Manchester United, I had only eight staff and dealt with most of the club admin. I wore numerous hats all in one day. Humanly speaking, things were simpler and more convivial. I remember how, back then, I knew the wives, children and even cousins of players like Steve Bruce and Gary Pallister. I knew everybody. Today, it's less straightforward."

What the Boss means is that he has learned how to handle agents. Some – such as Pini Zahavi, or the immensely powerful

Mino Raiola, with clients like Balotelli, Ibrahimovic and Robinho – are fearlessly up front with club management. For example, Mister Raiola had the nerve to say that Pep Guardiola (the coach of Barcelona) should be in a mental hospital. The relationship between the players and their coach has changed. They are less close, for the general well-being of each. The agent acts as a barrier and can be disruptive, making friendships fragile.

Although Sir Alex Ferguson is no longer my coach, I still call him "the Boss". When you meet such a truly successful individual, you must show respect. To give an idea of his character, here is an example. The Boss returned my call as soon as he received my SMS and agreed that I could interview him at 10 in the morning on his return from playing an away Champions League fixture. They had got back in from Bursaspor, Turkey, at five that very same morning. This overworked, harassed super-coach found time to see me.

Diana Law: "In his private life he is a very humble man. He owes his success to his dedication to work which he learned when he worked in the Clyde shipyards in Glasgow. His knighthood was awarded for genuine reasons: his patience, loyalty, passion, being a hard worker and a teacher and the other qualities that cancel out any flaws this specialist in the management of men may have. His strong character and talent are the hallmarks that make Manchester United renowned worldwide. The press only sees an angry, severe or victorious coach and ignores his great sense of humour, or how he will phone to give support to the manager of a team which has just been relegated."

Today, all footballers, especially his, are highly protected and surrounded by people who make money off their backs. It's as though the players are enveloped in thick, shiny viscous matter covering their skin and brain. It spreads, thanks to the daily massage of compliments on the little prodigy, like a profitable ointment, by the hangers-on in his entourage. Best be aware of these arse-lickers, because there are plenty of them about, especially at large clubs, the moment you're in the media. Real friends and real pros do exist, but it's not always easy to separate them out. I can understand how people become arrogant or nasty when they become famous because they have believed all the hype they've read about themselves. The moment you meet someone new, you get the impression that everything you do or say is extraordinary. You can tell bad jokes, but everyone will laugh regardless.

Lionel Messi could take a piss in the corner of Barcelona fan's living room and, more than likely, the response would be: "Hey, no worries, we'll clean it up for you. A hat-trick against Osasuna would be great. Have a good one, Lionel."

It's hard to keep your feet on the ground when you have to recognise who is who and why they are as they are. It's tiring and frustrating to have to uncover the genuine face of each different player, week in week out, and to understand better what makes them tick, one incident after the other. These observations change how you look at the world and the way you open up to it, as well as your relationships with other people. In times of trouble and strife few people will support you.

Sir Alex Ferguson: "The Manchester United squad now contains players from 20 different nationalities and cultures. Communication is very important in my role and those of my staff. I have had to adapt and focus on the personality of each player. I find it extremely interesting, especially when I remember how, years back, my team was composed entirely of British players. I have evolved. The differences between Brazilian, English or even French attitudes are obvious. You need to know how to motivate each individual, give them a slap on the back, or shout at them."

The Boss tells me that as he has a larger number of backroom staff, he has managed to establish a climate of trust and professionalism that I consider to be perfectionistic. I take the opportunity to ask him how, throughout his career, he has cultivated trust amongst his staff and his players. How has he created an atmosphere of peace and calm in a world of sharks?

"Louis, first, as I give them trust, they are always loyal to me. When it comes to a member of staff, I seek to know how he has mastered his method of communication with a player and then I let him do his job. I give trust to receive trust. As for the player who needs to talk or to confide in me, I give him time and he can be sure that what he says will always stay between four walls, I will not breathe a word to anyone. I think that's why it works."

I can confirm that, if needs be, the Boss's door is always open. I remember the period when I had injuries. I asked to see him, and asked him to help me to make my comeback as a young man who had to prove his talent all over again, as when I began in the game. He said: "Louis, are you OK? Listen to me. You'll come back fighting strong, that's all there is to it." It was the stimulus I needed, but he didn't have to say it. He'd done it again.

Sir Alex Ferguson: "Players today need more support because they are more fragile, more vulnerable. The media and public pressure can be destabilising factors for a generation who are paid large salaries."

Players are high maintenance and hard to control because of that thick, shiny, viscous, sticky matter coating their bodies, which thickens and becomes more slippery the more money, celebrity and transfer opportunities there are.

I observed how the Boss managed three different characters to achieve the same result a few years later. He looked for raw gems and crafted them to perfection. When they first arrived, aged 18, 19 and 17 respectively, they were motivated hard workers, but had yet to understand the philosophy of the club. From a technically gifted player, to an all-round player and a player dedicated to the team, he coached them to develop their skills and techniques to achieve maximum potential.

Cristiano Ronaldo became the only player in the world capable of scoring in virtually any position and in any way. As for Wayne Rooney, he has become one of the few who can do everything on the pitch and adapt his style depending on the opposition, or on the nature of the game: score a hat-trick, make two decisive passes, win more balls than a defender, shout at the referee and give the impression that everything is simple and there's nothing extraordinary about it. Up until he sadly became ill with colitis in December 2011, Darren Fletcher had become a symbol of consistency, of the collective, of precision and of winning. I'm sure he will be back.

Despite their very different characters, Sir Alex Ferguson recognised the need to give them time and advice tailored to each. Differences between generations and cultures from country to country are exacerbated by our consumer society. His great ability to teach and to trust the instincts of a player who wants to make progress means he is successful.

I recently watched Alexandre Jardin's film *Le Prof* ("The Teacher"). One scene struck me in particular and reminded me of Sir Alex Ferguson's method. A young teacher, during a disciplinary hearing, defends his style of teaching which is considered to be insufficiently academic. He then asks one of the people lined up to fire him to try out a test consisting of leaning forward to touch their toes in a standing position.

Please take a moment to get up and perform the same test. Yes, you dear reader, please stand up!

A member of the panel, aged about 50, gets up, surprised, and has a go. He cannot touch his feet with his hands which reach down the side of his body, but stop half way down his calves. His back is too stiff and inflexible; his legs and hands not long enough. Maybe yours are and you can just touch your toes, especially if you do yoga.

The young teacher then asks the 50-something what had stopped him from bending his knees to perform the task? This detail would have helped him to easily rest the palms of his hands on his feet. A child of five would have surely done it that way, because nobody would ever have taught him to keep his legs straight. With age, our habits tend to chip away at our thinking, our willingness and our instincts. Like the young teacher, Sir Alex Ferguson understands that we need discipline, but that indoctrination and rigid methods will fossilise over time and kill that crucial touch of madness or instinct and the desire to learn. He knows that players should be given the freedom to express themselves and grow each in their own way.

The example of Cristiano Ronaldo is a good one. In his early days at Manchester, he was a talented and already impressive footballer, but sometimes he'd thwart great passages of play by making over-elaborate or poorly executed moves. It would have been easy for Sir Alex to give him the legendary "Hair Dryer" treatment after a game when he thought Cristiano should have passed the ball instead of trying to shoot from an impossible angle, but that would not have been the solution. The patience, the time and the words of the former striker-turned-manager given to the young striker did the rest, because to have moulded him into a predictable player would have been a great mistake. Now he scores 50 goals a season. All great coaches have their style, and they all understand a player has his own story. A player needs time to be understood. Unfortunately, some coaches are fired because results take top priority over the player's success. This is hard for the player.

Michel Ebong, advisor to African players: "It's very hard for a player to cope with becoming an African football star and to manage the large amounts of money he is paid as he may have only just discovered the need for a bank account. Most African talent or young footballers come from a background of poverty and do not have good benchmarks to help them get a handle on the money they earn. They are not always ready for it. Picture a young guy who could not even afford to buy food who now finds himself with a salary that could change the life of thousands of people. The purchasing power of an African compared to a player in the West means he could build a new village for his family alone if he continues to play well."

The bling-bling aspect is hard to control in a young African player, because more often than not nobody in his entourage really dares to say anything that might cause offence, since staying in favour represents success and a better life. When the player goes into a spin, no one will stop him or put him back in his place. Very young, these guys become leaders, gods, a bank and a quick fix for many people. Sadly, no one can get a handle on the money they receive. It's as if they could buy everything they ever wanted and believe me, young players will do anything to prove they can. The money comes in so fast.

An extreme example of blinging-it is the practice of "*faroter*" which goes on in certain African countries. "*Faroter*" means showing off in front of people less well off than you, and is common in certain parts of Africa, but is shocking nonetheless. It is an ambiguous, unhealthy, degrading act which most people would be hard pushed to understand. Essentially, the rich kid shows off by throwing wads of money into the crowd and causes mayhem on the dance floor. Although African enthusiasm and *joie de vivre* may, in part, be behind this gesture, it is unhealthy even though people are up for it. This young African who has lived in misery and suffering is not teaching a lesson in respect to others. Money is important in this society, but even more so where poverty rules. Now that he is wealthy and the money in his pocket converts to a million central African francs, he gives a negative instead of a hopeful image.

Numerous players have fun blinging-it. They love to hear the engines of their supercars purr and wear the most expensive, ostentatious clothes. I was teased by my team-mates because I often dressed in Nike tracksuits rather than the latest designer gear to go to training. I like big cars and nice clothes, but so-and-so's latest collection doesn't make me jump for joy. Why go around looking like you're sponsored by Gucci, or Dolce & Gabbana? Especially in an all-male environment! As it is we see each other under the shower and that's enough. After training, most of us head home. Why bother to make such a huge effort all for five minutes as you arrive and another five as you leave? The headache of colour-co-ordinating is not something I have time for. If I'd played in Italy I would've been mercilessly mocked. Over there, every morning is a fashion show.

Truth is, sometimes it can be fun when a top club is after you during a transfer window, and you arrive to train in the latest Dolce & Gabbana jacket feeling like a million dollars. It's pure pride. You strut about like Wall Street's own Mr Bigshot in the hottest Franck Muller watch. It's a great way to restore, or boost, your confidence.

You say: "I got 50 per cent off, but my business is my business so I won't say where. Still, it's pure quality."

You take the mickey out of your mates, who give as good as they get.

You make an arrogant remark: "Hey, don't get jealous – know your place, sonny."

Laughter all round. Tensions ease up and the pressure for results lightens for a moment. It's a great way to get in the mood for getting out on to the pitch.

There are those millionaires who have money to burn, but do not want to pay like everyone else. Strange but true. Everyone likes a bargain. But then there are those millionaires who compete with each other to see who can spend the most, in a sort of game of rich man's one-upmanship. Many players expect special deals and gifts, but like those *nouveaux riches* from oil rich countries, they will also push the boat out and hit Paris or the Cote d'Azur with a crew of five cousins, an official girlfriend and a couple of replacements, a dozen friends and two chauffeurs to strip the finest stores in France. They book the 600m² Deluxe King Skyline Suite in the Hotel George V, that Paris landmark dating from 1928, and tip the luckier waiters €500. It's outrageous.

If you're a spendthrift, you'd better be rich like those millionaires who don't know what it's like to stumble across a £20 note when you're down on your uppers. It's better to remember what it was like to have no money and not take it for granted.

Each to his passion and his whims. A footballer doesn't have 50 things to do after training. He won't play tennis, do some gardening, go jogging, or go-karting. Because he's young he likes to shop, go nightclubbing or place bets at casinos and check out the top car dealers. Those who are more experienced and less foolhardy go fishing, play some golf, go to museums, do a bit of DIY, or play FIFA 2012 on their PlayStation 3.

Today everything moves faster in the world of football and there's more money, which was not the case when I started. Controversy and media hype have become the norm, as have multi-channel plasma TVs in the homes of football fans.

I spoke to Dan Donachie, the osteopath at Everton, who is the son of Willie, a former Manchester City defender who played for Scotland at the 1978 World Cup. Dan said: "My father sees the biggest difference today as being physical. Football is much faster thanks to the 1992 back pass rule which stops players from passing the ball back to their 'keeper for him to then pick up in his hands. Playing the ball back to the goalkeeper had become synonymous with time wasting. The intensity of matches increased as a consequence of the new rule. Another very obvious difference is how 20 years ago one game a week was broadcast compared to today, when even reserve games and matches at training academies are broadcast on several channels from different countries. TV coverage and revenues have rocketed." And consequently so has the pressure on players.

There are more pairs of eyes watching than ever before. Willie, an excellent player in the 1970s and 1980s, must find all these changes and the sight of young guys driving supercars in gold and diamond bling-bling jewellery annoying. This level of money around football did not exist back then. There may have been the same passion and number of stars on the field, but not the same marketing operation to accompany it all. The flash young player of the new millenium is seen by many more viewers and is recognised in the street by the baker, the postman, or even the tramp sleeping on an old newspaper which features the young star's exploits on the back page. This would make anyone big-headed. TV companies and sponsors spend fortunes to invade the homes of fans through football.

Zidane does not like to show off like some young players do. Flash jewellery isn't his thing. However, he admits: "To be with the family, I bought a beautiful boat. That way I'm not polluted by gorgeous cars, noise, articles about my game and billboards which imprison me in the persona of a famous soccer player. I like to isolate; to cut myself off from the world and just be with my family and friends."

So, to avoid spongers and the paparazzi he withdraws. This is the opposite of blinging-it. He enjoys life in his own private way. For this great talent to hang out on a big boat is less likely to upset the public than a 20-year-old who'll never win trophies driving a Lamborghini.

Some bling-bling footballers are so extreme and obsessed with their appearance and reputation that they wind people up. Invariably they haven't proved themselves in any great way, yet think that they are sufficiently top-flight for people to envy them. Rich or not, they will do anything to be believed, to be heard, to be seen. It looks as though they've made it to the top as they are under the spotlight. Some will go to a nightclub with a dozen mates. They shower beautiful girls with jeroboams of Moet & Chandon champagne. The £4,000, six-litre methuselah is not tasted but wasted over the body of Mam'zelle Starfucker who just made the footballer pay for it. She plays him to the hilt. In her £1,000 thigh-high boots and £500 hairstyle, she's super-hot to trot. When the waiter brings the huge bottle to Mr Bling he presents it to the club. The sexy girls in their Christian Louboutins at the other tables, and the gold-digger after a triplex apartment, are alerted to his presence: "Mmm . . . his gold card sure is loaded."

I remember the rumours about Djemba-Djemba having ten 4×4s in Douala and 30 bank accounts. He was in the Cameroon team that won the 2002 African Cup of Nations. We progressed together at Manchester United. He was a nice guy. But what about his entourage? Weren't there people who cared enough about this young guy trying to adapt to a new environment, to guide him and give him good advice? During his time at Old Trafford he splashed out so much that he relied on his bonuses to get by. When he left the UK he was drowning in a sea of debt. Guy Hillion, his first coach at Nantes, was quoted as saying: "He was touching. He used to get ecstatic about everything. One of the first things he said when he arrived was: 'I don't understand this. In France, I see money coming out of the walls.' He was talking about cash machines."

Generally, after two or three big seasons, too many sleepless nights and poor performances on the field can all bring the player close to losing his position and his salary. Then all the fun would be short-lived. His entourage needs to be strong enough to remind him of his most important objectives and bring him back down to earth.

Players' agent, Bruno Satin: "I find it harder to manage the new generation. They seem to have lost the burning desire of previous generations. Young guys once rushed to play outside. Now they go home like good boys and sit in front of their PlayStation or Wii. Most young guys don't only want to practise their favourite sport, they want what they see on TV. They want the new Messi Adidas F50s, the cars, the jewellery and all the rest."

An extreme obsession with appearances takes precedence over respect and serious hard work. Ego-management has become harder. Bruno Satin: "Going into a changing room full of pros used to be impressive. It generally took a month before a young player got used to rubbing shoulders with famous or older players.

It was, 'Hello sir, can I please leave the table?' Now that respect has gone. It's as though nobody and nothing can destabilise these kids. They come back from a game their chests puffed up with pride as if they had already notched up 50 games. Some of them are good kids, but society has a part to play."

Man or woman, nobody wants to appear vulnerable. It's as though the only way to succeed is to have a lot of nerve. Bruno Satin: "This is more pronounced in France, which I find disturbing. Perhaps it's one reason for the poor attitude of some young players as they do not listen and get big headed, fast. In Latin countries and even in England, there is still a certain respect for the coach and the club as institutions. There is nothing greater and more powerful than a club's history. The players just pass through. Nothing is stronger than the supporter and his love for his club. I don't think we make that clear enough in France." This may be a sweeping statement, but many French players who head abroad feel it. I do not know if the almost military training that I experienced has softened or if this new generation hungry for success refuse to be guided.

The moment I arrived at Everton in 2008, I felt the boundless passion and enthusiasm for the club from everyone there. The respect for the club's history, its culture and values must be expressed by each player on the pitch. Jimmy, the masseur, has the Everton club crest tattooed on his calf. The motto reads: "*Nil Satis Nisi Optimum* (Nothing But the Best is Good Enough)." Their greatest player was Dixie Dean, top scorer of the 1920s. Goodison is a special stadium which has hosted a great number of top flight matches. You can feel the spirit of many great sportsmen when you go on the pitch. It's a healthy club and I always felt the players were ambitious and wanted to improve. Its foundations are based on group effort as opposed to individuality. The team shows fighting spirit. Everton is an honest place and people are straight with you.

When I arrived at Tottenham Hotspur, I felt the same passion and culture of respect for the game, the players and the coach. I feel intensely supported by the fans. The respect for the legacy of a great player is so immense in this country that there is a bronze statue of Thierry Henry outside the Emirates Stadium. Nothing comes close to this in France when it comes to supporters and club bosses showing such appreciation. I can't see a statue of Zinédine Zidane going up outside the stadiums of AS Cannes or FC des Girondins de Bordeaux. Nothing in France honours the legacy of King Eric, who is adored by Man Utd fans.

As I progressed I enjoyed myself. The bling-bling phenomenon partly kicked off with Jacobs & Co. luxury watches, with their large quadrants and dials encrusted with diamonds. These innovative bejewelled timepieces launched the cool-to-show-it-off trend. Brands like Ed Hardy and Von Dutch and then Christian Audigier came on board and made a splash. Football players who want to be noticed now have a uniform look. Before, only the sports car hinted at the day-job of these too-young drivers. I'm not heavily into fashion, or jewels; for me it's property and sports cars – all beautiful cars in fact. At a young age I was occasionally recklessly extravagant.

At 20, my taste was for BMW and the lethal yet beautiful M3.

At 21, I turned Porschist, moving from a beautiful Carrera 996 to a Turbo which I kitted out like a batmobile.

At 27, I went for the Mercedes CLK and a rare racer from the DTM, German Touring Car Masters series.

At 30, I opted for the package deal: a supercar Audi R8 V10 Abt.

At 32, I just had to go for the Ferrari 458 Italia.

In an interview published in 2004, I said I would never drive that kind of car out of respect for my family, but I succumbed. I'm neither a gambler, nor a collector, or a bling-bling type of guy: just a lover of beautiful cars. I'm seriously lucky to be able to change them so often and not to have had bad crashes. I was a bit young to drive such big motors, but they weren't stolen, as many police officers liked to believe. The cops systematically took me for a drug dealer or a car thief.

Debate with self when pulled over by a cop:

What's the problem? Oh yeah, I'm black . . .

Uh . . . You don't often see a young guy who can afford flash wheels, do you?

Oh? Ah, I get you . . . so that's why I'm being pulled over.

Now I'm older I meet cops who are, more often than not, super-friendly and do their jobs properly. Cops like beautiful cars as much as footballers, but an inner-city guy wouldn't tell the same story as me.

I was hesitant about buying a red Ferrari, or the latest Lamborghini Gallardo. As well as being extraordinary vehicles, they are symbols of luxury in all their blazing splendour. I've always been wary of attracting attention and making people jealous. It takes very little for people to want stuff to happen to you. So I was mindful, but finally got fed up as I realised it made no difference. A passion is a passion, so run with it. I work hard to be able to afford these luxuries. My cars have been black with tinted windows since I was 20. I have fun and I'm hardly ever recognised.

Throughout his long career, Phil Neville, ex-England defender and Everton's skipper, has always been keen to maintain his good professional image. He's realised only recently the enormity of all that he has achieved. He has played for over 15 years at the highest level and won the biggest trophies. Despite this, he remains modest and does not brag about his successes. No doubt this is out of respect for the team and because of his determination to lead by example.

Phil Neville: "It's true that the issue about the sportsman's image in general bothers me, and I sometimes think I should do more of what I like and put it out of my mind, regardless of what people might think."

He refuses to set a bad example and believes that up-and-coming young players must be beyond reproach. He would not want to see a 20-year-old pitching up in a Lamborghini because he's just signed his first professional contract.

I can't disagree with him, even though I'm nuts about cars. In France, I once had the nerve to turn up to training in a Porsche, aged 21. Nothing was said, but I didn't play for three weeks. Certain players and the coach decided to make me pay for such blatant cheek.

Nev: "Louis, it's true that I had a go at enjoying myself with a Ferrari when I was at Manchester United in my teens, but I quickly felt uncomfortable because of my image as a 'man of integrity' that I work hard to maintain."

To my mind this is excessive since he is outstanding on and off the pitch. His wife recently gave him a wonderful birthday and wedding anniversary double whammy which, to my surprise, he did not sell. He kept the sport convertible and enjoys taking corners with the top down, even though it rains in Manchester where he lives at least 250 days a year. It's great to see him flourishing as he deserves it. His personalised license plate which reads an acronym of his name is fun. Great guy, great player, top professional, top wheels. Nobody has the right to force any of us to drive an electric car as a sign of respect or modesty. I could understand doing so for the environment and to counter global warming, but not to soothe somebody's wounded ego.

Bling-bling players are more than likely to have experienced something lacking in their childhood so they find ways make up for it. All these young stars who have sweated blood feel they have nothing to prove, or justify to anyone, least of all the grumpy neighbour and 50-something who can't bear seeing a kid behind the wheel of a butch Mercedes.

These young people are free to live how they choose, especially given where they have come from and all they've managed to accomplish. They are accountable to the club chairman, their coach and their fans but no one else.

People say: "They're just guys running after a ball in a field," or "It sucks. I slog my guts out for 40 hours a week . . . it'd take me a year to earn what that kid gets in one week just for kicking a ball . . ." Ra Ra Rupert in his diamond-design Pringle jumper is fuming as he and all the others who don't give a damn about football sit stuck in traffic for hours on the Fulham Road because Chelsea are playing at home. Not everyone likes football, but they are affected one way or another by this sport which is a hot topic in households across the world.

16
RACISM AND
OTHER TABOOS

he Independent: "Ferguson said that the re-emergence of the prejudice which beset the game 20 years ago has mystified him. 'I don't understand at all where it's coming from, to be honest with you, I don't understand it at all. This is a moment where we have to take stock and we should do something about it if it's surfacing again, and be really hard and firm on any form or shape of racism. There have been a couple of examples recently which is not good. In 2012, you can't believe it. It was obvious maybe 20 years ago and the improvements have been for everyone to see'."

Football has evolved and allows players of all races to flourish in the sport they love in a greater sense of security than previously. As the slogan says: "Football unites, racism divides."

I first experienced racism at the age of 13, the day I went to the Parc des Princes stadium in the smart south-western suburbs of Paris to watch Paris Saint-Germain. I will always remember my bittersweet feelings of fear and pride. I was with my father and my childhood friend, Domenico. We arrived a little in advance to avoid the traffic and find a parking spot. After leaving the car a couple of streets away, my father decided to get a coffee in a bar near the notorious Kop de Boulogne stand at the Parc des Princes, where PSG's hardcore and notoriously violent, right-wing supporters gather.

A bell rang as we opened the door. There was an almost imperceptible vibration in the air, an echo of voices from the back of the room, and a sense of surprise as heads swivelled to look at us. None of us paid any attention. As we approached the counter to place our order, a strange, heavy atmosphere enveloped us like a fog. I looked at my mate, but he seemed fine and was clearly excited about going to watch the match. The waitress and the owner were at the other end of the bar shushing a group of supporters. She whispered particularly insistently to a short, agitated guy who looked like a head boy. I noticed the embroidered PSG patch on his blue-and-red jersey. His face was so tensed up his eyes had almost disappeared beneath his frowning brows. We suddenly realised that everyone was staring at us.

Muttered phrases emerged from the shadows: "France for the French"; "Go back to Africa where you come from," along with other nasty comments.

We immediately realised they were Kop de Boulogne hooligans who are known for their racist tendencies and savagery. We had not yet placed our order. I assumed we'd head off, nice and quiet, but I had underestimated my old man's implacable temperament. The short, agitated man advanced towards us and threatened my dad. He had no idea that this was the worst thing he could do. My dad was steely strong. Even today, aged 33, I don't remember one instance, ever, of my father being intimidated by another man. I would have thought that a group of hooligans would change that.

There were lots of them and they were aggressive. But we quietly finished our hot chocolates. My father, unwilling to yield or be humiliated, showed great courage and pride. He was backed up by the owner of the bar. Accompanied by two children, my old man stayed calm, but ready to pounce. Answering insults with wisdom and intelligence can destabilise a whole group and exposes how racism is a belief underpinned by ignorance. It was reminiscent of the powerful aura of my old mate Kalagan from Sarcelles. After the game, we speculated as to what might have happened after our departure. As we passed by the bar, we noticed that it had been ransacked and the windows smashed. All because the boss had stood up for us.

England is probably the only country to have successfully

tackled overt racism in football thanks to funds the Premier League has invested in this fight. At the end of 1970s, West Bromwich Albion lead the way by fielding a talented trio of black players: Cyrille Regis, Laurie Cunningham and Brendan Batson. It was not until 1978 that the first black player represented England in the national team: Viv Anderson, the pioneer.

Today, although racial slurs are still heard, efforts are being made to deal with it, as I experienced at first hand when I was playing for Everton. A supporter was reported to a club steward by other fans disgusted by his racist heckling. He was expelled from the stadium and banned from football matches for three years. He called me a "fucking useless, lazy French bastard". It could have been worse. I find it hard to understand how harsher abuse is not always reprimanded.

Efforts vary from country to country. The will and intentions are not uniform across the board when it comes to fighting racism. The UK has a good reputation in the fight compared to other countries. Liverpool striker, Luis Suarez, was recently suspended for eight games and fined for racial abuse against Patrice Evra, but in 2004 the coach of Spain's national team, Luis Aragonés, who called Thierry Henry a piece of "n***** shit" was just fined €3,000.

Jean-Alain Boumsong, who's played for Rangers, Newcastle United, Juventus, Lyon and now at Panathinaikos: "Slow progress is being made, but the Italians will say openly what the French mutter under their breath. Despite the changes, racism runs deep in certain Latin countries."

Xenophobic fanaticism and hooliganism are like a ball and chain around the feet of this cosmopolitan team sport. Hooliganism is either expressed by fans fighting and wanting to smash the place up during, before, or after a match, or more seriously, by intentional organised violence involving gangs who attach them-selves to football clubs and fight with those of other clubs, some-times well before or after a game. Racism plays a part, but not always. Scaremongering by politicians on immigration exacerbates the situation in certain countries. In England there is a new generation of local organisations who fight against racism and the extreme right, like the Anti-Fascist Action group or the fanzine, *Marching On Together*. The idea of campaigning against racism in football is spreading into Europe.

I talked to a hooligan for this book, a hardcore gang leader, who told me that activities are on the rise. In England and other countries you don't often read about hooligans in the press. Since the 1990 Taylor Report, disorder linked to football has been "pushed" outside the stadium to other meeting points. So the groups are obliged to get better organised and are less easily controlled or arrested. The internet, mobiles and other technical devices like GPS make it easy for violent gangs to link up.

The hooligan: "I first got involved because of the adrenaline rush in the build up to a fight. I wanted to dominate the hooligan league just like my team. There are hooligans everywhere. Most clubs have several 'firms' attached to them."

A little later in the interview, I asked him if hooliganism equals racism. I must admit that his response instantly made me smile.

"I'm proud to say that my crew is not racist, we smash up everything in our way. But, yes, some crews obviously tie in with xenophobia. Racist ideology is present and we rub elbows with it, but we do not act on it. The rules aren't the same everywhere."

In other words he has racist attitudes, but does not act on them. The hooligan gave me some good advice: "If you go to a match without a scarf and a team jersey and wear neutral clothes and hang out in a group, it's more than likely you'll end up in a scuffle. Be vigilant."

Patrice Evra describes his arrival in Sicily over 10 years ago: "When I first went to training and produced a mobile phone from my pocket, my team-mates came up to me and started to give me advice about what the green and red buttons were for, as though I had no idea what 'to answer' and 'to hang up' meant.

I did not quite understand what they were on about; it was not really racism, more to do with ignorance. The penny dropped when I started watching Italian TV. Blacks were always shown wearing leaves and using wooden spears to hunt. That island was full of tolerant open people, but the way they live and talk and crack jokes is bad and disturbing for a black guy.

"Louis, people wanted to take photos of themselves with me, not because I was a pro, but because I was the only black footballer in the championship. I was a curiosity; an attraction like the lead character Ju/'hoansi in the film *The Gods Must Be Crazy*. If you remember, the bushman leaves the Kalahari desert and encounters Western civilization for the first time.

"I had to put up with monkey chants from the terraces and the worst insults. I used it all to give myself an inner strength. At first, my team-mates wanted to call me 'Nero.' I had to threaten to call them 'white shit' and make them understand that my parents gave me a name and surname."

For an Italian, to call someone "Nero" is not really racist. The term was used in America until the end of the 1960s. Even Martin Luther King, Jr., identified his own race as "Negro" in his famous 1963 speech "I Have a Dream". It just goes to show how far behind the times the Italians are, because that dates back almost 50 years! Its use is sometimes representative of a certain kind of humour, or an unconscious habit, but it's too close to the bone to be acceptable. Humour is debateable, but anything else is war. Racism exists everywhere and can come from anywhere.

Patrice Evra: "When I chose to play for France over Senegal, I was insulted and treated like a monkey who pulls down his trousers for the whites." Racism enrages all those who have experienced it.

Marouane Fellaini, midfielder for Everton: "Bro, I struggle to control myself and used to flare up fast. Sometimes all you can do is explode even though a second later you regret it because you know very well there are idiots out there from all kinds of backgrounds."

The surprised expression of customers in certain European boutique hotels, top-rated restaurants and five-star luxury beach resorts can be unnerving. It is not so surprising since the clientele which frequents these exclusive spots are generally privileged types – neither particularly cosmopolitan, nor non-white. To such an individual, the modern multiracial mix does not exist since non-whites are shut away, out of sight and out of mind, to rot in frustration in the high-rise estates outside the core of France's big cities. Life is tough enough as it is, so imagine being a young North African full of dreams and ambitions who has to fight against endless stereotypes.

More often than not, nowadays I'm one of the few black guys who can afford to stay in an exclusive hotel during the holidays, or dine at a three-star restaurant, so eyes widen as I enter the room. At first, it's a matter of pride for me that I represent success for the black inner-city community, or the countryside of Saint Anne in Guadeloupe. Then it becomes annoying, especially when there's a national debate in France backed up by surveys about whether or not the first black evening newsman on national TV, Harry Roselmack, is doing a great job and gets good ratings. To poll the public to find out if it's happy for a black guy to present the evening news instead of Patrick Poivre d'Arvor, one of the longest serving newsreaders in the world who Roselmack replaced, is disturbing. In light of this, it is interesting that Sir Trevor McDonald – the first black newsreader in the UK – who joined ITN in 1973 is the most popular newsman in Britain.

You have to accept and be proud of being black or yellow and benefit from it, in the same way that a woman uses her femininity like a trump card. At first, I was shocked to see Lilian Thuram – 1998 World Cup champion, campaigner against institutionalised racism and advocate of the teaching of black history – advertising Danone's creamy chocolate dessert. Ditto for tennis player, Jo-Wilfried Tsonga, advertising the chocolate bar, Kinder Bueno. For many, racism in the playground starts with black children being called "chocolate bar". Although causing offence may not be the intention of these big companies – who like to use famous people to advertise their products – there's a fine line to tread. But I now realise that if we turn down the few roles that come our way, we will not forge ahead. How to find the balance?

If it isn't racism that provokes hatred, it's religious fanatacism that wreaks havoc. Crimes, bomb attacks and hatred, coupled with a desire for revenge which permeates our daily lives and news bulletins. Atheism is flourishing because faith has lost its staying power. A few days after the attacks of September 11, a journalist asked Muhammad Ali: "How does it feel to share your religion with Osama Bin Laden?" To which he answered: "How do you feel about sharing yours with Adolf Hitler?" There are too many fanatics who have been brainwashed and are incapable of reflection. Hatred has invaded their every cell and not even the sight of a child smiling can soften such a mentality.

I dedicate this book to my ancestors. I say a big thank you to all those who have fought and who continue to fight any form of discrimination, to all our ancestors, black, yellow or white, who have enabled us to be free and to travel the world. I will never forget that they are the ones who endured slavery, war and humiliation. In comparison, very few of us have been whipped or have had to eat off the floor. Too many young people use the enslavement of their ancestors to justify violence, theft and disrespect. To be fed up with being exploited is justifiable, but to degrade our collective image is a bad move since violence begets violence. The fight goes on, and is not yet won.

It's important to remember every day how lucky we are. Racism should not be an obstacle for those in the inner cities but a motivating factor to get out, as it was for those who had no other choice but to fight. Black, white, yellow or mixed race, reach out a hand when one of you falls because once he's back up, when he spreads his wings he'll carry you with him.

Overt racial discrimination and intolerance has been tackled in Britain, unlike France, but look deeper and we still live in a society where there are pockets of racism and persistent economic inequality between whites and non-whites. France has a way to go. Many people fear difference and the unknown and often have intolerant or toxic ideas. We are all unique, and so have myriad ways of assessing, thinking and acting in the face of the unexplored. Diversity should be celebrated as something that enriches us all.

Freedom of thought and expression cannot be denied; therefore it is impossible to prevent people having racist thoughts and views. It is essential to act intelligently and to show a bigot that a non-European, non-white person is as good, attractive and intelligent as him. The eradication of racism does not only involve improving the image of certain races. For there to be no difference between us would be an impossibility, yet therein lies the difficulty for those who struggle daily.

I whisper to myself that a part of each of us is intolerant and potentially racist. We all have a self-protective reflex when a stranger enters our universe without permission, or without treating our customs and culture with due respect. I feel it when I see my cousins in Guadeloupe suffering from the high cost of living just because of a minority of wealthy landowners. We all feel injustice, but people often mix up the fear of foreigners, their politics or culture with the belief that race accounts for differences in human character or ability and that a particular race is superior to others.

Strangely, I have found that some blacks do not seem to like other blacks much, and whites even less. Certain Arabs do not like blacks and vice versa. Certain blacks do not like Jews and vice versa. Certain whites easily forget that some blacks, Jews, Arabs and Asians were severely damaged by colonialism and may have unconsciously assimilated their anger.

In some parts of Europe, flags bearing the swastika are displayed at matches and neo-Nazi skinheads shout racist slogans. Other agitators make monkey noises and gestures, or throw banana skins on to the pitch; they themselves are less evolved than the primates they imitate. I am pessimistic about our ability to change the thinking of these small-minded, ultra-conservative minorities. Obviously, to smash cars and rob old ladies and doctors' surgeries, whatever the motivation, is no way to fight racism and unemployment in the inner-city. But I do not believe in humankind's willingness or ability to eradicate this problem since corruption has become the order of the day: things are getting worse despite the efforts of so many.

Education, raising awareness of human rights and constructive use of independent media channels would be a start. It would be of benefit if people received a sound education based on reflection as opposed to learning everything by heart because there is such a mass of information to sift through. We need campaigning activists and people of the right mindset who can help others evaluate and change their thinking.

In France, the racial quotas row that broke out in April 2011 about limiting the number of dual-nationality players proposed by the French Football Federation (FFF) put the malaise over race in football under the spotlight. Mohamed Belkacemi, the Federation's National Technical Advisor, leaked details of the FFF's meeting on 8 November 2010 through a recording released on the Médiapart website, because he was amazed by certain comments made during the discussion. The story was that the French Football Federation was attempting to secretly implement a race-quota system in order to limit the number of players with dual-nationality in its national academies. A cap would be set on the number of players of different origins by limiting places in the academies in the 12–13 age range. The audio recordings released on the website included racial stereotyping and the debate veered off into a discussion about the physique of black players. The FFF authorised a full investigation into the matter and

National Technical Director, François Blaquart, was suspended pending the outcome of the investigation.

Other than being embarrassed, neither the politicians nor the public seemed particularly interested in this scandal, as though it wasn't their fight. It ended up being more of a damp squib than a bombshell. When Patrick Vieira, Lilan Thuram and others were asked for their opinions, the reaction to their comments suggested that speaking out against the shocking remarks made at the meeting placed their careers in football in danger.

Nicolas Anelka's words to British reporters in December 2010 about events during the World Cup in South Africa are pertinent: "People said there was a clan of black players in the French squad at the World Cup, and we then saw the true face of France. When France fails to win people start talking straight away about the players' skin colours and religious beliefs. When times get tough we find out what people really think. They said Franck Ribéry had hit Yoann Gourcuff – Ribéry the Muslim and Gourcuff the good French boy."

I was alarmed to hear that they were considering a national integration test at the age of 13, which players would have to pass to get into INF Clairefontaine. Or to hear of these other subtly discriminatory practices in order to get an idea of how a kid would choose their national team in seven years time and whether or not he would choose to play for France, even though he may not ever become a pro. I confess, I would have preferred to see the scandal break in 2012 during the presidential elections, as it would have been most revelatory to hear the excuses made for applying discriminatory practices and the double-talk of President Sarkozy, or that of other presidential candidates, while keeping law and order in the inner city is the focus of a flagship social programme. It would also have been interesting to see where Érick Mombaerts and François Blaquart at the National Technical Directorate (DTN) would have got to after a year of discussing the proposed changes. But of course Euro 2012 will be on at the same time as the presidential elections. It is essential that the French national team remain undamaged by this affair, especially since its renaissance orchestrated by national coach Laurent Blanc.

Whenever there is a heated debate in our society, there is usually a grain of truth in each side's argument. To have a genuine debate is good, but it is also dangerous since we're not talking about Spain, Brazil, or the Cameroon. France's revolutionary principles are an example to live by; a force for the good; a dream. The reality of a multiracial society is something which Marine Le Pen, the leader of France's right-wing Front National (National Front) party and her father, Jean-Marie, its founder and former head, must learn to live with.

One thing is certain, as Jean-Alain Boumsong says: "What was said during that meeting in November 2010 was serious and nobody could argue otherwise. I have children who I love and try to educate well, so I cannot hide behind my profession as a footballer and sidestep a subject like this. I had to explain and say how it is. So-called racists in France are underhand, so it's hard to confront or expose them. I'm not particularly militant, I just made observations about a situation that troubled and hurt a great many families."

The National Technical Board (DTN) and the president of the FFF, Noël Le Graët, must now rebuild, in mind and spirit, the young guys upset by the row at the 12 élite academies across France.

I was vexed and did not want to believe what had happened. I was sure it was all a misunderstanding. Like many people, I believed in the alleged transparency of both investigations set up by the FFF and the government to look into the quotas question, but nothing was revealed and everyone was cleared. It reminds me of how receiving one hour of detention outside school hours was not enough to stop me from messing about.

All I saw was a large black bubble disappearing noiselessly into the sky with more subtlety than Thierry Henry's handball against Ireland which gave France the opportunity to take part in the last World Cup. Titi suffered more than a 10-hour detention for his handball pass to William Gallas who then scored the crucial qualifying goal. He got it in the neck from all sides. The worst came from France. Politicians, athletes, journalists and fans accused him of tarnishing our country's image. A lesson was learned, for life.

Changes made over time make a difference, but stereotypes of all kinds are hard to shift at a fundamental level. The standard view is that human nature is averse to change and people will take the easy option if they can. Yet human nature is highly adaptable. We are all capable of both hate and tolerance. Overt racism in football continues to be successfully tackled, especially in England, but other behaviours remain in the shadows.

There was, of course, the scandal involving the then Sky Sports presenters, Richard Keys and Andy Gray, when their degrading off-air remarks about female lineswoman Sian Massey came to light. Many men behave like this amongst themselves, but it is unacceptable in the public arena. A man alone with a woman can be charming, but when he is surrounded by other men he often becomes boastful and uses aggressive language. Many men believe that the majority of women do not know the offside rule. Some, devoid of respect and class, wolf whistle after an attractive woman in the street. Worse, others will not agree to work under a woman. Men have teased the opposite sex with the same jokes for millennia. Women defend themselves as best they can and things are improving, albeit slowly; some are aiming for total equality. In France there are many more women in politics, on TV and in positions of responsibility than before. The one reservation I have is that women have hardened to protect themselves, but when the going gets tough they want to be treated as fragile, which is a kind of lifeline exclusive to them. Some have fun with male stereotypes. Fair enough.

Karen Brady, the other woman attacked by the duo on Sky Sports, is vice-chairman of West Ham United in East London. Gray and Keys mocked an interview she did about sexism in football. She is known for being an iron lady and was recently included in the list of the 100 most powerful women in Britain. I am confident that Ms Brady, who I do not know but whom I respect, especially for what she represents for other women, does not flinch from showing determination and strength in the macho, testosterone-filled world of football. Otherwise, she would not be taken seriously. It's likely she has had to demonstrate that she can be rougher and tougher, more cutthroat and invulnerable, than any businessman. Along the way, I'd imagine she has had to flay a few egos and has maybe taken pleasure from dominating the so-called stronger sex.

Sport is not the only difficult arena difficult for a woman to conquer. The financial heart of London, the City, is one of the most prosperous areas in the world but behind closed doors, women are frequently victims of sexist stereotypes. Ms Brady sets an example for a great many women.

Western women are comparatively lucky. In other countries, women are fighting for better economic participation, a good education, the right to vote, political power, help with childcare, and in some places, even the right to drive a car . . .

I am not a male chauvinist who considers himself superior to women. It is good that things are evolving, without forgetting the natural differences which exist between men and women. I must admit, I cannot see a curvaceous, blonde bombshell being a lineswoman or a referee for the simple reason that the purpose of these officials is not to be noticed. It would be a huge distraction and it would be hard for players to refrain from making cheeky comments.

I confess to being surprised when I see a woman at the wheel of a Porsche GT3, or a monster 4×4 Hummer, although more than likely she drives better than I do! My wife would be unlikely to support gender equality in the workplace, regardless of the circumstances, because if I were to come home one day and mention that my club had just recruited a cute new masseuse in place of Stu, my masseur at Tottenham, she would quickly become a super-agent and ensure I move on, even outside the transfer window!

I confess to being surprised by the extent to which advertising agencies will use pretty women to sell slimming products, beauty potions and lotions, deodorants, soaps and organic yogurt. In Italy and France, beautiful *naked* women are systematically used on advertising hoardings. It's subliminal marketing. I find it hard to see myself doing the shopping, making a stew, doing the dishes, or tidying up my wife's garage. Nevertheless, I consider myself to be attentive and romantic when it's called for. It's best to accept the different character traits, flaws and qualities of men and women even though there are exceptions to the rule.

I confess to enjoying the Challenge de France, the premier football competition for women in my home country, and seeing such power mixed with grace and finesse. It all began with the great Marinette Pichon who played professionally in America until 2004, and now with Olympique Lyonnais, the winner of the UEFA Women's Champions League in 2010/11. Just look at players like Brazil's Marta Viera da Silva, the Englishwoman Kelly Smith or Birgit Prinz, who played for FFC Frankfurt and the German national team before announcing the end of her career in August 2001.

The world of football has a mocking and frank mentality, so it is unrealistic to live in such an environment and expect to never face a harsh or nasty word. It is hard for a woman to work in a macho world where men feel the need to show themselves as conquerors and fighters, and to avoid being taunted by colleagues.

Homosexuality is a real taboo, so in football jokes get bad if the subject comes up. Rumours spread fast the moment a popular footballer is not seen with a gorgeous blonde on his arm, or is not known to enjoy champagne-laced, steamy nights.

Justin Fashanu was a pioneer. In 1980, aged 19, he was the first black footballer to be transferred for £1 million. Brian Clough, his manager at Nottingham Forest, mocked him, saying he was "a bloody poof!" He was the first, and so far the only, professional player in Britain to have the courage to come out as gay in 1990. He committed suicide eight years later. He found it much harder to deal with homophobia than racism in the macho world of football. I read recently in the *Daily Mail*: "Whether perceived to be gay or straight, he was always black and English football was not a pleasant place to be for men of colour in the 1970s and 1980s."

A recent survey shows that one in five gay employees consider their company's environment to be "hostile" and only 53 per cent risk coming out at work. This rate is even higher in the sports arena, because homosexuality provokes extreme reactions, mockery or embarrassment.

Graeme Le Saux, former defender for Chelsea and the England team, wrote in his autobiography: "I was like a bullied kid on his way to school to face his tormentors." For 14 years, Le Saux endured the taunts of his team-mates, other players and the fans yelling obscenities about his sexuality from the stands. And he was not even gay: he was married with kids! It was just because he was interested in the Arts, read *The Guardian* and was not part of the macho culture of the game.

The president of Paris rugby club Stade Français has made overtures towards breaking down some of these barriers through symbolic gestures. Introducing a pink away jersey was innovative. To produce a calendar entitled "Gods of the Stadium", featuring monumental, naked rugby players was a daring move. The calendar showed their "feminine side" and offered a great contrast to the physical brutality of the game. It attracted a new audience to rugby matches – namely women and gay men.

In 2009, former Wales and British Lions rugby captain, Gareth Thomas, joined the stars John Amaechi (basketball) and Donal Og Cusack (hurling) by revealing he was gay. He announced: "I and my sport were ready for it; I would not have done it 15 years ago. It's not about sexuality for me; it's about people who are brave and have been able to be who they want to be."

But football is resistant on many more fronts than rugby. There is a necessary caution in everything footballers do since they are so over-exposed in the media, whereas rugby players are afforded more privacy.

Homosexuality was legalised in England in 1967, but it wasn't until 1991 that Britain's first gay football team, Stonewall FC, was founded. In February 2012, all the Premier League's clubs signed up to the government's charter against homophobia, and the FA launched their anti-homophobia action plan: "Opening Doors and Joining In". Maybe there will be a sea-change in attitudes.

I confess that I would find it difficult in the changing room if a player "came out". Maybe it would take me a while to adapt and be candid in my jokes. Or would I move away because of being embarrassed – as much for him as for me? I would hope to be tolerant and not be responsible for a suicide like Justin Fashanu's. Why is football homophobic? Is it an irrational fear? Paradoxically, football has more effeminate-looking players than rugby. Many have fancy hairstyles, use gel and some even use male cosmetics!

Diana Law: "This behaviour is not unique to football because, as in many team sports, the sense of humour in the changing room can be lethal. Perhaps the real problem is not the team-mates of a player, but the opposition and the fans. The media would protect a gay player, but it'd be complicated."

Tim Cahill: "I grew up in a very tolerant family. No matter where you come from, what colour you are and what beliefs you have, as long as you are a good person that is all that matters. I try to educate my children so that they have decent values since today there are far more serious issues to deal with. I can imagine the difficulties a gay player would face in this macho world, so it's understandable if he prefers to stay in the shadows." The pressure and coping with abuse from the terraces would be a nightmare.

I am forthright. I love playing pranks and to have a good laugh. At Everton, there were certain traditions like at other clubs I've played for. At Finch Farm, Everton's training ground, if you closed the door of the lavatory it would be no surprise to get a bucket of water chucked over your head before your buttocks hit the seat. Picture David Ginola coming out of the cubicle with one side of his hair perfect and the other flattened and drenched like his copy of the French sports paper, *L'Equipe*: "Bollocks! Come on guys!"

Training games when you are only allowed two touches of the ball are fun, but best not play against me as I have very hard nails. The loser's ear is flicked by the winner's finger. And never leave your laptop in a changing room when Leon Osman, Tim Cahill or Phil Jagielka are present, as your menu will end up in Russian or Chinese. Worse, if they get hold of your phone they will send embarrassing messages to your coach, friends or wife.

There are thousands of funny stories like this from every club. For many players, the atmosphere of a changing room has an invisible aura which helps forge solidarity and self-confidence. When you feel good, the group knows. When you're brimming with confidence, you pass it on to your team-mates. Whether for good or ill, the group expresses itself and nothing stays hidden for long. Almost everything is known and said. We dream up rumours and speculation and laugh about them. The public does not laugh, but says what it thinks and repeats what it hears. It is blunt, malicious and tactless, especially when it comes from the opposition's fans. That's why, to my mind, I am lucky to be a heterosexual in football.

In trying to address this tricky subject I hope I have not come across as homophobic. But one thing is certain, I was not happy about Everton having to wear pink jerseys as part of our away strip for the 2010/11 season. It's a colour associated with softness, not manliness. Puppies and kittens in birthday cards often have pink bows around their necks. I told my boys they would never see me in that colour, but there I was in a pink Le Coq Sportif shirt – it felt absurd! Lol!

Have you seen yourself when you're drunk? Alcohol should be seen as a problem, but it isn't! Lol!

Alcohol is used by many fans as a release and to escape into a happy, carefree world. Many players drink for similar reasons. It helps alleviate the pressure of public scrutiny, money and fame and is a great way of celebrating a victory with friends. The culture of social drinking is still ingrained in the game. The problem starts when the bottle takes over. Footballing icons like George Best, Tony Adams, Robbie Savage and Paul Gascoigne battled with the booze. During an interview before he died from liver disease, George Best said: "People do not realise how I suffer from my alcoholism and they do not see the efforts I make. But I can't stop drinking. Unfortunately, because of this disease, I have not become the person I wanted to be. And I know I can never change anything." Gazza was England's star player in Italia '90 and Euro '96, but he lost everything after he succumbed to drink and depression. After rehab he is now rebuilding a new life. Tony Adams's Sporting Chance clinic in Hampshire offers support and counselling for players suffering from what is all too often not recognised as being a serious disease.

Some players like to live out Winston Churchill's famous quote: "I could not live without champagne – in victory I deserve it, in defeat I need it." The intensity of football today allows only a very few to go to town on the vodka. Twenty years ago preparation for a game went on around a table covered with bottles of beer and burgers. But alcohol is a very real danger to the modern footballer because the lifestyle pressures are so extreme. When players arrive for training still blotto from the night before, you might laugh the first couple of times, but as things go from bad to worse and their performance deteriorates it isn't so funny. When you're young, the body gets rid of the alcohol faster, so it can happen that a player is so drunk he stands up and pisses on the nightclub table, but the real test of endurance is the next morning. The older you get the longer it takes to recover from a hangover and your muscles hurt as much as your head. The nights are disturbed by your first child crying and you will long to head for the pitch with your team-mates. You, who were happy to stay at home before a match, will ask the coach to book the whole team into a hotel the night before the game so you get a good night's restorative sleep.

Gambling is a twin addiction to alcohol. Many players are suspended from banking privileges or casinos because they can no longer stop playing the tables. Some gamble a load of money and lose because there is no way of discussing their addiction openly. A casino boss said to me: "This is a good business for us, but we are often forced to show the door to guys who come 24 hours a day and the majority run out of money. It's like a drug. For us it's 'Banco' and we're quids in." Paul Merson, who played for Arsenal and England in the 1990s, spiralled into a life of addiction and ran up gambling debts estimated at more than £500,000.

To avoid temptation, we must always remember our objectives. The worst temptation of all is to accept money for the global big business of buying the result of a football game in advance or having a result manipulated by a corrupt referee. From Asia, Africa and the Americas to the West, football fanatics are obsessed with making money from matches and find ways to manage well-crafted cartels. FIFA recently revealed that there are 50 separate national investigations into match fixing underway. This kind of corruption is a terrible flaw in the sports world, devastating in its cumulative destructive power. For the beautiful game to lose its joyful playfulness and get destroyed by those seeking financial gain would be a tragedy.

17
STARS AND LEGENDS

Football has its stars, just like Hollywood. The big-name players are like A-list actors whose public image shines brightly. They are irreproachable and inaccessible, and make people dream. They are charismatic and are endowed with a unique know-how; they have exemplary careers underpinned by commercial viability. Their image is shaped and consecrated by the media. Superstars like Pelé, Zinédine Zidane, David Beckham, Cristiano Ronaldo and Lionel Messi are rare. They are so unique that they end up defining the game itself. Depraved habits are almost de rigueur for a rock star, but for a footballer they would lead to a career as short-lived as that of a reality TV star. He would soon slide down from the top of the pole as his extravagant lifestyle of partying, champagne and flirting with sexy girls in nightclubs becomes a habit, and his performance on the pitch would suffer. He'd be a shooting star, or not even that, shining bright but only for an instant. All stars are celebrities, but not all celebrities are stars.

How to become a football star? Simple . . . it takes talent, luck, almost superhuman tenacity and self-belief, and the "it" factor. It takes motivation, a touch of arrogance, hard work and passion for the glorious game. To achieve legendary status, a player needs to become a consistent source of inspiration respected by his team-mates and to accomplish stunning exploits. He must be in the right place at the right time and keep a cool head under pressure, despite his stellar success. These qualities are needed in abundance. Easy!

Best keep a receipt as proof. The whole world will believe that all the beautiful things you now have fell out of the sky and that you don't deserve them, or that it's a scam! I read an interview in the *Guardian* with Charles N'Zogbia who plays for Aston Villa, and he said: "When I go back to the neighbourhood, they look at me like a star. I tell them, 'I'm just like you, you can do it.' I see a lot of kids playing football and I say, 'I came from here and if I ended up being a professional, you can do it as well'."

Anything is possible, although not everyone can do what we see on TV. Professional football is anything but a dead end. Those who love the game for itself should go for it. But to those who are after the glory, the glamour, the luxury cars and extravagant lifestyle, make a U-turn and forget it.

The difference between a very good player and a megastar is immense. A stadium will be rammed with spectators just wanting to see him and his signature moves during his debut match for his new club. I have seen young girls and their mothers faint at the sight of Cristiano or Zinédine, the sort of thing you would have seen at a Michael Jackson concert.

Believe me, Cristiano Ronaldo always wanted to be a star. He has said as much and he has always worked to reach and stay at the very top of his discipline. He is fearless. His immense talent gives him an air of invincibility. But success does not come without a price. Everyone tries to stop him on the pitch, to catch up with the young prodigy and send him flying. Yet from one week to the next he consistently delivers the artistry and ferocity that make him untouchable, even though he has two arms and two legs like everyone else.

The only real recipe for success is to work hard; and more than everyone else. Cristiano worked at his free-kicks, dribbling and technical moves to the point that they were so polished they look like improvisations. He would weight train to the point where his muscles could take no more. He would push himself that extra mile in a match and try the seemingly impossible. To watch him train alleviates any criticism that could be levelled at him about his arrogance. He is who he is. Just remind yourself that few people in this world work as hard as he who proclaims himself to be one of the handsomest, wealthiest and best footballers. Watching him makes you realise how much more you still have to grow.

I much admire Samuel Eto'o, the former Inter Milan striker and captain of the national team of Cameroon, for the same generosity on the field. The way his confidence infects his teammates is incredible. He may be an excessive character off the field, but on it he is exemplary of team spirit and class.

I will always remember the last 16 match of the Champions League, Man United v Lyon, at the Stade Gerland in 2008. We were losing 1-0 when, in the second half, Carlos Tevez, who was on the bench, took it upon himself to get all fired up. Annoyed that we had not equalised, he was convinced he had what it took to break the deadlock. By the power of his attitude, he compelled Alex Ferguson to bring him on. His body language read: "Let me on the pitch and I'll smash us home." His insistent glances at the Boss did the trick. You can guess what happened. This is being a great player, and a huge contrast from the infamous Manchester City v Bayern Munich Champions League clash in 2011. Michael Schumacher, Tiger Woods, Michael Jordan, Lionel Messi, Usain Bolt, Mike Tyson, Roger Federer, Sébastien Loeb, the eight-times World Rally champion, all have or had this ability to make a break for the border. They defy logic and go for it 100 per cent, and then some.

Ambition motivates you to achieve excellence. For some it is a matter of pride; for others it's to think big. In France, ambition is often frowned upon, whereas in other cultures it is respected. Ambition is a key to success. Jealous people spit on success, luck and hard work that is recognised and rewarded.

To be a star is to represent a dream for a child, an old man or a family; a poor, sick or handicapped person; even a bored billionaire. It is to represent the collective vision of a country. Many people dream of becoming, mixing with, or raising a superstar. A billionaire may be rich but not necessarily popular; he is rarely recognised in the street, except perhaps when he draws up in front of a Louis Vuitton boutique in his Rolls-Royce.

Even when you get to the top, you still dream like you did when you were on the bottom rung of the ladder. You always want more, and fewer problems. Playing top-level football brings with it happiness, privileges and exceptional relationships. You can't ever get enough. I dream of pulling off another left-foot strike like I did in the 2009 FA Cup Final at Wembley, Everton v Chelsea, 25 seconds into the game. But this time my ultimate dream goal would not make FA Cup history for being the fastest goal in a final, more likely it'd be the winning goal in an historic final for my club.

All the goals I have ever scored are important to me and I love them all, so to choose the best one is impossible. I would like to notch up even more: in training, for my club, in cup games, friendlies, the Champions League, or for France. To score a goal gives you an indescribable burst of happiness and strength.

To reach the stars is playing in the UEFA Champions League and lifting that 8kg cup with the big ears. It's participating in the World Cup with great players. Holding the 25kg Premier League trophy aloft felt fantastic. I would have loved to lift more of those weighty trophies.

To reach the stars is to have had the privilege of representing my country, specifically that overseas region of France: Guadeloupe. It is to have worn the same French jersey as Zinédine Zidane when he passed the ball to me to score the first time I played for France in an international friendly against Belgium in 2004.

To reach the stars is to have fans whom I adore and to whom I say thank you. It's winning games and scoring important goals. It's rubbing shoulders with great personalities. It's smiling from ear to ear as I drive to work. It's visiting beautiful places with my family or my club. It's leading a privileged life and career thanks to my hard work and my talent.

To reach the stars is seeing my kids watch me play on TV, proud of their dad. It's freeing my parents from problems and securing my children's future. It's helping young people and those in need in an intelligent way. It's being one of the many sponsors of the European Leukodystrophy Association (ELA): a duty and responsibility that means I keep my feet firmly on the ground.

In football, the knocks are violent and unexpected.
A player's career is short and paradoxical.
Everything moves fast.
In a flash, you go from being a young pro, to a retiree at 35.
You go from being a young unknown, to a worldwide star.
From missing a shot to a legendary bicycle kick.
From being a zero to a hero.
From being a joker to a family man.
From being the outsider to the skipper.
From being "lazy" to a phenomenon.
From being "a bloody black" to the best striker.
From having a girlfriend to being married to a WAG.
From being an innocent to a millionaire seducer.
From having no degree to being an example of social success.
From owning a 15sqm studio to a large villa.
From driving a Volkswagen Polo to a Mercedes SLR.
From travelling EasyJet to private flights.
From staying in the Holiday Inn to Burj al Arab in Dubai.
From drinking Schloer to Moët & Chandon.
From the neighbourhood to the stars: the inner core stays the same.
Petit Louis has grown up, but he still plays like a child.

18

NON, JE NE
REGRETTE RIEN

Now that I've taken you on a safari through the world of football and shown you its ups and downs, pitfalls and pressures, pains and pleasures, the risks and the big bucks, the privacy and the media intrusion . . . if you ask me would I do it all again, I'd answer: "Yes! YES!"

If you really want to become a pro, here are some key tips to remember, courtesy of me, my wife, and my team-mates who joined me on this journey.

When you're footie-mad . . .

"Keep in mind that football is a game: have fun. Win, share and pass on the joy of doing it all together."

Louis Saha

"Accept the hard times so that you appreciate even more when your dreams come true."

William Gallas, Tottenham Hotspur

"Accept discipline and rules because they are a fact of life on the pitch. Otherwise, you'll find yourself losing out because the system is so powerful; and you'd just be wasting your time."

Zinédine Zidane

"Do not hide on the pitch. Having confidence in your team-mates boosts your own confidence."

Sir Alex Ferguson

"Having a difficult injury early on in my career made me realise the importance of weight training and doing exercises in extra time. I learned the meaning of the expression: 'Better be safe than sorry'. So when I'm less motivated, I think back to the times when I couldn't train 'cause I was hurt and felt depressed because I couldn't play to inspire myself."

Joleon Lescott, Manchester City

"Make an effort and sacrifices from day one without needing anyone to motivate you. Do extra training when nobody is looking."

Patrick Vieira, former French world champion who played for Arsenal, Juventus, Internazionale and Manchester City

"To be a predator on the pitch, you must be obsessed with your objective. Mine is the goal."

Djibril Cissé, Queens Park Rangers

"Make spectacular performances as often as possible. Seize your chance."

Patrice Evra, Manchester United

"Trust is the foundation-stone of a high-level player. A touch of arrogance is the nucleus of a phenomenal player. Practice expressing these traits well in a match."

Louis Saha

"Don't be pushed around when you feel you deserve your place or the opportunity to play, especially if you give all of yourself in training. Make your coach understand where you are coming from in an intelligent way, so that he won't make his choice lightly. He might not change his mind, but he won't hold it against you because it will show him your determination. Don't forget: respect for your coach is all-important."

Louis Saha

"To be overwhelmed by determination and fight to the very end, you need to maintain good relationships, underpinned by loyalty, with your team-mates and coaches."

Luis Boa Morte, Orlando Pirates, South Africa

"Ask your coach to sit down with you and look at a video of one of your matches so you can both analyse it and note down what you need to work on. It's a simple way of focusing on what you need to do to make progress."

Louis Saha

"Your dreams are non-negotiable. Be realistic, but do not readily agree when someone tells you that you won't make it."

Mikel Arteta, Arsenal

"In order to have no regrets, work harder and take more pleasure than anyone around you."

Phil Neville, Everton

"For African players, try to be a role-model, or an ambassador, in your way, especially by giving your all in everything you do. Believe in work well done, with pain as your companion. There are opportunities for everyone in Africa; the African must believe in himself."

Yakubu Aiyegbeni, Blackburn Rovers

Health: the most precious thing in the world

Dr Olivier Fichez, sports physician, private practice:

"Football is a sport involving violent rotational pivot contact and sudden changes in direction. Trauma sustained on the field must be reduced by physical preparation: wearing suitable footwear with insoles if necessary, a good diet, healing sleep supplemented by appropriate pain-free stretches.

The foot is the player's main tool, so he must take great care of each one. The body of a high-level footballer is a machine; you need to know how it works if you want to use it properly. Read the instruction manual!

Food is like fuel for a Formula One car. If you put lead in the engine, it explodes. Vegetables, meat, fish and all kinds of carbohydrates like rice, pasta and cereals eaten as part of a varied diet are essential. Obviously alcohol and fast food are totally unsuitable. Proper hydration allows for a high level of effort and performance, as does taking food supplements (omega 3, vitamins, etc).

Each player is physiologically different and requires special monitoring. You need to know the muscle mass, endurance, speed, flexibility and skeletal system of the player in question if you want to help him advance. Making progress to the next level needs to be done intelligently and according to his qualities. You should listen for the signals sent by the body.

Avoid cocaine and ecstasy; drug tests are no joke. These chemicals stay in the blood for six months. Hair analysis for cannabis, cocaine and heroin is a common practice in America."

"They say that sex before a match is not recommended due to the release of certain neuropeptides which mean you relax after the act."

Louis Saha

Media mania

"If you want a private life, you can have one, but you can't also sign contracts with certain types of magazines and newspapers. A choice has to be made because the press is aggressive, and when you accept that kind of deal, your private life means nothing in their hands."

Diana Law, press officer for Manchester United

"A player should surround himself with top-quality, reliable, honest professionals so he can benefit successfully from his image."

Djibril Cissé

"Try to speak correctly when you are interviewed and anticipate traps. Do not forget that a translation can be used to create controversy. Journalists can easily misinterpret an interview to their advantage."

Louis Saha

"Man is venal, but not all men are malicious. Not all readers are gullible; some do not believe what they read in newspapers."

Julien Laurens, *Le Parisien*

"Society is conservative and based on moral judgment."

Georgia de Chamberet, BookBlast Ltd – editor & translator of this book

"Public life, private life . . . Fight temptation, vice and imposters."

Louis Saha

"Do not allow your private life to interfere with your football, otherwise neither one will function at full capacity."

Luis Boa Morte

"Choose your friends, agents and clubs wisely."

Bruno Satin, authorised agent for the FFF, French Football Federation, and head of IMG, International Management Group

"Never forget where you come from, especially if it's from below. This will help you move ahead and stay on top."

Tim Cahill, Everton

Venus and Mars

"If possible, a player's wife should have an occupation. Rather than to provide for her family, this financial independence gives her a measure of recognition. She can use her money to indulge her player with small pleasures, invite him out to dinner and give him gifts."

Aurélie Gillet-Saha

"When a woman spends the day doing nothing, conversation dries up fast and life becomes monotonous – so be interesting! The PlayStation has become a player's best ally to help him relax and ease the tension, to the chagrin of his wife who would happily sue Sony. When our five-year-old boy was asked: 'What is daddy's job?' he answered, 'He plays with PlayStation!' (His dad did his training while he was at school, so he thought his work was done on the games console!) Now he is nine, he aspires to the same career. For the welfare of the family, we mutually agreed to ban everyone from playing video games during the week."

Aurélie Gillet-Saha

"Learn some technical terms such as 15-15 and VO2max [endurance training drills] to determine how tired your player will be when he gets home from training. He will come home wiped out. Don't count on your footballer for entertainment. A player who enjoys browsing in a shopping centre is a rarity. He will not be in the mood to satisfy his bored wife and will do nothing but nap after such intense physical exercise."

Aurélie Gillet-Saha

"Love from a long distance is hard to maintain as temptation is everywhere. Facing up to suspected adultery and choosing to look people in the eye, or not, when the tabloids run headlines is tough. You have to be dignified and unforgiving if it becomes chronic."

Aurélie Gillet-Saha

"Learn to fight the WAG's enemy number one: other women! To do this, take good care of yourself and pamper your man so he does not look away. If you have a flawless self image, other women are less attracted to your man as contenders will be more easily discouraged in front of an Adriana Karembeu [who recently separated from her husband, Christian Karembeu, the retired French international footballer and scout for Arsenal]. Take care of your man, your family and your home. Avoid making scenes, be understanding when he is tired, stressed or is feeling down. Do not be too demanding. Know when to take a step back, all the while staying supportive and do not resent being his punch bag at times. Be vigilant yet trusting."

Aurélie Gillet-Saha

"Learn to recognise and avoid certain players: those hard nuts who use their position to gain easy success with women, or the type who goes out every weekend before and after a match, or the heavy drinker who blames alcohol when things go wrong."

Aurélie Gillet-Saha

"Do not believe rumours, or what is written in the press. When in doubt, check it out for yourself."

Aurélie Gillet-Saha

"Do not get too used to delegating, or being overly assisted. Doing a maximum of things yourself is the best way to keep your feet on the ground and deal with 'retirement'."

Sandra Evra

"Stick to your values despite the disconcerting world around us. Be humble and do not project a negative image that could boomerang back at you [this is also valid for players]."

Karen Distin

"At retirement your network of friends will shrink, so don't be surprised. Try to keep your true friends, those you had before you became 'the wife of . . .'"

Sue Ellen Jager

"Always remember that the lifestyle of 90 per cent of footballers is ephemeral (unless you're married to Ronaldo!) and their career ends fast, so income falls off. Try not to get used to spending lavishly. Weigh up your expenses against what is 'normal' and make provision for the future. It's great to experience extraordinary things and enjoy a luxurious lifestyle, but it can become a dangerous habit."

Aurélie Gillet-Saha

Money makes the world go around, the world go around, the world go around . . .

"Choose the people around you wisely because your strength at critical moments partly lies in them. If they are honest and thoughtful, they will never guide you towards bankruptcy."

Vincent Saha

"I've noticed that at retirement 90 per cent of people struggle to pay even one bill. If you are given the opportunity to practice the sport you love and earn a living, go for it! Be happy and enjoy helping others less fortunate than you."

Philippe Christanval, former French international who played for Monaco, Barcelona, Marseille, Fulham

"Always remember that a career goes too, or very, fast so if you are lucky enough to be paid a good salary, don't forget that, from one day to next, it could stop."

Vincent Saha

"The first and last thing to remember: the choices we make build our future, so always be vigilant."

Louis Saha

ACKNOWLEDGEMENTS

First off, I took great pleasure in writing this book and would like to thank everyone who participated and helped this exciting project come to fruition. I want to thank my mother, whom I adore, for showing me love, kindness and devotion. I thank both my parents for having me. They taught me about parenting and making priorities. They built a stable, interdependent family and I learned to share with my brother and sister, who I love even more as time goes on. I thank my wife, Aurélie, who I am still trying to impress with football, or this book, although it created discord and tension more than once because of all the time I spent on it. I thank her for being who she is and what she has endured with me, as I'm a right prankster!

I also thank Laura Doyle and Georgia de Chamberet who, besides becoming my friends, revealed to me the world of writing and a wonderful passion. I became a so-called writer without claiming to be an avid reader. While I wrote this book in its entirety, they guided me like a child learning to walk. Thanks also to Charles Biétry and Pat Evra for writing glowing testimonials. And to Darren Baker for his wonderful cover illustration over which he took so much time and trouble. Thank you to my team-mates, coaches, scouts, opponents, fans, friends and all those who have crossed my path and enabled me to learn so many wonderful things. Thanks to: Pat, ZZ, Titi, Willy, Sylvain D., Diana, Ji, Sénateur Michel, Double D, Tim H., Tim C., Felly, Phil

Nev, Richard B., Sendo, Carlos Tevez, Edwin, JL, Kolo, Yak, Jonathan B., Nino, Bruno S., Boum, Djib C., Miky, Olive, Président Christanval and Sir Alex Ferguson.

To all of you, I ask you to remember that a book isn't written in a day and not to focus on small possibly negative details, but more on the substance and information that may be of interest. The rest is whatever you make of it. A book cannot be everything to everyone. Pass it on.

Half the money raised by this book will be donated to the European Leukodystrophy Association (ELA) that fights against the debilitating brain disease. Zinédine Zidane is its most famous sponsor. (www.ela-asso.com)

This book is supported by the Institut Français as part of the Burgess programme. (www.frenchbooknews.com)